1984

The
Misunderstood Child

The Misunderstood Child

Understanding and
Coping with Your Child's
Learning Disabilities

THIRD EDITION

Larry B. Silver, M.D.

Clinical Professor of Psychiatry
Georgetown University
School of Medicine

THREE RIVERS PRESS

NEW YORK

No book, including this one, can replace the services of a qualified health professional. Please use this book to help you communicate more effectively with your child's doctor so your child will get the best care possible.

Grateful acknowledgment is made to Dutton Signet, a division of Penguin Putnam, Inc., and International Creative Management for permission to reprint four cartoons from *It's a Teacher's Life* by David Sipress. Copyright © 1993 by David Sipress. Rights throughout the British Commonwealth are controlled by International Creative Management. Reprinted by permission of Dutton Signet, a division of Penguin Putnam, Inc. and International Creative Management.

Published by Three Rivers Press, New York, New York. Member of the Crown Publishing Group.

Random House, Inc. New York, Toronto, London, Sydney, Auckland
www.randomhouse.com

THREE RIVERS PRESS is a registered trademark and the Three Rivers Press colophon is a trademark of Random House, Inc.

Originally published in paperback by Times Books in 1998.

Printed in the United States of America.

Library of Congress Cataloging-in-Publication Data
Silver, Larry B.
The misunderstood child : understanding and coping with your child's learning disabilities / Larry B. Silver.—
3rd ed. p. cm.
Previous eds. with subtitle: A guide for parents of children with learning disabilities.
Includes index.
ISBN 0-8129-2987-X (pbk.)
1. Learning disabled children. 2. Parent and child.
I. Title.
RJ506.L4S55 1998
618.9285889—dc21 97-51664

ISBN 0-8129-2987-X

9 8 7 6 5 4

Third Edition

The third edition of this book is dedicated to the Learning Disabilities Association of America and to its over sixty thousand professional and parent volunteers, who have made such a great difference in the lives of children, adolescents, and adults who have learning disabilities. I am proud to have been an active member since 1969.

The joy of learning is often a nightmare for more than 10 million normal, bright, intelligent children—just because no one has recognized their learning difference. Understand their frustration—and begin to understand the problem.

Let no child be demeaned, nor have his or her wonder diminished, because of our ignorance or inactivity. Let no child be deprived of discovery because we lack the resources to discover his or her problem. Let no child—ever—doubt self or mind because we are unsure of our commitment.

—NATIONAL CENTER FOR LEARNING DISABILITIES

When I wrote the first edition of this book in 1984, public school programs for children and adolescents with learning disabilities were reasonably strong. I focused on the role of the parent and family in helping this son or daughter. In 1992, when I wrote the second edition, budget cuts had already begun to affect the services provided to those students with learning disabilities. I again focused the book on parents and families, keeping all of the previous material, only updated. But I stressed even more the need for parents to be *informed consumers* and *assertive advocates*. It was harder to get what each student needed, and the most knowledgeable parents were most likely to succeed.

This third edition is fully updated. I also added new information based on the very productive past ten years of research. I believe this edition will be as helpful to parents and families as the previous two editions. But there is a different tone in many sections of the book. The budget cuts to school systems have had a significant impact across public education in the quality and quantity of education provided. For those with special needs, the budget cuts are even greater. For those with special needs who have no visible evidence of a disability—like children and adolescents with learning disabilities—our children—the budget cuts have hit the hardest. A school system cannot avoid helping a student who is visually impaired or hearing impaired or who is in a wheelchair. But our children look normal, so it is easier to create a philosophy that justifies providing fewer services. Many students with special needs are now placed in a regular classroom with minimal services and often with a teacher who is not trained to address these needs. Such an approach is referred to as "inclusion." This philosophy—inclusion—must be a philosophy based on balancing the budget. There is no research to suggest it is a philosophy based on evidence that inclusion works. For some, inclusion is adequate. For many, the lack of a trained teacher and the lack of necessary support services result in disaster. This edition stresses even more the need for parents to learn how to help their son or daughter. It also stresses the need for today's parents to pick up the work of previous parents in fighting for what our kids need.

Interestingly, for those of us concerned with learning disabilities, it is the best of times and it is the worst of times. Significant research done over the past ten or so years has contributed to our understanding of the processes involved in reading disabilities and other learning disabilities. We know more about attention deficit hyperactivity disorder (ADHD) and about treatment. We know more about the brain and how it develops and how development might go wrong. Through the major effort of parent volunteers, our law—the Individuals with Disabilities Education Act (IDEA)—was saved from possible changes that would have justified even less help for our children and adolescents.

Yet, because of budget restraints, it is the worst of times. We see an erosion of services for our youth in schools and for our adults as they move into their postsecondary lives. For some children, the services available in our public schools are fewer today than they were before passage of Public Law 94-142. And too many of our adults have not found a way to succeed.

As with the previous editions, my primary goal has been to help parents understand their child or adolescent with learning disabilities and/or ADHD and to use this knowledge to create the type of family and school programs that maximize growth toward a happy, successful life. I hope this edition helps you to be that special parent and to have that special family.

CONTENTS

Contents

Understanding Learning Disabilities and Related Disorders

A Road Map for Understanding Learning Disabilities

A learning disability is a neurological disorder. That is, it is the result of a nervous system that has been "wired" a little differently. The brain is clearly not damaged, defective, or retarded. But, in certain areas, it processes information in a different way than it is supposed to. There are other problems relating to brain function that might exist along with learning disabilities. We call these comorbid problems.

It is important for you to know of these related problems. Many children, adolescents, and adults with learning disabilities will also have one of these other problems. These problems, too, must be found and addressed. This book will focus primarily on learning disabilities. However, these related, or comorbid, problems will also be explained.

You might find it helpful to have an overview or road map for making sense of these problems. I'll go into each issue in greater detail in later chapters. Parents sometimes tell me that no one seems to know what is wrong with their child; every professional they see has a different label or diagnosis. Often, the problem is that the child does have several areas of difficulty and each professional focuses on just one of them.

For many children, something affects the brain early in development, often during the first part of pregnancy. When this happens, it is unlikely that only one area of the brain is involved. Several areas might be affected. To make it easier to study these individuals, professionals separate out each possible problem area and put a label on it. So, depending on which areas of the brain are involved, the person will have different disorders.

For at least 50 percent of individuals, this developmental impact is the result of the genetic code. The problems run in the family because the genetic code tells the brain to wire itself differently. We do not have a full explanation for the other 50 percent. I will discuss some of these possibilities in Chapter 3.

Before I become specific, let me explain another important theme. The brain is immature at birth. It constantly grows as new wires are activated and fired. We call these changes maturational spurts. This growth takes place throughout childhood, adolescence, and early adulthood. Each maturational spurt affects the brain the way installing new software affects your computer; suddenly the computer can do things it couldn't do before. So, too, with each firing of new wires in the brain, the brain can do things it could not do before. As each new area becomes activated, there are two possibilities. It may be that the wires in this area were not affected prenatally and are wired "normally." Thus, when this area of the brain begins to work, the individual suddenly can do things that were difficult before. However, it is possible that when this area of the brain begins to work, it will become apparent that this area is also wired differently. Only, we had no way of knowing until the area began to work. For this individual, new problems arise.

This is the reason that some children struggle and struggle, then suddenly master things that were difficult before. Professionals working with the child at that time often get the credit for the change. You've heard the story: Mary struggled with reading for several years. Finally, she got Mrs. Jones as a teacher and within a month she was reading. This is also the reason why some children improve in one area only to discover another area of difficulty.

The cortex, or thinking part of the brain, has many functions. I will discuss four basic functions: language skills; muscle (motor) skills; thinking (cognitive) skills; and organization skills (executive function). Any or all of these areas might be wired differently.

Miswiring of the Brain

If the area of the brain that is wired differently relates to language functioning, the person will have a problem called a language disability. The first clue often is a delay in language development. The child is not speaking at all by age two, or by two and a half or three the child is using only a few words. Some may speak no better by four. If a speech and language therapist works with this child, it might be possible to speed up the development of language. There is a sigh of relief. Then, by four or five another problem becomes clear. This child may have difficulty processing and understanding what is being said (receptive language disability) or might have difficulty organizing thoughts, finding the right words, and speaking in a fluid and clear way (expressive language disability). More help is needed.

As this child enters the early elementary grades, another problem might become apparent. The first task in reading is language-based. The child must recognize units of sound (phonemes) and connect these sounds to the correct written symbols (graphemes). There are forty-four phonemes in the English language. Each letter has at least one sound; vowels have two sounds (a short and a long sound); certain combinations (*sh, th, ch,* etc.) have their own sounds. There are thirty-six graphemes in the English language (*A* through *Z* and *0* through *9*). To read, you must "break this code" by learning what sounds go with what symbols and sounding out words. Many children with a delay in language development, and later with receptive and/or expressive language problems, have problems learning to read in first grade. Spelling is the reverse process. You must start with the language in your brain and connect it with the right symbol by writing on the page. Thus, many children with reading problems also have problems with spelling.

Some children have a delay in language, receive help, improve, and never have another problem. Others might improve but show up later with receptive and expressive language problems. With help, these later problems improve and the child has no further problems. Others progress into reading problems. It just depends on whether the next area of brain activation is also wired differently.

If the area of the brain that is wired differently relates to the use of our muscles, we see what is called a motor disability. For some, the primary problems relate to the ability to coordinate and use teams of large muscles (gross motor skills); such kids have difficulty with running, jumping, or climbing. Others might have difficulty coordinating and using teams of small muscles (fine motor skills). They have difficulty learning to button, zip, tie, color within the line, use scissors, use eating utensils, and, later, use a pencil or pen to form letters and write. Still others might have a broader pattern of motor problems called sensory integration disorder. Now, in addition to problems with gross and fine motor planning functions, they might have difficulty making sense out of information coming from nerve endings in the skin. They might be very sensitive to touch, or they might misread temperature or pain. They also might have difficulty processing information from their inner ear (vestibular system), information the body uses to determine its relation to gravity. Thus they have difficulty with movement in space or position in space. Which of these many possible motor problems are present will depend on the areas of the brain involved.

If the area of the brain that is wired differently relates to the processing of information for learning, we call it a learning disability. In some ways, this division of the cortex is artificial. If an individual has a learning disability, more than one area of the brain is involved.

In terms of human evolution, the most recent addition to the cortex is the sophisticated area of the brain that acts like the chief executive officer in a company. This area carries out what is called executive functions. It orchestrates behaviors. This is the area that assesses a task or problem, decides how to tackle or solve the task, orchestrates the necessary activities or functions, continually makes midcourse changes or corrections, and eventually reaches a successful conclusion. If this area of the brain is wired differently, a person has difficulty with organizational planning and with carrying out tasks successfully.

This problem with wiring might extend beyond the cortex. There is an area of the brain that is often called the area of vigilance. This area of the brain is found in animals and primitive humans as well as in modern humans. It is the area that allows us to be a hunter. It controls the ability to sit very still so that you do not scare away your prey, the ability to track your prey and not to be distracted by any background activity, and the ability to strike just at the right time.

Picture, for example, a frog sitting on a lily pad (so you won't think this is only a human trait). Not a muscle moves or the fly will go away. The eyes track the fly. And, just at the right moment, the tongue comes out and catches the fly. Some children have problems with the wiring of this area of vigilance. As a result, they might be hyperactive, distractible, or impulsive. We call this disorder attention deficit hyperactivity disorder (ADHD).

You can now see why some children have a learning disability. Others might have a language disability or sensory integration disorder. Still others might have ADHD. Many might have one, two, three, or all four of these problems. Such children don't really have multiple disorders. They have multiple manifestations of the initial underlying problem that resulted in areas of the brain being wired differently.

Problems with Modulation

With the dramatic new methods for studying the brain, other problem areas are starting to make sense. Another area of the brain that might be affected is called the modulation area. This is the area that maintains emotional or psychological balance or equilibrium, avoiding extremes. If any specific area is involved, we will find a problem with modulation of a specific function. Such problems have been there since birth.

Some people have problems modulating anxiety. They have a history since early life of being high-strung or anxious. Over the years, the focus of their anxiety may change, but the central theme is a high anxiety level. They might be afraid to go to sleep alone at night. Later they might have a fear of being in part of the house alone or a fear of bees or a fear of something else. As these children move into adolescence or adulthood, they might develop a full-blown anxiety disorder. Some may have so much difficulty regulating anxiety that the level gets too high and triggers a physical (fight-or-flight) response. They have a panic disorder: They break out into a sweat; their heart pounds; they feel weak.

Another regulating problem relates to the ability to modulate anger. These children have been irritable and angry since early childhood. They have always had tantrums. As they get older, they show a specific form of difficulty regulating anger called intermittent explosive disorder. When they get angry, they don't just have a tantrum or pout or slam doors. Rather, they have a very short fuse. Sometimes they explode so fast you don't know for sure what caused the explosion. Once they pass over their threshold, they lose control. They yell, scream, curse, hit, throw, threaten. They act in an irrational way and cannot be reasoned with. Sometimes they seem paranoid, saying people are trying to hurt them. The episode lasts up to fifteen minutes or more. Then it ends almost as abruptly as it began. Once it is over, they may be tired and want to rest or sleep. They usually don't want to discuss what happened and seem confused about their behavior. Later they might feel remorse about what they did. These are the Dr. Jekyll–Mr. Hyde children.

Some may have difficulty modulating moods. They seem to have been unhappy or sad most of their life. They are moody or depressed some of the time or all of the time. Some will go on to develop a depressive disorder. A very few, in adolescence, may show difficulty modulating not just the down side (depression) but the up side (excitement, manic behavior). They might develop a bipolar disorder (formerly called manic-depressive disorder).

Another pattern of behavior that seems connected to these modulating disorders relates to the ability to regulate thoughts and behaviors. Some will have difficulty controlling their thoughts and experience the need to rethink over and over a thought or thought pattern (obsessive behavior). Others feel they must do certain things or they will get too anxious. They know "it is silly" but cannot stop. They might need to touch things a certain way or number of times. They might need to check and recheck things (for example, if the front door is locked or the stove is off). They might need to do certain patterns or rituals. This disorder is called obsessive-compulsive disorder.

There is one last area of difficulty with modulation that may or may not turn out to be part of this pattern. However, this problem is a comorbid condition and relates to difficulty regulating certain motor functions. Persons with this problem experience clusters of muscles contracting, causing what are called motor tics. Others may experience the need to say certain sounds or words, called vocal tics. These individuals have a tic disorder or a specific form of this problem called Tourette's disorder.

Our brain is a beautifully functioning, fascinating part of our body. It has many functions. If something affects this brain early in development, this impact will cause areas of the brain to develop differently. Depending on which parts of the brain are involved, a person will develop different problem areas. We have a name for each.

This road map will help you understand your son or daughter. Or, if you are an adult, it will help you understand yourself. As you read this road map, you will see many familiar trails or sites. It is not unusual for children, adolescents, or adults to have one or more of these disorders. The more disorders a person has, the more likely it is the person will have even more. So, it is not uncommon to find a child with learning disabilities and ADHD. This same child might have a tic disorder or an obsessive-compulsive disorder, or be overly anxious, or have trouble regulating anger.

The primary focus of this book is on learning disabilities. However, each of these related disorders will be discussed as well. I hope this road map helps you orient yourself as you travel from chapter to chapter.

Your Task as a Parent

Victor was a disaster in elementary school. He never sat still or paid attention in class, yet his teachers passed him along from grade to grade. By the fourth grade, when he was ten years old, he still read at a first-grade level, and his math skills were no better. The school at last evaluated him and concluded that he had learning disabilities. The report also described Victor as "hyperactive" and "distractible." Despite this evaluation, Victor went into a regular fifth-grade program. There, his classroom and academic performance became even worse, and he also grew much more unpleasant and provocative at home.

By the time he finished the sixth grade, Victor could only be described as impossible. At school, he did everything he could to get kicked out of class: he hid under desks, threw objects, and crawled around the floor barking like a dog. All of his disruptive tactics succeeded. His classmates thought he was funny, and he spent more time banished from the classroom than he spent in it.

The more trouble he got into at school, the more his parents tried to punish him at home. Soon the family was in chaos. When Victor rebelled against the limits his parents set as punishment, the parents fought with each other about how firm to be in enforcing them. His brother, already humiliated by Victor's behavior, spent more and more time at a friend's house to avoid the fighting at home. When the parents went to the school to try to get to the cause of the problem, the principal told them that Victor's emotional disturbance probably stemmed from their own marital distress. She told them that the school could not be responsible for family problems and suggested that they go for psychiatric help. No one mentioned the fourth-grade evaluation.

By the time the parents did seek a private psychiatric evaluation, Victor was almost thirteen years old. During the interviews, Victor's behavior shifted between quiet depression and open hostility. When quiet, he spoke of "being stupid." He made such statements as "I can't read good; I can't do anything good. Maybe I'm just dumb." He saw himself as "bad." He was "ruining the family." He would add, "Maybe they should just send me away to school so I won't cause so much trouble." When he became hostile in the session, Victor joked around, tried to break items in the office, and threatened to leave the room.

A new educational evaluation, updating the one done in the fourth grade, revealed multiple learning and language disabilities. Victor was three years behind in most academic skill areas. Psychological testing revealed a superior intellectual potential with a verbal IQ of 132, but a below-average performance IQ of 98. Everyone who took part in the evaluation saw Victor as hyperactive and distractible. The recommendations included (1) placement in a full-time special education program, (2) individual and family therapy, and (3) a trial period on a medication for his hyperactivity and distractibility.

I met with Victor to review the findings. He paraded in, joking about what "some dumb teacher" had done. I put my arm around his shoulder and said, "I want to let you know what all of the tests show. You know, now that I understand your problems, I really admire you. I'd probably have thrown in the towel years before you did." Victor sat down looking sad. But he followed me with interest as I reviewed his strong and weak areas, interrupting to make comments such as, "You mean, like, when I read a page but forget what I read, or I start to talk to someone and halfway through I forget where I started?" I then discussed the IQ test, subtest by subtest, showing him how particular learning problems interfered with his ability to successfully answer questions. I emphasized how bright he was, despite his experiences in school.

Later in our interview, I told Victor that I thought he had become the class clown to cover up his feeling like a "retard." I told him that I didn't blame him, but that he could expect better of himself. Then I explained the proposed plan for special help. He understood what I described, but refused to go along with it because he didn't want to go to a different school than his friends. I also explained why I wanted him to try medication and described what it could do. He didn't like that idea either, but he agreed to try it "for a few days." As he left my office, I reassured him that I understood the pain and frustration he had gone through and that I really wanted to help him. He smiled and held out his hand. We shook hands and Victor left.

I reviewed the full evaluation and the series of recommendations once again in my meeting with Victor's parents. They seemed relieved to gain a better understanding of their son's difficulties, but were angry with the school and with themselves for not doing something sooner. They agreed with all of the recommendations.

The next meeting was a family session with Victor, his brother, and his parents, and the maternal grandmother who lived with the family. We reviewed the whole evaluation again. During this session Victor behaved very provocatively, eventually forcing everyone to get angry with him. I pointed out to him what he was doing and the effect it was having, but he continued with his irritating, disruptive behavior.

After a series of meetings with the personnel at Victor's school, during which all of the data were again presented and discussed, it was agreed that he would go into a self-contained special education program. He was to remain in the program for the next three years, although we did not know that then.

Victor's problems were serious, but not as severe as those of many such children and certainly not hopeless. If you have a child with learning disabilities plus possibly attention deficit hyperactivity disorder (ADHD) in your family, no doubt you recognize some of the elements in Victor's story. You can probably tell a more vivid, dramatic, and agonizing story yourself. If the child with a learning disability is *your* child, no doubt you also know just how Victor's parents felt—their denial, frustration, anxiety, depression, guilt, and despair. And you probably recognize best of all their anger—anger at the circumstances and, perhaps above all, anger at their own bad luck. The parents' anger is as easy to understand as the child's, however different. Unfortunately, understanding falls short even of a first step toward a remedy. All of the energy that goes into this anger must be rerouted toward educated action—patient, unremitting, effective action.

Victor's case is not typical—there is no "typical" child with learning disabilities—but it is not unusual either. Although caught late, Victor's problems were caught in the nick of time. Let us now return to Victor's story.

Victor resented being placed in the special education program. Initially, he fell back on his old clowning act. But, in the new program, each time he had to be removed from class, someone sat down and discussed his behavior with him. The theme was "You don't like it here, but how are you ever going to get back to regular school if you don't stay in class long enough to get the help you need? You're bright, and you can overcome your problems, but you can't do that until you are willing to work *with* us rather than *against* us." Victor's teacher also tried to point out the probable causes for his misbehavior. When he knocked over the desk, the teacher would say, "I guess it's easier to get mad at the desk than to get mad at yourself because you can't do the math. How about picking up the desk so we can sit down and I can help you?"

I started Victor on a stimulant medication (discussed in Chapter 16). His overactive behavior lessened significantly, as did his distractibility. Both his teacher and his family noted a calming effect. His father commented, "Victor went fishing with me, and for the first time in his life, he quietly sat and enjoyed himself." His mother marveled over a family dinner during which Victor did not jump up and down once. More important, Victor noted a change. He enjoyed the relaxed feeling. He tried to explain the decreased distractibility. "You know what it's like when you are in a room and the refrigerator goes off. Suddenly you realize how much noise it makes. Well, the medication makes my head quiet. I never realized how much noise was going on up there." He remained on medication from that point on with no objections.

Victor's general stormy behavior, however, lasted throughout most of the first year. During this time Victor was in both individual and family therapy. The therapist saw Victor once a week and the family every other week. Although Victor had plenty of work to do on his own, most of the effort during the first year went into working with the family. The parents had to regain control of both Victor and their family life, and with the therapist's guidance, they established a behavior modification program, including a point system of rewards for Victor and a time-out room where he went when events got out of hand. They also had to find ways to recognize and fill their own needs. Obviously, they had to learn to support each other through the crisis with Victor, but they also had to occasionally get away for a weekend, even if only to stay with friends in town. As therapy progressed, they learned how to speak to Victor candidly and clearly, reflecting back to him just how his behavior seemed to them and just how they reacted to his behavior, much as the teacher did. In the therapy, Victor's brother also received the support he needed. Encouraged in the belief that Victor had no right to abuse him or to embarrass him in front of his friends, he too learned how to protect his own interests and to deal more honestly with Victor. Unlike in the past, his parents supported him in these efforts.

The first year was hard work. Victor made little obvious progress, but they all felt good about the direction in which they were heading. During the summer, Victor continued to attend psychotherapy sessions and to take the prescribed medication.

The first week of the second year in the special school went especially badly. Victor was very angry. He wanted to be back in public school. He could see that it would be difficult for him to attend his old school, but he still wanted to be there. Then, slowly, he accepted reality. Increasingly he would answer his teacher's reflective comments with "I know! I know!" In therapy, the sad, frightened Victor was most often present. As he struggled with his anger, frustration, and helplessness, he also began to accept the idea that his future was up to him. If he was willing to work, his family and special education teachers would work very hard to help him. If he resisted, fought, or played games, his family and teachers would stick by him, but he would not make progress. Frequently, now, he asked to review past test results, especially the IQ test. He wondered at times if more medication would make him better sooner.

Victor began to work at school. He stopped a lot of the clowning behavior, and he learned that he could talk about his feelings rather than act them out. For example, one afternoon after a very frustrating hour of work on reading, he waited until the rest of the class went to gym and then sat down on the floor near the teacher's desk and cried. His teacher sat still and did nothing. Finally Victor said, "I'm just a retard. I'll never learn this stuff. You're wasting your time. My brain is just too dumb to learn." His teacher put his arm on Victor's shoulder and just listened. Then he told him how glad he was that Victor felt safe enough to share such personal thoughts with him and that he could talk about his feelings rather than acting them out. He also told Victor that the work was indeed hard, but he reassured him that he was bright and would make it.

Victor made up two years of academic work during his second year in the special program. His attitude at home improved, and he formed a good relationship with his father. He returned willingly to the program for the third year and continued to make progress. At his request, the individual therapy and medication continued.

The next year Victor returned to his local high school, taking only an hour a day of extra help in the resource room. He continued to need the medication. He completed high school and was accepted in a college that had a special program for students with learning disabilities. He decided to become a special education teacher. Whatever he does, I have no concerns about Victor's future.

We can never know how much better off Victor might have been had he received earlier help. Perhaps help came at just the moment when he was ready to make use of it. We will also never know what else Victor's parents could have done at an earlier stage, or if what they did do could have been better. Putting ourselves in their place, however, we can certainly suppose that knowing more sooner would have helped them to manage their distressing situation more effectively. The energy they spent doing their best might have gone into more productive activities than punishing Victor, the family, and themselves.

If you need not imagine yourself in the shoes of Victor's parents because you are already in them, I shall do the best I can to help you. I wish I could promise to give you a total understanding of learning disabilities, ADHD, and other related problems, but I can't. The human services field is full of highly trained, concerned, responsible professionals, but many of the phenomena that they see every day cannot be explained. I can promise you this, however, if partial knowledge is not quite power, it is at least the equipment you must have to fight for the best attention and treatment you can get for your child or adolescent.

What you must do is fight for the right attention. In a very unusual way, you are a consumer of services. These services may not be easily found, and they will rarely be thrust at you. They are there, however. Your daughter or son will be their most important beneficiary, but you are the child's only agent in this matter. As your child begins to benefit from the right kind of attention, so will you and your family.

The point is that as soon as you recognize your situation, you must do everything in your power to become an *informed consumer* and an *assertive advocate* for your child or adolescent. No one and no single agency—not your family physician, your child's teacher, the school, or anyone else—is as vitally concerned as you are, or as informed as you can and must be.

A child or adolescent with learning disabilities and possibly ADHD confronts a series of Herculean tasks laid out over a long, long course. But the rewards are virtually certain: Your daughter or son can improve, can learn to learn, and can grow toward becoming a normal, happy adult. That success depends on you—on your action, assertion, perseverance, and advocacy. The task of getting help for your child or adolescent may be smaller than the task that is facing your son or daughter, but it is compelling and immediate. It will take all of the strength and determination you have and more. It will baffle and frustrate you, but it will eventually bring reward.

The task, however, is inescapable, imminent, and above all, ultimately yours alone. I hope this book will help your child and your family.

Basic Information to Understand

To help your daughter or son most effectively, you must first have a fair understanding of the problems. It may help you, initially, to realize that 10 to 20 percent of the average school-age population have trouble with academic work. There are many possible reasons. Most fall into several broad categories: (1) some have mental retardation—that is, they have below-normal intellectual capacities, and therefore they will always function below normal levels academically; (2) some have emotional problems that interfere with either their ability to learn or their availability to learning (because disruptive behaviors lead to removal from class); and (3) some have average or above-average intelligence, but still have academic difficulties because of the way their brain functions. Although such children may have problems with vision, hearing, or both, their learning problems are not caused by these impairments. People with learning disabilities fall into this third group. They represent about 10 percent of most of the school-age population.

As discussed in the first chapter, children and adolescents with learning disabilities may have one or more of a group of associated neurological disorders. About 20 to 25 percent will have attention deficit hyperactivity disorder (ADHD). In addition, some may have a motor tic disorder or Tourette's disorder. Others may have an anxiety disorder, obsessive-compulsive disorder, anger control problems, or depression. Some may have two, three, or more of these difficulties.

Most students with learning disabilities develop emotional, social, and family problems because of the frustrations and failures they experience. These emotional, social, and family problems are referred to as "secondary" to emphasize that they are the consequences of the academic disability and not the cause of the academic problems. The most frequent pattern seen is:

Learning disabilities
Attention deficit hyperactivity disorder (ADHD)
Secondary emotional, social, and family problems

Each of these difficulties will be discussed in this book. Before doing this, I would like to discuss several key questions often concerning parents as they begin down the diagnostic and treatment planning path.

1. What do the terms used to explain my child mean?
2. Do more boys than girls have these problems?
3. What causes these problems? Who, or what, is to blame?

What Do the Terms Used to Explain My Child Mean?

What shall we call this child or adolescent or adult? Everyone seems to have a different name for people with this group of behaviors and problems. In general, there are several reasons for the confusion on labels. First, as our understanding of these problems evolved over the past fifty or more years, different labels were used. With new knowledge, these labels changed. However, some professionals still use the old terms. Second, each professional group that works with these students has its own terms reflecting its specialty. For example, a learning disability specialist and a speech-language therapist might use different terms for the same problem area.

Let me take you through a quick look at the history of our understanding of these problems, reviewing some of the different labels that have evolved throughout the years. Prior to the 1940s in the United States, a child who had difficulty learning was considered to have mental retardation, to exhibit emotional disturbances, or to be socially and culturally disadvantaged. In the early 1940s, a fourth group was identified, children who had difficulty learning because of a presumed problem with their nervous system. The initial researchers noted that these students had the same learning problems as individuals who were known to have brain damage (for example, after trauma or surgery to the brain). Yet, these students looked normal; thus, researchers concluded that the students also had brain damage, but that the damage was minimal. The term *minimal brain damage* was introduced. Gradually, however, observations and testing revealed that no evidence of damage to the brain could be found in most of these children. Indeed, research information began to point to the idea that the cause of the problem lay in how the brain functions—that is, the problem was physiologic and not structural. All of the brain mechanisms are present and operable, but some of the "wiring" is hooked up differently and, thus, does not work in the normal way. Scientists created a term to suggest this concept of faulty functioning. The prefix *dys*, which means "difficulty with," was incorporated, and the term *minimal brain dysfunction*, or *MBD*, came into use. The literature on MBD described such children as having (1) learning difficulties, presumed to be due to a dysfunctional nervous system; (2) problems with hyperactivity and distractibility; and (3) emotional and family problems that were considered to be a consequence of the first two sets of problems.

From the 1950s through the present, professionals from a number of different disciplines intensively studied the problem of MBD. Because each discipline trains its specialists and subspecialists differently and uses a different vocabulary, each investigator described what he or she found somewhat differently. Much as in the story of the blind men who studied the elephant, each described only part of the subject. Only now have we been able to see what the whole elephant looks like.

History of Learning Disabilities

Educators specializing in children with academic problems—the special education professionals—studied the learning problems. Initially, they used labels that had been established for many years in schools of education to describe the primary presenting problems. Thus, children who had trouble with reading because of language-based problems had *dyslexia* and were called dyslexic. Children with writing problems had *dysgraphia* and were called dysgraphic. Trouble with arithmetic was called *dyscalculia*. Other special educators found these terms too general and not helpful. They decided that they had to look for the specific reasons for the trouble with reading, writing, or arithmetic. These professionals began to look for the underlying learning difficulties that explained the academic skill difficulties. The term *learning disability* was finally selected and has become the primary term used today.

If the student has difficulty receiving, processing, and expressing language, the term *language disability* would be used. Speech-language therapists would use such terms as *receptive language disability*, *central language disability*, or *expressive language disability*. Special education professionals might call the same problems auditory processing, pragmatic language, or demand language disabilities.

A special education professional might refer to a child's difficulty with motor planning activities as a fine motor or gross motor problem. For these problems occupational therapists might use the term *motor dyspraxia*. They might identify other problems and refer to the total clinical picture as *sensory integration disorder*.

History of ADHD

Other professionals studied those children who were described as hyperactive and distractible. The first official term established in 1968 in the medical classification system for these children was *hyperkinetic reaction of childhood*, and with it came the concept of the hyperactive child. The description noted overactivity, restlessness, distractibility, and a short attention span. In 1980, the term was officially changed to *attention deficit disorder*, or *ADD*, to emphasize that distractibility with a short attention span was the primary clinical issue and that hyperactivity or impulsivity also might be present. Different terms were used for two subtypes: *ADD with hyperactivity* and *ADD without hyperactivity*. A child needed only to have one of the three behaviors (hyperactivity, distractibility, or impulsivity) to be diagnosed.

In 1987, the official classification term for these children changed to *attention deficit hyperactivity disorder*, or *ADHD*, to reflect that although distractibility is the primary issue, hyperactivity is also an important factor of the disorder. Again, a child could have any of the three problems and be diagnosed with ADHD. The child did not have to be hyperactive.

In 1994, the official classification changed again. The same term was used, *attention deficit hyperactivity disorder*. The term *inattention* was substituted for *distractibility*. Three subtypes were established: (1) mixed type, for individuals who are hyperactive, inattentive, and impulsive; (2) inattentive type, for individuals who are primarily inattentive; and (3) hyperactive-impulsive type, for individuals who are primarily hyperactive and impulsive. Despite these changes, many professionals and parents like to use the term *ADD* for children who are only inattentive (distractible) and the term *ADHD* for children who are also hyperactive. It is important to remember that the only official term that can be used on reports or other records is *attention deficit hyperactivity disorder (ADHD)*.

These changes in names over the years do not reflect ambivalence on the part of the professionals who develop these classifications and guidelines. They reflect the rapidly expanding knowledge of this disorder.

History of Emotional, Social, and Family Problems

Mental health professionals studied the emotional, social, and family problems often seen with children and adolescents with learning disabilities. In addition to describing these problems, these professionals clarified a very important issue. For the individual with a learning disability, the emotional, social, and family problems were not the *cause* of the academic difficulties. These problems were the *consequence* of their academic difficulties and of the resulting frustrations and failures experienced. This is a very important concept that will be discussed throughout the book.

Where Are We Today?

The term *minimal brain dysfunction* is no longer used. In its place, the different components are identified and labeled individually using current terms. The treatment plan would address each of the individual problems. Thus, today a child who used to be diagnosed with MBD would be identified as having:

Learning disabilities
Attention deficit hyperactivity disorder (ADHD)
Secondary emotional, social, and family problems

Now to return to our question: What shall we call these children? If the child or adolescent or adult has informational processing problems that are neurologically based and that result in difficulties mastering academic skills and strategies, he or she will be identified as having a learning disability. If this individual is hyperactive, inattentive (distractible), and/or impulsive, he or she will be identified as having ADHD. (As will become clearer later in this book, learning disabilities and ADHD are two separate but related disorders.) Further, if emotional, social, and/or family problems exist, it becomes critical to determine if they are the cause of the academic difficulty (this is not the type of child or adolescent discussed in this book) or if they are the consequence of the learning disabilities and/or ADHD.

Don't let different professionals who use different terms confuse you. Nor should you be confused by books you read that use different terms. Often, these terms suggest that the professional had trained at an earlier time and has not kept up with the progressive changing of concepts. If you are at a meeting for your child or adolescent and the professionals are debating whether your child has dyslexia or a learning disability, understand that the professionals come from different schools of thought or that they have not kept up with the field. Both terms refer to your child's reading disability. If you hear a term at a meeting or see a term in a report and you do not know what it means, don't be embarrassed to ask for clarification. It is your son or daughter. You need to know what these professionals mean.

Do More Boys Than Girls Have These Problems?

Until recently, the literature on learning disabilities suggested that the ratio of boys to girls with this disorder is between 5:1 and 9:1. Many theories have been proposed to explain why more boys than girls have learning disabilities. None of these theories fully explain this observation. Recent studies suggest that there is no difference in the numbers of boys and girls with learning disabilities. Researchers studied and tested the total kindergarten population of a school system and then followed the children through their educational years. They compared the children who met the criteria for a learning disability based on their studies with the number of children who had been tested by the school system and found to have learning disabilities. Whereas the ratio of boys to girls in the school-identified population (that is, those the school had singled out) was closer to the 5:1 ratio often cited in the research literature, the ratio of boys to girls found with learning disabilities when all children were tested by the researchers was 1:1. As many girls as boys were found to have learning disabilities.

There are two possible reasons for these differences. First, there is a referral bias. Boys who are frustrated in school are more likely to act out than girls. Girls are more likely to withdraw and be quiet. Consequently, more boys are referred for testing and, thus, identified. The other reason relates to possible test bias. Many of the tests used to diagnose learning disabilities were designed and standardized on boys. It is possible that there are differences in the way boys reflect their learning disabilities as compared to girls. Thus, the test used today might miss certain types of problems found with girls. Efforts are underway to minimize these biases.

Learning disabilities appear to be as common among girls as among boys. However, until the two problems discussed above are corrected, the number of boys found in special education programs may continue to be significantly higher than the number of girls.

The same ratio of boys to girls is noted for ADHD, at least 5:1 in favor of boys. Studies are currently in progress to clarify if these figures also might reflect referral or test bias. Another factor is that children and adolescents with hyperactivity and/or impulsivity are more likely to be noticed, referred, and diagnosed. Those with only inattention (distractibility) are less obvious and more likely to be seen as uninterested—"airheads" or "space cadets"—and missed. It is possible that more girls than boys have the purely inattentive form of this disorder; thus, more girls with ADHD are missed than boys. This possibility has not yet been clarified.

What Are the Causes of Learning Disabilities?

Once parents become aware that they have a child or adolescent with a learning disability and have accepted this reality, they immediately ask, "How could this happen? Why did it happen? Why me?" It is as if knowing the cause of something implies knowing its cure. Or, for some, knowing the cause offers something to blame for the problem or something to avoid so that it won't happen to someone else in the family.

The answer to the question of the cause of learning disabilities or of ADHD has not yet been determined. Most research suggests that for most individuals something affected or influenced the brain during pregnancy, probably early in pregnancy. In about 50 percent of children, research shows that what is affected is the genetic code that "tells" the brain to wire itself differently. That is, these problems run in the family. For the other 50 percent, we have a lot of information and leads, but no firm answers.

When a sibling, mother, or father, or other family members have learning disabilities and/or ADHD, it is easier to assume a familial cause. For the other 50 percent, there might be many ideas, but there cannot be closure on the cause. We will have to wait for more research.

What we do know is that the brain is wired differently. For many years the literature referred to learning disabilities as "presumed" to be neurologically based. The research of the past decade or longer is so definite that the word *presumed* is no longer needed. The strongest evidence comes from microscopic studies of the brains of individuals who were known to have learning disabilities and who died of such a cause that the brain was not affected. In each brain studied, specific areas of the brain were found where cells had migrated out to their first developmental site in the brain but stayed there and did not migrate to the usual primary site seen in the fully developed brain. In addition, many of these cells were disconnected. That is, the nerve cell sent out extensions that were to connect with a specific area of the brain. But these extensions were "loose" and never connected. The sites of these faulty migration and wiring patterns match the areas of the brain known to be involved in such language-based learning skills as reading.

Another area of research that is confirming the neurological base for learning disabilities involves brain imaging. Methods for studying the brain as it functions by brain imaging techniques have been around for over twenty years. However, these techniques required the use of radioisotope-tagged chemicals. Thus, they were not used for research with children or adolescents. A new technique for brain imaging, the functional magnetic resonance imaging (MRI) method, does not require the use of radioisotopes. Thus, it is now possible to study the brain as it functions. Children can be asked to read, for example, and the patterns of brain activity can be compared between boys and girls and between children with learning disabilities and children without. Using this technique, researchers are mapping out the neural architecture for reading a printed word. Researchers can locate the site in the brain that becomes activated when letters are identified. Then, in sequence, they can observe the sites where the process of attaching the correct sound(s) to the letters occurs, then the sites where the different letters are blended, and the sites where meaning is applied to the letters (words).

These imaging studies show a difference between children with learning disabilities and children without learning disabilities. These studies have revealed another surprising difference. The areas of the brain involved with reading are different in men and women. Both use the same sites. However, men only use these sites on the left side of the brain whereas women use these sites on both the left and the right sides of the brain. The full meaning of these findings is not yet understood. It might explain why women tend more often than men to compensate for their reading disability.

The 50 Percent with a Familial Pattern

About half the children with learning disabilities have family members with this disability.

Genetic Patterns

Studies suggest that as many as 50 percent of children with learning disabilities have inherited this brain pattern. The genetic code results in the brain wiring itself differently in specific areas. The disability

runs in families, with brothers or sisters, a parent or parents, and extended relatives of a parent having a similar problem. This same statistic appears to be true for ADHD.

Family studies, twins studies, and adoptee–foster home studies support the importance of a genetic factor. For example, there is an increased risk for these disabilities in parents or children who have relatives who have these disabilities. If one of a pair of identical twins has a learning disability or ADHD, the other twin is much more likely to have these problems, whereas a fraternal twin would be less likely than an identical twin to have these similar disabilities. The familial pattern appears to be clear. Although researchers are getting closer, the specific genetic markers or pathways or processes are not yet known.

The current thinking is that where there is a familial pattern, the genetic code instructs the brain to wire itself differently, resulting in learning disabilities. If the genetic code instructs other cells to develop without the ability to produce the normal amount of a specific neurotransmitter, the result is ADHD.

There is a related area of genetic study that might someday help us understand another possible cause of learning disability. Our genetic process takes place through specific units of function called chromosomes. Each chromosome is made up of specific units called genomes. Each genome has a specific task in instructing the body to develop. Increasing studies on these genomes have identified specific genomes that are related to specific functions or specific genome defects that result in specific diseases.

Each genome is made up of a specific number of basic proteins called amino acids. These amino acids are laid out in a very specific way. One concept is that something might influence a genome, causing one or two amino acids to shift position on the chain and changing the specific pattern of the genome. This shift might result in faulty development for the area controlled by that genome. It might someday be clarified that some forms of nonfamilial learning disabilities are the result of such an accidental shift.

Adoption

Another interesting observation that has been documented on several occasions is that the number of adoptions of children and adolescents who have a learning disability is five times higher than would be expected in the general population. The same incidence has been found with ADHD.

One could speculate about the parents of children placed for adoption or about the possible risk factors that were experienced by these children during pregnancy and delivery. The incidence may be higher for children who were adopted from economically underdeveloped countries and from poverty areas within these countries. Mothers in these places often receive minimal or no care and may have been malnourished. The baby is often malnourished during the weeks or months before adoption. Proper intake of the appropriate foods, especially protein, is critical during fetal life and during the early months of life if the brain is to develop properly.

At this time, the reasons for such a high incidence of these disabilities with children who were adopted remain unknown. It must be remembered that the statistics cited refer to the number of children with learning disabilities who have been adopted. These figures are very different than looking at how many children who have been adopted have learning disabilities. It is suspected that the percentage would be similar to that in the general population. Parents should not be discouraged from adopting children. However, they might try to learn as much as possible about the birth parents, the pregnancy, and the life of the baby between delivery and placement.

The Other 50 Percent of Children

About half the children with learning disabilities do not have family members with this disability.

The Chemical Systems of the Brain

The brain is made up of trillions of nerve cells, each of which communicates with other specific cells. This communication has to take place in such a way that only one other cell, the right cell, is stimulated. Each cell produces minute amounts of a specific chemical that passes across a microscopic space (called a synapse) and stimulates the next, correct cell. These chemicals that transmit messages from one nerve cell to another are called neurotransmitters. Once this neurotransmitter crosses the synapse and stimulates the other cell, another chemical process occurs that neutralizes or breaks down the neurotransmitter. How does this work? Each nerve cell releases a specific chemical with a specific structure. The chemical passes over thousands of cells. The cell that is supposed to be stimulated has a specific site on its surface, called a receptor site. When this specific chemical (neurotransmitter) passes over this specific cell, it connects with this specific receptor site and the new cell is stimulated. This neurotransmitter system is fascinating and allows each nerve cell to stimulate only the nerve cells it is supposed to stimulate.

The brain produces many different types of neurotransmitters. We know of about fifty. It is estimated that there are as many as two hundred. This new knowledge of the neurochemistry of the brain has resulted in a rapid expansion of knowledge of brain function and dysfunction. As will be discussed in Chapter 16, ADHD appears to be the result of a deficiency of a specific neurotransmitter in a specific area of the brain. Certain types of depression are the result of a deficiency of another specific neurotransmitter in another area of the brain. No data suggests that a neurotransmitter factor might be the cause of learning disabilities.

There are other chemical activities related to the developing brain and an expanding body of knowledge on these activities. These chemicals control brain and behavioral interactions. New research at the molecular level on the genetic process of transmitting messages from the heredity-carrying gene to the developing brain offers much promise for clarification. Specific chemical messages, called neuroendocrines, travel to the brain throughout fetal development. Each binds with a particular cell or cell group that has the correct receptor site for this chemical. This binding results in the growth of these cells. Each day different sites are stimulated to grow in a very exact and orchestrated complex process, slowly weaving together the networks of nerves that make up the human brain.

Could these genetic messengers be affected or influenced, resulting in a differently functioning brain? Could this explain learning disabilities? Might certain drugs or other chemicals interfere with the biochemical messenger process, resulting in the absence of brain growth for that particular unit of time when that messenger should have been active? And would such a block during a brief time affect other brain growth that should link later with this area of non-growth? Research in molecular genetics and cellular biology offers promise of such answers. With these answers lies hope not just for understanding but for prevention or possibly for treatment concepts.

One set of studies was of enough concern that the information resulted in prevention efforts even before all of the facts were known. It was found that 80 percent of pregnant women in the United States took over-the-counter or prescription medications during pregnancy or at the time of delivery. It was not known which of these medications crossed through the placenta into the fetus nor what effect these chemicals might have had on the chemically driven genetic process described above. Further, some of the medications used at the time of delivery could, after delivery, no longer pass back to the mother to be metabolized by her liver. Thus, they remained in the infant's blood for a longer period until the immature liver could metabolize them. Could these medications explain the more subtle changes found in the brain or in other organ systems with children? The answer is not available. However, as a preventive effort, pregnant women are advised to take no medications during pregnancy, and there is an increasing effort to use no medications at delivery, with encouragement for women to use more natural childbirth methods.

Another area of research supports the possibility of a chemical blockage as an explanation for the faulty wiring present in children with learning disabilities. To explain this research, I need to explain in more detail how the brain develops. As the initial cells of the developing brain begin to evolve, new cells multiply and then migrate out to new sites in the brain. These cells migrate out beyond where they will be in the ultimately developed brain. More cells are produced than will exist in the "finished" brain. Once these cells reach their temporary position in the developing brain, they send out nerve endings toward the area of the brain to which they are to connect. If the nerve ending establishes a connection, the cell survives. If the nerve ending does not establish proper connections, the cell does not survive. Once this process is finished and the proper number of cells are present, these cells migrate again back toward their place of origin. Once they reach their ultimate location, the migration stops. The proper number of cells, each connected to their other correct areas of the brain, are then in place.

As mentioned earlier, microscopic studies of the brains of individuals with learning disabilities show a consistent pattern. The process of migration was interrupted. Areas of the brain were found where cells had migrated out to their first position but had not migrated back to their proper site in the brain. In addition, all of the cells that did not form a connection did not disappear. There were too many cells, and some had nerve endings that did not connect with other cells. There was clear microscopic evidence of "faulty wiring."

One line of thought is that in people with learning disabilities, the genetic code does not orchestrate the neuroendocrine system correctly, resulting in the dysfunctional pattern. Another thought is that a chemical present in the developing fetus temporarily interferes with or blocks this process, resulting in a disruption and a dysfunctional pattern. This second idea is linked to the discussion of medications taken during pregnancy or at delivery.

Fetal Development

As already discussed, events or experiences during pregnancy, at the time of delivery, or soon after delivery can affect the developing brain. Socioenvironmental factors also can have a negative impact. Examples include poor nutrition, absence of prenatal care, metabolic or toxic factors, infections, or stress. Each can result in difficulties during pregnancy, premature delivery, and low birth weight. Studies, for example, show a relationship between low birth weight and prematurity and later academic difficulties or later hyperactivity and distractibility. Only, there is no consistent pattern. Many children who are premature or of low birth weight do not develop learning disabilities.

Two major national collaborative projects are in process, one in the United States and one in England. Children have been followed since the mother first learned of her pregnancy and volunteered for the study. Multiple studies have been done during certain age periods and extensive observational information has been accumulated. These children are approaching adulthood.

Studies done at age seven (second grade) and at age ten (fifth grade) identified those who were having academic difficulties (for any reason) or who showed evidence of hyperactivity, distractibility, and/or impulsivity. Through a study of the data on each child, efforts were made to statistically find patterns or correlations with specific factors.

It must be noted that such data are suggestive at best and that factors such as socioeconomic status were not factored into the results. The information at both age periods found a suggestive correlation with the following factors: maternal cigarette smoking during pregnancy, convulsions during pregnancy, low fetal heart rate during the second stage of labor, lower placental weight, breech presentation, and a specific type of inflammation called chorionitis. Also noted was a history of the mother drinking alcohol during the pregnancy. In these cases, the amount used was two or three drinks a day, far less than that consumed with a more serious disorder called fetal alcohol syndrome.

Although there is not a firm association between these factors and problems found with the children, preventive efforts are in effect. Pregnant women are told not to smoke or drink during the pregnancy. Proper nutrition throughout the pregnancy is stressed. Mothers are told not to use over-the-counter or prescription medications during pregnancy or at the time of delivery unless the medications are essential and they are directed by the physician to do so. Although the final results are not in, these preventive efforts seem more than appropriate.

Metabolites and Toxins

Metabolites are chemicals naturally seen within the body. Toxins are chemicals present in the body that are not naturally there. Metabolites include glucose, specific hormones, electrolytes, and other chemicals. For each, there is a normal range of expected levels. If the level is too high or too low, there can be difficulties. There are no specific studies relating learning disabilities to either high or low levels of these metabolites. However, all of the facts are not yet in.

Toxins in the blood and brain during pregnancy, during the early months of life, and, for some, throughout childhood can result in brain dysfunction or brain damage. The toxin most studied is lead. Depending on the amount present, the period of development when it is present, and for how long it is present, the result could be mental retardation, learning disabilities, or milder forms of academic difficulty. Many other toxins are being studied.

Substance Abuse

Studies of substance abuse during pregnancy are distressing. As many as 50 percent of the babies of mothers who used crack cocaine during pregnancy show evidence as they grow of learning disabilities, ADHD, and impulse problems. The data on other drug use during pregnancy is not as complete, but the pattern appears to be the same.

Recent studies show that the problem is not just with a mother who uses drugs or alcohol during pregnancy. Evidence now shows that if the father is using drugs or alcohol at the time of conception, the genetic patterns of the sperm might be affected, resulting in difficulties with the fetus and with the future baby.

Problems at Delivery

Many studies have been done to find the impact, if any, later in life of complications during delivery. The long-term impact of such factors as a long labor, the use of forceps, the position of baby, and fetal distress is unclear. There is no direct correlation.

Fetal distress noted at delivery that persists over minutes and a bilirubin level that persists above the accepted safe level are factors that seem to suggest a higher likelihood of learning disabilities later in life. However, here too there is not a direct correlation.

Factors in Childhood

The impact of malnutrition, metabolites, and toxins have been discussed. Infections such as encephalitis can result in changes in the brain, resulting in learning disabilities. Trauma can result in structural changes and academic difficulties.

Fascinating findings from brain research offer another view both of brain development and the potential for brain dysfunction. Key to much of this developmental research is that the electrical and chemical activity of the brain cells change the physical structure of the brain.

At birth a baby's brain contains one hundred billion nerve cells (neurons), roughly as many neurons as there are stars in the Milky Way. Also in place are a trillion cells that protect and nourish the neurons, called glial cells. But while the brain contains virtually all of the nerve cells it will ever have, the pattern of wiring between them has not stabilized. Researchers suggest that the brain lays out circuits that are its best guess about what's required for vision, for language, for every function. Now it is up to neural activity—no longer spontaneous, but driven by a flood of sensory experiences—to take this rough blueprint and progressively refine it.

During the first year of life, the brain undergoes a series of extraordinary changes. Starting shortly after birth, a baby's brain produces trillions more connections between neurons than it can possibly use. Then, through a process that involves competition, the brain eliminates connections or synapses that are seldom or never used. The excess synapses in a child's brain undergo a pruning, starting around the age of ten or earlier, leaving behind a mind whose patterns of emotion and thought are, for better or worse, unique.

Deprived of a stimulating environment, a child's brain suffers. Children who don't play much or are rarely touched develop brains 20 to 30 percent smaller than normal for their age. Rich and stimulating experiences result in many more synapses per neuron.

Experts now agree that a baby does not come into the world as a genetically preprogrammed automaton or a blank slate at the mercy of the environment, but arrives as something much more interesting.

Nature is the dominating factor during this phase of development, but nurture plays a vital supportive role.

To relate this research to what was discussed earlier, changes in the environment of the womb—whether caused by maternal malnutrition, drug abuse, or a viral infection—can wreck the clockwork precision of the neural assembly line. Also, the instructions programmed into the genes can affect this developmental process.

What this research makes clear is that the genes control the unfolding of the brain. However, as soon as the neurons make their connections and begin to fire, what they do begins to matter more and more. Experience becomes critical. There is a wealth of new knowledge on the importance of this experience on the developing brain. Those wires that are stimulated persist. Those wires that are not used disappear.

For example, when a baby is born, it can see and hear and smell and respond to touch, but only dimly. Over the first few months of life the brain's higher centers explode with new connections. By the age of two, a child's brain contains twice as many synapses and consumes twice as much energy as the brain of a normal adult. Experience influences this wiring process. Each time a baby experiences something (like a sound or touch or sight), tiny bursts of energy shoot through the brain, weaving neurons into integral circuits. Decreased experience or the lack of experience can result in a brain that is less developed or worse.

Where all of this research will lead us is mind-boggling. Certainly, it raises questions not only about child rearing but about the critical role of day care centers. How it might clarify issues relating to learning disabilities is not known. Early and frequent interactions and stimulation (sounds, sights, touch) significantly influence brain development. Parents and child care workers need to know this.

We do see one possible clinical problem that might best be explained by this new developmental knowledge. A higher percentage of children with language disabilities had a history of frequent ear infections over months or years of early childhood. Until treated, hearing might be impaired. Is it possible that reduced hearing during certain critical periods of early development influenced the brain's ability to develop the sites needed to distinguish the subtle differences in sound we discussed earlier, the phonemes? Might this impact on development have resulted in the language problems? We do not know the answer yet.

Other Possible Factors

Studies to date have not shown a consistent relationship between learning disabilities or ADHD and such variables as birth order, number of siblings, times the family moved, family income, mother's age, mother's educational level, or father's educational level.

It is suggested that there may be cultural factors involved. It is true that there are cultural and bilingual factors that might influence the quality of education received or the level of academic accomplishment reached. It is important to realize that these difficulties related to cultural, bilingual, or socioeconomic factors are not the result of a neurologically based processing problem. These difficulties are not a learning disability.

In Summary About Causes

We know a lot. We also know very little. We understand many possible causes of learning disabilities. We do not have a definite answer yet. Until we do, we cannot speak in terms of prevention or cure, only of hope for preventive efforts and better treatments.

Learning disabilities result from a brain that is wired differently. Once this wiring happens, we do not know how to rewire or correct the problem. Thus, at this time interventions involve "habilitation." (We cannot say "rehabilitation" because a function was not lost that has to be relearned.) Habilitation involves special education, speech-language therapy, remedial reading specialists, occupational therapy, and many other interventions to be discussed throughout this book.

ADHD does appear to be the result of a neurotransmitter deficiency in a specific area of the brain. At this time we cannot correct the nerve cells involved and cause them to produce more of this neurotransmitter. But, as will be discussed in Chapter 16, we do have medications that increase the level of this neurotransmitter in this area of the brain and that can temporarily relieve the hyperactivity, distractibility, and/or impulsivity.

Basic Concepts to Remember

As you go about seeking treatment for your child or adolescent, keep these four ideas firmly in mind. You will need them to understand everything that happens to you from now on.

1. Your child or adolescent does not have mental retardation, nor is he or she primarily displaying emotional disturbances.

2. Your child or adolescent probably has a group of difficulties often found together. The most common are learning disabilities and ADHD and the secondary emotional, social, and family problems. There are others that you will learn about in this book. Know which of these problems your son or daughter has. Each must be addressed to make progress.

3. Learning disabilities are *life disabilities*. These disabilities do not interfere just with school, they interfere with every aspect of your child's or adolescent's life—at home, with friends, in sports, in activities. You must learn to understand every aspect of your youngster's disabilities and how they affect him or her in all of these areas, as well as how they affect you and the other members of your family.

4. You must learn to build on strengths while understanding and compensating for weaknesses. If possible, try not to magnify the weaknesses.

Your child's problems may seem overwhelming. But you must keep in mind that although this condition is unfortunate, it is not the worst thing in the world. Many people can help you understand more, not only about your situation and that of your child, but about what remedies will work. You must know as much as possible about what to ask, whom to ask, and what to demand. The people you meet will help you learn more about what they can do and about what your child can do. Only you are motivated enough to push for appropriate testing and constructive remedies. Only you know your child well enough to see that he or she gets the best help you can find. When you are ready to give up, remember that you do not have this luxury. Your child cannot afford that luxury on your part.

I will try to provide you with the understanding, knowledge, and other information you will need to help your child. You must be your son's or daughter's informed consumer and assertive advocate. No one can be more concerned about or involved with your child or adolescent than you. Ready or not, the job is yours. This book will help you accomplish your goals.

4

The Specific Learning Disabilities

All of us have areas in which we readily learn. A few of us even seem to excel in limited areas with very little apparent learning—thus, the "natural" athlete, the musical "genius," the "gifted" artist. All of us also have areas in which our abilities will never be more than average and a few areas in which we cannot seem to learn anything. Children, adolescents, and adults with learning disabilities have areas of strengths and average ability too. These individuals, however, have larger areas, or different areas, of learning weakness, than most people. Each person with a learning disability displays a different pattern of strengths and weaknesses. You must learn as much as you can about the whole pattern that your child displays—the disabilities, of course, but also the abilities. What your child can do, and may indeed do well, is just as important as what she or he cannot do because it is these strengths upon which you must build.

You may have suspected a learning disability before your daughter, say, entered school. This concern became real when she failed to learn the basic skills taught in first or second grade. Depending on the types of learning disabilities, some students will do well until third or fifth or sixth grade. Only then will their disabilities interfere with academic success.

Your daughter may have read letters backward or confused certain letters or numbers. Or she may have misunderstood what you said or have been slow in developing speech or muscle coordination.

In order to help you understand learning disabilities, let me outline a simple scheme describing what the brain must do in order for learning to take place. The first step is *input*—getting information into the brain from the eyes and ears primarily but, as I will discuss later, from other senses as well. Once this information arrives, the brain needs to make sense out of it—a process called *integration*. Next, the information is stored and later retrieved—the *memory* process. Finally, the brain reacts through talking or using our muscles—*output*.

The brain does a great deal more than this, of course. Any learning task involves more than one of these processes. However, this simplified scheme will do for our purpose. It will give you a structure for understanding learning disabilities. Once again, then, the learning processes are:

Input
Integration
Memory
Output

Input Disabilities

Information arrives at the brain as impulses, transmitted along nerve cells called neurons. This information comes primarily from our eyes and from our ears. This input process takes place in the brain. It does not pertain to visual problems, such as nearsightedness or farsightedness, or to any hearing problems. This central input process of seeing or hearing or perceiving one's environment is referred to as perception. Thus, individuals who have perception disabilities in the area of visual input are labeled as having *visual perception disabilities*, and those with disabilities in the area of auditory input as having *auditory perception disabilities*. Some children have problems with one area of input; some have both kinds of perception disabilities; and some may have problems when both types of input are needed at the same time. An example would be seeing what the teacher writes on the blackboard while listening to the explanation of what is being written.

Visual Perception Disabilities

Your son may have difficulty in organizing the position and shape of what he sees. He may see letters or numbers as reversed or rotated. A *u* might look like an *n*; an *E* might look like a *W* or a *3* or an *M*; a *6* like a *9*. He may confuse similar-looking letters because of these rotations or reversals: *d*, *b*, *p*, and *q* may be confused with one another. All children show this problem until about age five and a half or six. This confusion with position or input becomes apparent when the child begins to read, write, or copy letters, numbers, or designs.

Another child might have what is called a *figure-ground* problem—that is, difficulty in focusing on the significant figure among all the other visual inputs in the background. Reading requires focusing on specific letters or groups of letters, and then tracking from left to right, line after line. Children with this disability may have reading difficulties. They skip words or lines or read the same line twice. Many life situations require figure-ground ability. For example, a child is told to pass the saltshaker but has difficulty finding it among the many dishes and platters on the table.

Judging distance is another visual perception task that can be poorly functioning. These individuals have a *depth perception* problem. Information is received from each eye and combined to create three-dimensional vision. Your child may misjudge depth, bumping into things, falling off a chair, or knocking over a drink because his hand got to the glass before he expected. What you see as carelessness may actually be just this type of perception error.

There are other types of problems associated with visual perception disabilities. These occur when several areas of perception are needed at the same time. While playing in an open field or gym, your child may become confused and disoriented because of trouble organizing his position in space. Or perhaps the child may have difficulty understanding left and right or up and down.

One very common type of visual perception disability relates to doing activities when the eyes have to tell the hands or legs what to do. This is called a *visual-motor* task. When such information is unreliable, activities like catching a ball, jumping rope, doing puzzles, or using a hammer and nail become difficult or impossible. To catch a ball, the eyes must first focus on the ball (that is, visual figure-ground). The child must then keep his eyes on the ball so that his brain can use depth perception to perceive the correct position, speed, and path of the ball and then tell the various parts of his body—legs and arms—exactly where to move and when to move. A child who has difficulty with figure-ground or who misperceives distance or speed may have difficulty catching, hitting, or throwing balls. Thus, he may not do well with sports that require such quick eye-hand coordination (baseball or basketball). For similar reasons, this child might have difficulty with jump rope, four-square, or hopscotch.

Auditory Perception Disabilities

As with visual perception, children may have difficulty with one or several aspects of auditory perception. Some may have difficulty distinguishing subtle differences in sound. Ours is a visual society; so when I mentioned subtle differences in shapes earlier, you knew I meant the twenty-six letters in the alphabet and the ten shapes in our numerical system (0–9). There are forty-four units of sound in the English language, called *phonemes*. Each letter has a sound. Vowels have two sounds, a short and a long sound. Certain combinations, like *sh, th, ch,* have specific sounds. A child with this disability may have difficulty distinguishing subtle differences in these phonemes. She might confuse words that sound alike: *blue* and *blow, ball* and *bell, can* and *can't.* I might ask her, "How are you?" and she might answer, "I'm nine." This child may have thought I said "old" instead of, or in addition to, "are."

A child may have difficulty with auditory figure-ground. For example, the child might be watching television in a room where others are playing or talking. When you call out to her from another room, you might be into your third point before the child distinguishes your voice (i.e., figure) from the other voices and sounds (i.e., background). With this disability, it seems that the child never listens or pays attention. Intuitively, you might learn early that it helps to have eye contact before speaking. You might learn to go into the room, call the child's name, and wait until you have eye contact before you begin to speak.

As another example, I recall observing Mary in her fourth-grade classroom. She had been evaluated and found to have learning disabilities, one of which was an auditory figure-ground problem. One day when I was observing her at school, she was at her desk reading a book. Other children were talking in the back of the room. There was noise of movement in the hall and the usual noise of recess through the open window. The teacher suddenly said, "Children, let's do our math. Open up your book to page thirty-eight and do problem five." Mary looked up to listen to her teacher as she heard "problem five." She looked around and saw the others take out their math book. So she did the same. She then looked over the shoulder of her friend to see on which page she could find problem five. Mary thought she was being a good student. At that moment her teacher shouted, "Mary, stop bothering Jan and get to work." The teacher then looked at me sitting in the back of the room and said, "See what I mean. She never pays attention." Mary was confused and hurt because she did not know what she had done wrong. (How many times has your child done something to upset you and then said in all sincerity, "I didn't do anything.") This was the only brain she had ever had, and she did not know that it was different. She only knew that she was trying hard and suddenly the teacher was angry with her. The teacher was frustrated with Mary because she did not yet know of Mary's disabilities. Later, I explained the problem to the teacher and suggested how she could use Mary's strength (visual figure-ground) to compensate for her weakness (auditory figure-ground). When the teacher wanted to give the class instructions, she would first say, "Class, may I have your attention." (She did not want to embarrass Mary by calling out only her name.) She watched until Mary was looking at her. Then she gave the instructions. She was building on Mary's strengths to compensate for her weaknesses. This approach is called accommodation.

Some children cannot process sound inputs as fast as other people can. Most special education professionals call this problem an *auditory* lag. Speech-language therapists might call this problem an *auditory processing* problem or a *receptive language* problem. It is as if these children have to concentrate on what they are hearing for a fraction of a second longer before they understand it. Then they refocus on what is being said. Only by now they have missed a word or phrase. Soon they cannot keep up and become lost. For example, a teacher might explain something in class. A child misses parts of what was said and is confused. She asks a question. The teacher becomes annoyed and says, "I just explained that. Why don't you pay attention?"

Sensory Integration Disorder

How does the brain know how to orchestrate muscle activities? For example, when a person is tying a shoe or writing on a page or hopping, how does the brain know exactly which muscles or joints to use in what way in the proper sequence? We call this ability motor planning, as different from muscle strength. There are four basic sensory inputs needed to provide the brain with the information needed. If these sensory inputs are not performing correctly or the brain has difficulty integrating these inputs, the individual has a *sensory integration disorder*. These four inputs are:

Visual perception
Tactile perception
Proprioceptive perception
Vestibular perception

Visual perception was already discussed.

TACTILE PERCEPTION.   There are nerve endings in our skin that relay information about touch. Some are near the surface and respond to light touch, and others are deeper and respond to deep touch or pressure. Some children misperceive messages from these nerve endings and have a *tactile perception* disability. They are tactilely defensive. Such a person is sensitive to touch and may perceive it as uncomfortable or even painful. From early childhood he will not like being touched or held. The tighter you cuddle, the more the child cries. This is frustrating to the parent and to the infant. Later, this child may complain of the tag on the back of a shirt, only like to wear soft and loose clothes, say the elastic in his underwear or belt is too tight. This child might wear socks inside out, complaining that the seam bothers him or might prefer to keep shoes off. He sits in class but is fidgety, rearranging clothes, moving tags, or taking shoes off. The scalp is very rich in these nerve endings. This child might cry and be upset when you wash, brush, cut, or comb his hair. Children with tactile perception disability seem crazy, and their behaviors are hard to understand until the reason behind them is explained.

Parents learn early that they cannot grab, hold, or touch their child without warning. If the child volunteers to climb into your lap, it is all right. If you want to touch the child, however, you have to announce what you will do and come toward his face so that he can prepare. If you come up from behind and touch him, the child might jump away. You might have learned that such children prefer deep touch. You squeeze hard and rub deep when you hold your child.

Some children with tactile sensitivity feel defensive and try to avoid people getting too close. They walk around the edges of groups, don't like to sit with the class during circle time, lag at the back of lines. This child might be walking down the hall when another child accidently brushes against him, and respond as if the touch were a major blow and hit the other child.

Some children with tactile defensiveness feel deprived of touch. Thus, they might seek touch when they are in control. They might go around the room hugging or touching other children. This is not to say that all young children who do this have sensory integration disorder, but such a possibility must be kept in mind, especially when the other behaviors associated with this disorder are noted.

PROPRIOCEPTIVE PERCEPTION.   There are nerve endings in our muscle fibers, ligaments, and joints that tell us which muscle groups are relaxed or contracted and which parts of which joints are bent or extended. These proprioceptive nerve endings inform the brain of muscle tone, muscle and body movement, and body position. These inputs help the individual to adapt to his or her environment and to hold the body upright. This information also helps the brain orchestrate complex motor planning activities such as writing. If your daughter is having difficulty with this sensory input, she may be confused with her body in space and may have difficulty with muscle tone and maintaining posture. She will have difficulty changing her body in order to keep from losing balance. She might have difficulty with motor planning involving groups of large muscles (gross motor activities) such as running, jumping, hopping, climbing, or with motor planning involving groups of small muscles (fine motor activities) such as buttoning, zipping, tying, or writing.

Some children with this disability feel deprived of proprioceptive input. They might seek such input by jumping or stomping feet, or bumping into the wall.

VESTIBULAR PERCEPTION.   There is an organ system in each inner ear called the semicircular canals. The nerve endings in these systems inform the brain of head position, thus body position in space. This information is essential for handling the impact of gravity and maintaining the correct position in space. It allows you to stand on one leg and maintain balance or to ride a two-wheeled bicycle and maintain balance. If your son has a *vestibular perception* disability, he will have difficulty with body position in space. These problems may result in difficulty climbing on a jungle gym or riding a two-wheeled bike. He may become anxious or uncomfortable with sudden changes in body position. It is this system that helps the brain maintain the necessary tone to maintain body posture against gravity. Thus, some children with this disability have weak upper back muscles and prefer to rest their head on the desk or to lie down from time to time.

Some children with this problem feel deprived of vestibular stimulation. They might try to create such stimulation by spinning in a chair or swinging in a swing. Some may sit or stand and rock their body forward and back.

THE INTEGRATED SYSTEM.   Sensory integration disorder refers to individuals who have combinations of the above-described problems. The gross and fine motor planning problems may be most obvious. The other problems are more difficult to observe unless you know to look for them. An occupational therapist can evaluate this individual, clarify the problems, and provide the essential therapeutic interventions.

Other Sensory Inputs

Children and adolescents with learning disabilities might show difficulty with other sensory inputs. There is no research yet to validate this possibility, but the clinical observations are there.

Some seem very sensitive to taste. Food tastes different or funny to them. They are picky eaters and complain about foods most people like. Others may be sensitive to *smell*. They complain of smells you do not pick up. They avoid a certain area because "it smells funny."

Some children seem not to be as sensitive to *temperature* as others. They go outside in the middle of a cold winter without a coat and seem to be fine. Some may be less sensitive to *pain*. They hurt themselves and appear not to notice.

Children with these sensory sensitivities were not put on this earth to drive you crazy. Their problems are real and must be understood and accepted.

Integration Disabilities

Once information coming into the brain is registered, it has to be understood. This is a complex process. Let me try to explain it before I go into the specific integration disabilities. To do this, let me ask you to do something for me. I want you to print the following three symbols in your brain:

d o g

No problem with visual perception; so it is correctly printed in your brain. There are at least three things you would have to do to make sense out of, that is to integrate, these three symbols. First, you would have to place the symbols in the right order, or sequence the inputs. Is it

d-o-g or **g-o-d** or **o-g-d**

or what? Second, you have to infer meaning for the word from the context in which it is used. For example, "the dog" and "you dog" have very different meanings. In one case you are identifying a pet, and in the other case you are insulting someone. Thus, you have to abstract meanings from these words. Finally, you have to take this word now that it is recorded properly and you know what it means, as well as all the other words that are pouring into your head plus the many memory tracks being stimulated by these words and pull them all together or organize them in a way that can be understood.

The process of integrating inputs or of understanding what your brain has recorded, thus requires three steps:

Sequencing
Abstraction
Organization

Your child might have a disability in one area or more. For example, since inputs are processed through both the visual and the auditory pathways, some children might have a visual sequencing disability or an auditory sequencing disability. So, too, the other integrative tasks might involve one input mode and not the other.

Sequencing Disabilities

A child with such a disability might hear or read a story; but in recounting it, she may start in the middle, go to the beginning, and then shift to the end. Eventually, the whole story comes out, but the sequence of events is wrong. Or a child might see the math problem as

$$16 - 3 = ?$$

on the blackboard but write it on the paper as

$$61 - 3 = ?$$

Or, a child might see

$$2 + 3 = ?$$

and write

$$2 + 5 = 3$$

The child knows the right answer but gets the sequence wrong. She knows the math concepts but makes careless errors in calculation. Spelling words with all of the right letters but in the wrong order can also reflect this disability.

A child might memorize a sequence—the days of the week or the months of the year or the times table—and then be unable to use the sequence. He can recite the months of the year; however, if asked what comes after August, the child pauses before answering, "September." When asked about the pause, the child describes going back to January and moving forward to get the answer. Using the dictionary can be very frustrating. The child has to recite the alphabet each time to know if finding the next letter means going up or down the column.

A child with a sequence disability might hit the baseball and then run to third base rather than to first or might have difficulty with board games that require moving in a particular sequence. When setting the dinner table, he or she might have difficulty remembering where to properly place each item. The child may also have difficulty with the sequence of dressing. Parents walking into the child's bedroom in the morning do not know whether to laugh, cry, or bite their tongue. The child may have his pants on but is holding his underpants. Or she might have her blouse on and be holding her undershirt.

Abstraction Disabilities

Once information is recorded in the brain and placed in the right sequence, one must be able to infer meaning. If children with learning disabilities have abstraction difficulties, they usually have a mild form. Abstraction is such a basic intellectual task that if the disability were too great, the child might be functioning below normal level.

Some children do have problems with abstraction. For example, the teacher might be doing a language arts exercise with the class. The teacher reads a story about a police officer and then begins a discussion of police officers in general. The children are asked if they know any men or women who are police offices in their neighborhoods, and, if so, what do they do? A child with an abstraction disability may not be able to answer such a question. She or he could talk only about the particular officer in the story and would not be able to generalize to all law officers.

I remember observing in a regular classroom. The teacher was working with four children at one table. The rest of the class were at their seats doing independent work. I was observing a child who had an abstraction disability working with the teacher. Two children in the back of the room began to whisper to each other. The teacher looked up and said, "Class, will you please be quiet." The child with the abstraction difficulty looked up, seemed annoyed, and complained, "I was not talking." The teacher agreed and explained that she knew he was not talking but that she was referring to the class in general. He became more upset. He had taken her statement literally. If the class was talking and he was part of the class, she meant that he was talking. And he was not talking. He continued to protest about being accused of doing something he did not do.

Older children, adolescents, or adults with abstraction problems may not understand jokes, either. They do not know what is so funny and when to laugh. They may be confused by puns or idioms. They seem to take things literally and to misunderstand what is said.

Organization Disabilities

If your daughter has difficulties with organization, you will not need a formal evaluation to know. Look at her notebook and papers, locker, desk, or bedroom. She is "disorganized" in all aspects of life. The notebook will be a mess with papers in the wrong place or shoved in or falling out. She will lose things like books or coats or pencils or forget things. Homework gets done, but somehow it gets lost or forgotten and is not turned in. The child's bedroom is a disaster no matter how many times you have cleaned it or told your child to keep it clean. This person might have difficulty organizing time and planning. She has difficulty planning the time needed to do homework or planning ahead to be on time.

This student never seems to bring home what she will need to do for homework. The teacher might use an assignment sheet, but it

does not help this child. There is chaos in the morning as your daughter tries to get everything together to take to school.

Information, once recorded, sequenced, and understood, must be integrated with a constant flow of information and must be related to previously learned information. We find some students who have difficulty breaking a whole concept down into its parts and other students who have difficulty pulling pieces of information into a whole concept. As an example of the difficulty of going from the whole to parts, consider a child who reads a book. He can discuss the book in general, giving good information. However, then he might have difficulty answering specific, detailed questions from the book. On the other hand, a child who has difficulty going from parts to the whole might read this book and provide great detail about everything that happened in the story. However, when she is asked what the theme of the book was or who the lead character was, she might not know. Students who have no difficulty going from the whole concept to parts often do well with essay examinations. Students who have difficulty taking pieces of information and recalling the whole concept may have difficulty with multiple choice examinations. (Witness the student who does very well in high school, writing beautiful papers and essays, who then bombs on the Scholastic Aptitude Test. The SAT is multiple choice.)

Some individuals have difficulty organizing their thoughts before speaking and seem to ramble. Others have difficulty organizing their thoughts to put on paper. They explain what they want to write in great detail and then write a confusing paper with all the facts included but in the wrong order or disconnected.

Memory Disabilities

Once information is received, recorded in the brain, and integrated, it must be stored and later retrieved. This storage and retrieval process is called *memory*. There are two types of memory—short-term memory and long-term memory.

Short-term memory is the process by which you store and hold information by the method of concentration and repetition. The information is available while it is being attended to but might be lost once this attention is removed. For example, when you call the infor-

PEANUTS reprinted by permission of United Feature Syndicate, Inc.

mation operator for a long-distance telephone number with the area code, you get a ten-digit number. Most people can retain these numbers long enough to dial the number if they dial right away and nothing interrupts their attention. However, if someone starts to talk to them in the course of dialing, they might forget the numbers. Similarly, a person might go to the store with five items in mind to buy. No list is needed. But by the time the shopper gets to the store, so many different impressions may have intervened that he or she has forgotten some of the items. Remember in high school or college when you studied for an examination by "cramming"? You shoved all of the facts into your head by reviewing over and over. You studied up till the minute the exam started. You probably did well. Then, weeks later, you started to study for your final. You looked at your notes and reacted as if you had never seen them before. This is short-term memory.

Long-term memory refers to the process by which you store information that you have often repeated. You can retrieve this information quickly by thinking of it. For example, you can come up with your current home address and telephone number quite readily by thinking about them.

If your child or adolescent has a memory disability, it is most likely a short-term one. Like abstraction disabilities, long-term memory disabilities interfere so much with intellectual functioning that a child who has such a disability is more likely to be functioning below normal.

It may take ten to fifteen repetitions throughout several days for a child with a short-term memory problem to retain what the average child might retain after three to five repetitions on one occasion. Yet, this same child might have no problem with long-term memory. He or she will surprise you at times by remembering in great detail things that happened years ago that you have forgotten.

A short-term memory disability can occur with information learned through what one sees, *visual short-term memory disability,* or with information learned through what one hears, *auditory short-term memory disability.* Some may have one form of the disability; others may have both.

Your child might read through a spelling list one evening and really seem to know the words (because she is concentrating on them). The next day she has lost most or all of the words. Similarly, a teacher might review a math concept in class until your child understands and remembers it (because she is concentrating on it). Yet, when it is time to do the math homework that night, she has forgotten how to do the problems. If a parent does the first problem, bringing the memory back, the child can then do the rest. Likewise, this student might read a page and remember it, read the next page and remember it, and the next and the next page. Then, the child gets to the end of the chapter and does not remember what she read.

If your daughter has this disability, you learned the hard way that you cannot give more than one instruction at a time. If you say "Go upstairs, wash up, get into your pajamas, then come on down again for a snack," forget it. She will not remember that many instructions at once.

Or your son might make you angry by constantly stopping in the middle of telling you something and saying "Oh, forget it" or "It's not important." If so, it is possible that he has a short-term memory disability. He starts to speak, knowing what he wants to say. However, partway through, he forgets the flow of ideas. It is embarrassing to say, "I'm sorry. What was I saying?" It is easier for him to say "Oh, forget it."

Output Disabilities

The brain communicates information either by means of words (language output) or though muscle activity such as writing, drawing, gesturing (motor output). An individual with a learning disability might have a *language disability* or a *motor disability.*

Language Disability

For our discussion, let's focus on two types of language used in communication—spontaneous language and demand language. You use spontaneous language in situations where you initiate whatever is said. Here you have the luxury of picking the subject and taking some time to organize your thoughts and to find the correct words before you say anything. In a demand language situation, someone else sets up a circumstance by asking you a question or for a comment. You then must respond quickly. Now you do not have as much time to organize your thoughts or to find the right words. You have only a split second in which you must simultaneously organize, find words, and answer more or less appropriately.

Children with a language disability usually have no difficulty with spontaneous language. They do, however, often have problems with demand language. Special education professionals usually call this a demand language disability. Speech-language therapists call this problem an expressive language disability. This inconsistency in speech ability can be striking and confusing. A youngster or adult may initiate all sorts of conversations, may never keep quiet, in fact, and may sound quite normal. But, put into a situation that demands a response (e.g., "What did you do today?" or "What is the answer?"), the same person might answer "Huh?" or "What?" or "I don't know." Or she or he might ask you to repeat the question to gain time, or may not answer at all, appearing not to be paying attention. If the child is forced to answer, his or her response may be so confusing or circumstantial that it is difficult to follow. She or he may sound totally unlike the person who was speaking so fluently just a minute ago. This confusion in language behavior often puzzles parents and teachers. A teacher might put a child down as lazy or negative because the child speaks all of the time in class; however, if called on to answer a question, the child often will say "I don't know."

Motor Disabilities

We discussed motor output problems earlier in another context. Let me review again. The individual with a learning disability might have difficulty coordinating groups of large muscles (arms, legs, trunk); this is called a *gross motor disability*. Or the person might have diffi-

culty coordinating groups of small muscles (e.g., hands); this is called a *fine motor disability*.

Gross motor disabilities may cause your child to be clumsy, to stumble, to fall, to bump into things, or to have trouble with generalized physical activities such as running, climbing, jumping, or riding a bike.

The most common form of a fine motor disability shows up when the child begins to write. The problem lies in an inability to get the many muscles in the dominant hand to work together as a team. Her handwriting is poor. The child awkwardly holds a pen or pencil and writes slowly; thus, her hand gets tired. She seems not to be able to get her hand to write as fast as her head is thinking.

Watch your dominant hand as you write something. Notice the many detailed fine muscle activities that it takes to write legibly. Writing requires a constant flow of such activities. Now place your pen in your nondominant hand and try to write. You suddenly have a writing disability. If you go very slowly, writing is tedious but your handwriting is legible. But how frustrating it is for your mind to be so far ahead of what you are writing! If you go at a regular pace, however, your hand aches and your handwriting immediately deteriorates. Shape, size, spacing, and positioning—everything about the handwriting looks awful no matter how hard you try.

A child with a fine motor disability goes through this all of the time. How many times have you said to your child, "If you take your time, your handwriting will be better. When you rush it becomes too sloppy." How did it feel for you when you slowed down to compensate?

Some may have this fine motor problem only with writing. Usually, however, the child has a broader problem called a written language disability. In addition to the problems with the mechanical aspects of writing, he has difficulty getting his thoughts out of the brain and onto the paper. He may have difficulty with spelling, grammar, punctuation, or capitalization. The child seems to know more than he writes about. Often, the child can edit and correct his own errors once written. The difficulty is in the outflow of information. The same child who gets 100 on spelling tests may misspell the same words or simpler words when writing.

A written language disability is very frustrating and can be very serious. Most schools do not grade you on what you know but on what you put down on a piece of paper. If you cannot copy from the board fast enough, take notes when the teacher is talking, or write in class, you have a problem. Of necessity, homework requires writing. Maybe this is why your child or adolescent resists doing homework. Think of copying from the board. First, you have to look at the word (visual perception). Then, you have to retain the word while you look down to write (visual short-term memory). Finally, you have to copy the word on the paper (fine motor). Children with disabilities in these areas may have to copy one word or letter at a time, never finishing the work.

Establishing Your Child's Profile

The learning process is much more complex, but this simple input-integration-memory-output model for describing learning disabilities should be more than adequate to help you understand the many problem areas. When you read professional reports or sit in on conferences, these are the terms you'll hear used.

The important thing is that you must know your son's or daughter's specific profile. Each child, adolescent, or adult with a learning disability will have a different combination of disabilities and abilities. You must know your own son's or daughter's areas of learning disabilities and abilities.

Look at the checklist of learning disabilities below. Do you know where your child's disabilities lie? Where are his or her strengths? You must know this information in order to learn how to build on strengths rather than magnify weaknesses when selecting chores, activities, sports, or camps. You must know this information and how to best help your child with his or her homework. If you cannot complete your child's profile, ask the special education member of the school team to help. Or ask the individual who did the testing to help you translate the results into this type of information.

Learning Disabilities

INPUT

Visual perception
Auditory perception
Sensory integration

INTEGRATION

Sequencing
  Auditory
  Visual
Abstraction
  Auditory
  Visual
Organization
  Auditory
  Visual

MEMORY

Auditory short-term memory
Visual short-term memory

OUTPUT

Demand language
Motor
  Gross motor
  Fine motor

In Chapter 3, I noted that for about 50 percent of children and adolescents with learning disabilities, such disabilities appear in a familial pattern—that is, the problems are inherited. This means that there is about a 50 percent possibility that one parent also will have a learning disability. As you learn about your child, you might say, "That's me." This may be the first time in your life that you understand why you have had so much difficulty in school or in life. If so, learn about yourself. The new knowledge will be valuable. It may help you rethink your past and some of the experiences you have had. This knowledge may be needed when help for your son or daughter is discussed. As one mother once told me, "You keep telling me that I have to help my son be more organized with his work. But, I have not been organized one day of my life. How can I help him when I have the same problem?"

Learning Disabilities and the School Curriculum

It is helpful to understand the general progression of the curriculum through school. This overview might explain why some students begin to have difficulty in the first grade, others in the third or sixth or ninth. Although each school system establishes its own curriculum for each grade, there is a similar theme for all.

In first grade, children are taught the basic skills. In reading it is phonological awareness: that is, the ability to attach the correct sound to each symbol and then to blend these individual sounds into a word. (The teacher assumes that between prekindergarten and kindergarten, you will have learned the graphic symbols—*A* through *Z* and *1* through *9* plus *0*.) In writing, the basic skill is learning to print each letter of the alphabet, first in lowercase and later in uppercase. In math, it is learning the basic concepts of numbers: first, that we use a base 10 system in math; second, that numbers can neither be created nor made to disappear (called the "conservation of numbers"). These concepts lead to addition and subtraction.

Second grade is usually used to consolidate the skills taught in first. Basically, no new skills are taught. Thus, if you are not fully at grade level at the end of first, your teacher might use second grade to improve these skills.

Third grade is very important because a major leap is made. The first weeks are spent in review. Then, the teacher assumes that you know your basic skills. Thus, the focus shifts to using these skills. The issue is no longer Can you read? but What have you read? You read a book and explain what you read. It is no longer Can you write? but What have you written? You write journals and book reports. Spelling, grammar, punctuation, and style of writing become important topics. The teacher assumes that you know the conservation of numbers. Multiplication and division are introduced. Thus, if you enter third grade without solid basic skills, you will start to struggle by November, following the review period. The year will become more and more difficult.

Fourth and fifth grades are spent expanding on the use of skills. Gradually, having or learning the skills is not the issue. These abilities are used to study subject matter—history, science, geography, etc. If the abilities needed in third grade are not solid, fourth and fifth will be difficult.

Sixth, seventh, and eighth grades—middle school—focus on subject content. Teachers assume that you have both the skills and the ability to use these skills. If you are weak in one or more of these skills, you will struggle. In general, the subjects are taught in a structured way, with a focus on teaching learning strategies and study skills. Because each student now has five to seven teachers and subjects, if you have problems with organization, you may have difficulty managing the classes and assignments.

In high school the focus continues to be on topic areas. Your teachers present the material with the assumption that you know good learning strategies and study skills. Thus, if you have organization or executive functioning disabilities, you may struggle.

We can see that students who have learning disabilities that interfere with mastery of basic skills may begin to have difficulty in first and second grade. Students who have the ability to learn the basic skills may have areas of disability that interfere more with reading comprehension, written language, or higher math concepts. They will struggle in third. Students with learning disabilities that primarily interfere with organizational skills might not struggle until middle school. And students with difficulties in the executive functioning areas might do well until high school.

In Summary

Each individual will have his or her specific profile of learning disabilities and learning abilities. This chapter provides you with the knowledge and vocabulary to understand your son's or daughter's learning disabilities. It is essential that parents fully understand the areas of disability and the areas of ability. As will be discussed in more detail in Chapter 15, you must learn to build on the strengths while minimizing the impact of the weaknesses.

5

Learning Disabilities
Are Life Disabilities

As you read the previous chapter on the specific learning disabilities, the impact of these disabilities on class participation, mastering academic skills, and learning successful study skills may have become apparent to you. Learning disabilities definitely are school disabilities. However, it is equally critical for parents and for other adults who work with these children and adolescents to understand that learning disabilities are life disabilities. The same disabilities that interfere with reading, writing, and arithmetic also will interfere with sports and other activities, with family life, and with getting along with friends.

The special education professional must know your son's or daughter's areas of learning ability and disability in order to develop the necessary educational program. You also must know your son's or daughter's areas of learning ability and disability to know in what sports or activities he or she is most likely to succeed, what chores to assign, what camps to select, and what decisions to make in countless other crucial daily situations. Knowing these strengths and weaknesses, you can use this understanding to maximize your child's growth and success and to minimize frustration and failure within the family and in the outside world.

One other reality about learning disabilities: Once the wiring is laid down differently, it does not correct itself. Learning disabilities are lifetime disabilities. The child with a learning disability will become the adolescent with a learning disability, will become the adult with a learning disability, and will become the senior citizen with a learning disability. The disability does not go away. At each stage of life, the disability presents a new type of demand.

Let me use the same input-integration-memory-output model to illustrate what I mean. My purpose is to sensitize you to this reality so that you can understand your child's experience of life.

Input Disabilities

A child or adolescent with visual perception difficulties may have problems with sports that require quick eye-hand coordination, such as catching, throwing, or hitting a ball. The ball could be a baseball, basketball, volleyball, or football. In order to have this eye-hand co-ordination, the first task is to look in the right direction and to spot the ball. This activity requires visual figure-ground skills. If the child has a disability in this area, she may not spot the ball and will stand there as the ball hits her or hits the ground. The second task is to keep one's eye on the ball. This enables the brain to use depth perception to track the ball and to inform the body, legs, arms, and hands where to be at the right time to catch the ball. Individuals with visual per-ception problems might play these sports poorly and, thus, avoid them. They might intuitively have learned that they do best in sports that do not need, or that require only minimal, eye-hand coordina-tion (e.g., swimming, soccer, certain track and field events, horseback riding).

What about jump rope? First, the child must spot where the rope hits the ground (visual figure-ground). Then, he must focus on this spot while running toward the rope so that his brain can use depth perception to inform the body when and where to jump. You can see the potential problems with four-square, hopscotch, and other activities.

Individuals with depth perception problems may fall off their seat, bump into things, or misjudge the distance to a drink and knock over the glass. They may be confused by large, open spaces such as gyms, parking lots, and shopping malls.

A child or adolescent with an auditory perception problem might misunderstand what adults or friends say and thus respond incor-

PEANUTS reprinted by permission of United Feature Syndicate, Inc.

rectly. This child may have difficulty knowing what sounds to listen to when there are competing sounds. Such a child might miss what is being said to her by parents or friends because she was listening to one sound (maybe the television or stereo) and did not realize that another sound had started (a friend talking to her). If the child has a delay in processing speech (auditory lag), she may appear not to be listening or to be staring into space. This is the individual who is often called an "airhead" or a "space cadet."

Remember that auditory processing problems can create problems with sports as well. The coach is yelling instructions, and this child is not paying attention or not understanding what is being said.

Integration Disabilities

Individuals with sequencing problems may confuse the steps involved in playing a game, might hit the baseball and run to the wrong base, or might have difficulty getting into uniform. Imagine a basketball coach explaining a practice drill to a child who cannot remember the sequence of tasks involved.

Much humor is based on subtle changes in the meanings of words or phrases. An individual with abstraction problems may miss the meaning of jokes and be out of place with friends. In a crowd, there is no problem. When everyone else laughs, it is time to laugh. However, in a one-to-one situation, the joke teller might get angry because the listener did not laugh. Puns and slang expressions cause problems as well. Some individuals with abstraction problems appear to be supersensitive or paranoid because they take everything literally.

Organizational problems often create family conflicts. Not only is the bedroom disorganized, but things may be left around the house. The child doesn't bring the necessary books and papers home from school; the right work never gets back to school. Coats are left or lost. Friends, too, become annoyed because this child never remembers what or where to do things.

Some children and adolescents are so disorganized that they cannot do their homework unless someone is there with them, helping to structure and organize the work. Parents may get angry with this child, thinking that he or she is too dependent on them and will not work unless they work with him or her. Teachers may complain that the parent is doing too much; yet this parent knows that without this help, the child gets little done.

Memory Disabilities

Children and adolescents with short-term memory disabilities can have problems communicating and in social interactions. They may meet someone they know but forget the person's name. You give a series of instructions, and your child follows only one or two. A friend calls up annoyed, telling your child, "I thought you promised to meet me after school and walk home with me."

An activities director or sports coach may give your child a series of instructions, and he or she can't remember all of them. Remember that drill most coaches use in basketball: The coach says, "I want you to form two lines, line A and line B. Now, the first person in line A dribble up and shoot the ball. The first person in line B retrieve the ball and bounce pass it to the next person in line A. Then, each of you get into the back of the other line. Now start." The player with an auditory short-term memory problem will be confused or in the wrong place and the coach will yell.

Output Disabilities

The inability to write quickly and legibly or to spell can be a problem in playing certain games, performing some activities, taking telephone messages, or writing a note to a friend. People laugh at your child's mistakes or assume he or she isn't smart.

Motor coordination difficulties can cause problems with buttoning, tying, zipping, playing certain games, cutting up food, even getting food into the mouth rather than on the face. The child looks and acts differently in so many life tasks.

Expressive language problems make communications with family and friends difficult. Individuals may have problems with small talk or with interacting in a conversation. Often, they appear to be shy and avoid talking or being with people for fear of saying the wrong thing and appearing foolish.

Learning Disabilities *Are* Life Disabilities

Unless parents and other important people in the individual's life understand the disabilities, everyone experiences frustration. Your child cannot do certain things well and gets rejected, yelled at, punished, or all of the above. He hears, "If you just tried harder, you could play baseball as well as the other kids" or "If you would only practice more, you wouldn't make so many mistakes" or "How could you have forgotten to tell me that you were supposed to be at your friend's house a half an hour ago?"

Parents become angry and feel frustrated as well, saying "No matter how many times I tell him to do something, he doesn't listen" or "Your room is a mess again. You cannot go out until you straighten it up" or "Why don't you look where you are going" or "You are such a mess. Why don't you look at what you are doing so you won't be such a disaster walking around the house."

Success in sports is essential for peer acceptance as a child. Clumsiness and poor eye-hand coordination can be painful to the child and can be lead to peer rejections. What does it feel like to be this child or adolescent? Let me have Jill explain. She wrote this essay and sent it to me shortly after starting college at a school with a special education program. We had worked together since late elementary school, and she understood her learning disabilities. It was this knowledge of herself that helped her describe her life. I present her letter to me exactly as it was written.

I think that when I was born I was put in a rocket ship and taken to another planet—earth. I never felt that I was like anyone else here. From the time I was five, I can recall feeling like an outsider. I first remember feeling like an alien when I tried to communicate. People would raise their eyebrows and make other facial expressions of confusion when I tried to express myself. I was aware of starting a sentence in my head but only the last half came out of my mouth. I know how E.T. must have felt. It was like I was speaking another language and thinking on another wavelength. Constant rejection created feelings of isolation and isolation created anger and anger created self-defeat. I could not judge time and was anxious about being late. I never got a joke (no matter how simple) because it was abstract, and I could never get myself or my work in order because of my sequencing problems. Printing was murder because of my perceptual problems and my spacing was the worst. I could never remember anything but the first part of a direction and the noise level of the then popular "open classroom" drove me crazy. I always wondered how everyone got everything the leader said but me. Definitely wrong planet!

I found one accepting person to be friends with and stuck to her like glue. Most of my anger at my environment and my inability to control it or even to make sense out of it was directed at my parents and my brother because I knew they couldn't leave me like the others, no matter what I did. Once I kicked a hole in the wall because I couldn't find my shoes and that proved how dumb I really was. Only a moron could lose their shoes—I wanted to kick myself but was at least smart enough to choose the wall instead. It was so hard getting through everyday life; things that other people automatically did required constant thought and concern for me. To protect myself, I build a wall around myself.

I could only handle myself and my needs. No one else mattered, not my family or friends. My family was angry at my self-centered ways. I was the black sheep—the alien—the different one. I never understood why everyone was so angry at me. Why didn't they understand that I was just surviving? My daydreams were of me in a rough and choppy ocean where a storm was raging. I was all alone in the middle of a great black sea. It took all of my strength just to stay above the water. I had no energy left to call for help or even notice if anyone else was around. That's how my life was. I had to be self-centered to survive.

School was no haven. The teachers said I was unmotivated and not paying attention. Some even yelled at me and physically shook me. One teacher who really thought she understood learning disabilities would say, "Does everyone understand?" And then she turned to me, as the class followed her gaze, and said, "And do you, Jill?" I suddenly felt my antennae's sprouting from my head. Everyone knew I was different when I was taken from the room for tutoring and later I had to lie about special teachers and the "resource room" (a place for the "slower kids"). In school, it's every teenager's nightmare to be different. By high school my conversations had improved to the point were I was accepted as an "airhead" but I still had to keep my secret "help room" a secret. With careful planning I could sneak into the resource room just as the bell rang and everyone was out of the halls. Talk about being different—when someone asked who my English teacher was, no one knew her because only "SPEDS" (Special Education students) had her and normal kids didn't know she existed.

High school was a turning point. I started noticing things. Dr. Silver, a psychiatrist, who really understands how to explain learning disabilities, made me aware of ways to compensate for my shortcomings. I began to read people from their faces and body language. If their faces looked confused, I would say, "Did I say something wrong?" Or, I would make a joke. Sometimes I would just start over. Dr. Silver showed me how to use little tricks to get around my disabilities like leaning forward to concentrate on a professor's lecture and this also helped force out disturbing background noises. Dr. Silver explained that with my auditory discrimination problems, bars with large crowds would become very difficult social meeting places for me. I feel like I'm there, people are there, music is there but I'm in a plastic bubble separated from everything. All of the noises, the conversation, the band, the glasses clinking—all are amplified and blended together like a senseless drone. I can't hear anyone's conversation because I only hear parts of what they say and none of it makes sense. I try to fill in the missing parts but my answers must be off the wall from the reactions I get. I keep thinking in the middle of everyone having fun, "Scotty, beam me up. Get me out of here!"

At college, there is a wonderful learning disability program, the term L.D. has come to mean learning desirable to me. I have found my planet! People like me do exist and they aren't crazy. We even joke about being L.D. Its like a private club and its not unpopular. At dinner, if someone forgets their silverware there is a chorus of "L.D., L.D., L.D." and a knowing smile of acceptance. Once, four of us got lost driving to a dance and my friend, the driver said, "Oh, no! Four L.D.s and no one has a pencil." She quickly assigned one part of the directions to each of us. "You remember the first part, you the second, and you the third." We all laughed at ourselves. At this college I cannot use L.D. as an excuse. I found that in real life no one really cares if I'm L.D. They only care if I don't try. Its results that count, not excuses. I really wanted to be a radio d.j., but I knew that with my disabilities it would be impossible. How could I "cue" records, answer phone requests and check scripts all at the same time. But, guess what? The girl voted "Biggest Airhead—Class of 1984" just got her F.M. license. Everyone from professors to students had quizzed me whenever they saw me. No one let me quit.

Life is still not a breeze. My friends, who say they understand, still get mad when I say I can't listen to the radio, talk, and hear directions at the same time. They still can't believe it when I go left when they say right. Actually, I have more trouble understanding why I do the exact opposite, but I know I'm not dumb or an airhead. That's how my brain works or doesn't work. That's me. I'm not different. I'm special! No one is more sensitive to others than I am. I am my own friend and I have recently begun to feel better about myself and to like myself. I am having success. I will be an L.D. forever. It will never go away, but each day I learn to handle another thing or work something out and things get better for me. How many people can say that?

As Jill so beautifully teaches us, *learning disabilities are life disabilities.* The work never stops.

Learning Disabilities *Are* Lifetime Disabilities

As discussed earlier, the child with a learning disability will become the adolescent with a learning disability, will become the adult with a learning disability. Our goal is to help the individual address the needs at each phase of development and to provide the self-knowledge and advocacy skills to address the next phase of development.

Again, I would like to use an example from my clinical work to illustrate the lifetime aspect of learning disabilities. I first met Lynn when she was at the end of her tenth grade. As of this writing, she is thirty-four. I have known her for the past eighteen years. As I tell her story to date, please understand that she solved most of her problems on her own. I only saw her when there was a crisis that she could not resolve on her own. Often, a session or two with me would give her the clarity and direction it took to solve a developmental crisis, allowing her to move on.

I first saw Lynn at the end of her sophomore year of high school because she was depressed and abusive to her sisters. She did make the family dysfunctional because of her temper and explosions at her two sisters. I also learned that she had done poorly in school since second or third grade. Her parents were told by teachers during third grade that Lynn might not be as bright as her sisters. Thus, her parents shouldn't expect as much from her. By high school, her grades were very low. She was often yelled at or punished for her grades and not infrequently "grounded" for whole marking periods until her grades got better. Lynn was very social and popular. She enjoyed her friends and relied on them for support and help. To take away her social life was to take away her one positive part of life.

By the end of the tenth grade she was discouraged and felt defeated by school. She felt that she was a failure to her parents and an embarrassment to her family. Her rage at her sisters was because they were so smart and successful and she was not. During my early meetings with Lynn we discussed school. She told me she hated to read and didn't understand what she read. Her handwriting was poor as were her spelling, grammar, punctuation, and capitalization. Her math skills were limited and not at the level needed to do high school math. She was disorganized with her materials, tasks, thoughts, and writing. Yet she had an excellent vocabulary and discussed school and her problems with great awareness and ability to communicate.

Because I suspected Lynn had a learning disability, formal testing was done. She was found to be very bright (verbal IQ of 132) but with significant learning disabilities. All of her school problems now made sense. Lynn was relieved and motivated to accept help. Her parents were less comfortable with the findings. They had to rethink and relearn about their daughter. They were angry with the school system for "misleading" them and for not doing the testing earlier.

Lynn spent the remaining two years of high school receiving intensive special education tutoring and classroom accommodations. Because of her low self-esteem and poor self-image, I saw her in individual therapy over this period of time. By graduation, she was no longer depressed, was working hard in school, and was confident she could make it.

She went to a four-year college with a special program for students with learning disabilities and did well. I did not hear from her for several years. Then, a call. Could she come in? She told me that she just graduated from college. "Now what do I do? I have a college diploma so I can walk around my neighborhood and show that I am smart. But what do I do for the rest of my life with a college degree and no skills?" We had to work on her future. After some vocational counseling, she chose a career track where she could use her verbal and social skills. She could then use specific software material on the computer to help her compensate for her disabilities. She is now a very successful professional in her career.

I did not hear from Lynn again for several years. One day she called to ask if she could come in. "I have this serious boyfriend. . . . We are in love." I said I was pleased. She went on, "But I can't fake it any longer. He gives me a *TV Guide* or movie list and says what should we do? The other day we were driving on the expressway. He handed me a set of directions and asked me to be the navigator. He gives me a book to read and wants to discuss the book. If I tell him about my disabilities, he won't like me anymore."

We had to discuss her lifelong fear of disclosure. She believed that if people knew she couldn't read or write well, they would think she was dumb and no longer like her. We had to work through her fears. She role-played what to say. The boyfriend didn't run away. In fact, I was invited to their engagement party. The teamwork had already started. She opened the presents, and he read the cards.

A few years later Lynn called again. "Help. I'm pregnant." I smiled and told her how happy I was for her. "No," she replied. "What do I do if my baby has learning disabilities too?" We spoke of the possibility that this might happen. "But," I said, "if this baby has your learning disabilities, we will pick it up in preschool. He or she will not have to wait till high school to get help." She was only slightly relieved.

I got other calls over the next years. "What do I do when my daughter can read at a higher grade level than I can? How do I explain to her why I can't read? What do I do when she gets past fourth-grade math? How do I help her write her papers?" We met over several sessions and helped work on her concerns. They were real. She needed to know how she would address each problem with her daughter. Again, the fear of disclosure.

Last year I got another call. "Help, I think we might get a divorce." I met with Lynn. Over several sessions the theme began to make sense. She was naturally very disorganized. In order to survive, she had to be superorganized. With a career, husband, two children, and other demands, she had to be almost rigid to survive. Dinner had to start at 6:00 P.M. and end by 6:30. The dishes had to be done by 6:45 so that she could give her two daughters a bath, get them ready for bed, read to them, and get them in bed by 8:15 P.M. She had to be free by 8:15 in order to complete her many work and home tasks for the evening and to have time to organize the next day. Her poor husband. He would get caught in a traffic jam and arrive home at 6:10 P.M. rather than at 5:50. She would blow up and scream at him for ruining her life. Her anger could last for days. If he got a work-related phone call or had to make a phone call just after dinner and was not available to help for five minutes, she lost control again. He could not take any more. She was convinced he just "did not understand."

I shifted to marital therapy. Quickly stated, the main issues needing work related to helping him understand her learning disabilities to a greater degree than he had known. She also began to see just how rigid she had become. With this understanding, he was able to make several changes in his work and time schedules. If he were running late, he would call. She began to relax a little bit and to accept that there was such a word as "compromise." It took months of work. Their relationship improved, and they continued to work on the problems on their own.

I do not know how many times Lynn solved her own problems. I suspect there were many occasions when she could reflect and work out solutions. I only know the times she called me. I have no doubt that Lynn will call again someday as she reaches another developmental phase of life. Learning disabilities *are* lifetime disabilities.

T W O

Related Disorders

Attention Deficit Hyperactivity Disorder (ADHD)

As I mentioned in Chapter 1, about 20 percent of children and adolescents with learning disabilities also have attention deficit hyperactivity disorder (ADHD). The statistics for the reverse are even higher. Of all children and adolescents with ADHD, between 30 and 50 percent will have a learning disability, depending on the criteria used to define learning disabilities.

These disorders are related but are not the same. It is important to clarify if your son or daughter with learning disabilities has ADHD. Learning disabilities are processing problems and interfere with an individual's *ability* to learn. ADHD is a disorder that makes the individual *unavailable* for learning. However, the individual is able to process and learn when he or she is able to sit, attend, and be available for the learning process.

This chapter will describe in detail what ADHD is and is not. Some of the material in this chapter will be reviewed in later chapters, expanded to include discussion of the evaluation process and treatment. Thus, you may find parts of other chapters redundant; however, I believe this duplication necessary in order to establish a concept in this chapter and then build on it later.

What Are ADHD Behaviors?

The official classification system identifies the essential features of ADHD as having developmentally inappropriate degrees of inattention, impulsiveness, and hyperactivity. Although many persons with ADHD show problems in each of these areas, some will have only one or two of these behaviors. It is not necessary to have all three behaviors to have ADHD. For example, a child can be relaxed, even downright lethargic, and still have ADHD if he or she is inattentive.

Let me describe each of these three behaviors. I will illustrate how each might be seen over the life span.

Hyperactivity

The hyperactive child is rarely one who runs around in circles or up and down the hall, unable to stand or sit still. There *are* some young children like this. However, most young children with true hyperactivity display squirmy, fidgety behavior beyond the norm. Some part of the body is always in motion, often purposeless motion. They might be sitting in the chair but with one knee on the floor. They might rock the chair, possibly going back too far and falling. Their fingers are always tapping or playing with something. Their legs are often swinging. Parents report that this child never sits through a meal without getting up or down. By late childhood or adolescence these behaviors might be less noticeable or better controlled. By adulthood, if the behaviors persist, many find jobs or careers that are compatible with the behaviors. They go into fields of work where moving around is expected. They avoid jobs that require sitting at a desk all day.

Inattention/Distractibility

Children with ADHD will be inattentive because they are distracted. As a result, they have a short attention span and have difficulty staying on task. For children and early adolescents, the most frequent challenge is blocking out unimportant stimuli in their environment. They are distracted by auditory and/or visual stimuli. If they are auditorily distractible, they will hear and respond to sounds that most would hear and tune out. Teachers report that if someone in the back of the room is tapping a pencil or whispering or if someone is walking in the halls, others will ignore the sound but these children must turn and listen. If someone is talking in another room or a basketball is being dribbled on the playground, these students look up and notice. At home, these children might react to minor sounds like a floorboard cracking, the dog's tail wagging, traffic outside, or someone on the telephone.

A person who is visually distractible might pay attention to the design on a rug, a picture, or poster. You leave your child in the morning to get dressed. When you return, he is playing with a toy, distracted from dressing by the toy. You send this child upstairs to do something, and he never returns. On the way, the child saw something and began to play with it; then he saw something else and began to use it. Outside, this child will notice birds flying, clouds going by, trees moving and not stay focused on the appropriate activity.

By later adolescence or adulthood, these persons might evince another form of inattention or distractibility. Some have difficulty blocking out their internal thoughts in order to focus on what they should be attending to. In general, there are two types of internal distractibility. Some complain that their mind *drifts*. They daydream all of the time. They are talking to someone and suddenly realize that their mind has wandered and they weren't paying attention. It is clear that they are not avoiding something stressful because this drifting occurs everyplace, even when they're relaxed and with friends. Others complain that their mind *jumps*. They describe having many thoughts at once and not being able to block out the unwanted ones. They are trying to listen to or do something and thinking of two or three other things at the same time. Sometimes they make a comment based on one of the other internal thoughts, and people wonder why they changed the subject. Some adults with ADHD describe doing something, and then being distracted by another thought so that they drop what they are doing and move to something else. Then another thought and another jump to another activity. Their life is full of incomplete piles of unfinished activities.

Some children and adolescents with auditory or visual distractibility appear to be able to attend to certain tasks for long periods of time. You question if they are really distractible if they can spend hours watching television or playing a video game. These tasks are usually ones that are enjoyable with high motivation. To attend, they learn to hyperfocus. They often appear to be in a trance. You cannot reach them unless you touch or shake them or stand between them and the activity they are focused on. Some adolescents with auditory distractibility seem to study best with music playing in the background. You wonder how they could be distractible if they do their homework with music. Many will tell you that the music is like white noise. This steady sound blocks out all of the small sounds that distract them (people talking, phones ringing).

Young children with auditory and visual distractibility might show sensory overload when in a busy, noisy place (shopping mall, birthday party, circus). They become irritable and upset, and complain about the noise. They may hold their ears and want to leave.

Impulsivity

An individual with impulsivity appears not to be able to reflect before he or she talks or acts. Thus, this person doesn't learn from experience, since he or she cannot delay action long enough to recall past experience and consequences. She or he may call out without raising a hand or may blurt out something or interrupt the teacher while he or she is working with another student. At home, this child or adolescent might interrupt parents when they are on the phone or talking to someone else. Older individuals with this problem may say something before thinking and hurt someone's feelings.

This child's actions may be impulsive as well. He gets upset and pushes or hits. She wants something and grabs for it. This child acts quickly and may run into the street or away from mother in a busy shopping center. Adolescents may use poor judgment in their actions. Adults might buy something without considering whether they can afford it or quit a job before having another. All may be seen as having poor judgment or being accident-prone.

How Is the Diagnosis of ADHD Made?

There are many reasons why individuals might be hyperactive, inattentive/distractible, and/or impulsive. ADHD is the *least* common reason. Just because a child cannot sit still or pay attention in class, we cannot assume that the child has ADHD.

The most common cause of any of these three behaviors with children, adolescents, or adults is anxiety. When you are anxious, you can't sit still or pay attention. You may be irritable and snap at people. Children, especially, become very restless when they are anxious. So a child with a learning disability might be very fidgety and active during a reading or writing exercise but may be very relaxed and calm the rest of the class day.

The second most common cause of hyperactivity, inattention/distractibility, and/or impulsivity is depression. Some can have an agitated depression. They are restless and cannot focus on or attend to anything. They appear irritable. Others may have a withdrawn form of depression and have difficulty attending or relating to people. Both forms of depression can cause one or more of the three behaviors associated with ADHD. A child's parents might have just separated, and the child appears to be inattentive in class. An adolescent breaks up with his girlfriend and is fidgety and inattentive.

The third most common cause of these behaviors is a learning disability. A child with an auditory perception problem will appear to have auditory distractibility. If he finds some work difficult or hard to understand, he appears not to be paying attention. Or the anxiety caused by the stress of academic performance might result in his hyperactivity or inattention. A child with sensory integration disorder

might be uncomfortable because of tactile sensitivity and squirm or
fidget in class.

How, then, does the clinician make the diagnosis? The answer will
be discussed in Chapter 14. You will learn that the diagnosis is made
primarily by the clinical history.

How Long Does ADHD Last?

For many years we believed that all children with ADHD "outgrew"
it by puberty. This was wishful thinking. Studies now show that
about 50 percent of children will improve around the age of puberty.
There appears to be a maturational spurt in the frontal cortex that
helps the brain compensate better. But 50 percent will go into adolescence with their ADHD. About 30 percent of children will continue to have ADHD into their adult life.

There are no ways to predict the path a child will take. If a parent
says, "I had all of those problems, but they went away during high
school," we have a clue. If a parent says, "I had all of those problems
and still do," we have another clue. But these are only clues, never
certainties.

What Causes ADHD?

ADHD is a neurologically based disorder. How it is manifested is influenced by age, sex, and psychological makeup as well as by social
and cultural factors. As will be discussed in great detail in Chapter
16, the neurological problem relates to a neurotransmitter deficiency
in specific areas of the brain.

As with learning disabilities, there is a familial pattern in about 50
percent of the individuals who have ADHD. The specific genetic
theme is not yet understood.

Each of the possible causes of learning disabilities discussed in
Chapter 3 might cause ADHD. Any of the kinds of impacts on the
developing brain described might result in this problem.

How Is ADHD Treated?

As will be discussed in great detail in Chapter 16, the treatment of choice is the use of specific medications that appear to raise the level of the deficient neurotransmitter. Once the level is where it should be, the behaviors lessen or disappear. There are other important nonmedication treatments that will be discussed as well.

It is important to clarify if the individual has a learning disability or ADHD or both. Special education will help students with learning disabilities but will not improve the ADHD. Specific medications will treat the ADHD but will not improve the learning disabilities.

7

Modulating Disorders and Tic Disorders

Some children have difficulty modulating and regulating anxiety, mood, and anger. Some may have difficulty modulating their thoughts and behaviors, resulting in obsessive-compulsive disorder. Others might have an involuntary muscle contraction problem, or tic disorder.

The Modulating Disorders

To function, the brain must be able to modulate or to regulate specific functions in order to maintain a balance or equilibrium and to avoid extremes. These modulating tasks appear to be regulated using the same areas of the brain and the same neurotransmitter: *serotonin*.

These areas modulate anxiety, anger, and mood. Thus, difficulties in modulation will result in difficulties with one or more of these feelings. The individual might feel anxious, have difficulty controlling anger, or feel depressed. Obsessive-compulsive disorder appears to be another of these modulating disorders. Here, the person has difficulty modulating or regulating specific thoughts or behaviors. Characteristic of these modulating disorders is that they are chronic. That is, they have been noticed since early childhood. With each of the modulating disorders there appears to be a high frequency of a familial pattern, often up to 50 percent. Parents or closely related relatives have or have had the same problems.

Since children and adolescents with learning disabilities and/or attention deficit hyperactivity disorder (ADHD) have a higher likelihood of having one or more of these modulating disorders than the normal population, it is important for parents to understand each. By knowing what it is, how it is recognized and diagnosed, and how it is treated, parents can be sure that their daughter or son sees the right professional and receives the right help.

Problems Modulating Anxiety

Anxiety is that emotional uneasiness associated with the anticipation of something bad happening or of danger. We distinguish it from fear, the emotional response to real danger, although the body's response to each is the same. Anxiety is a common life experience. You are driving down the highway and notice a flashing red light in your rearview mirror. Your first response might be to feel anxious: Your heart starts to pound, and you may begin to sweat. Then, the police car passes you and drives on, and you relax. The anxiety was that you might be pulled over for speeding. Anxiety is a normal feeling prior to taking a test or prior to being examined by your family doctor. However, anxiety also can be part of many psychiatric and other medical disorders.

Each person might experience anxiety differently. The most common responses are listed here.

BEHAVIORS EXPERIENCED WHEN ANXIOUS

Related to the heart: palpitations, rapid heartbeat, increase in blood pressure, flushing or pallor.

Related to breathing: feeling of shortness of breath, increased rate of breathing.

Related to the skin: blotching, rash, increase in skin temperature with sweating, funny sensations felt in the skin.

Related to the muscles: mild shaking (tremor), muscle tension, muscle cramps.

Other physical behaviors: headache, chest pain, overalertness, startling easily, insomnia, nightmares, dizziness, fainting, urinary frequency.

Other psychological behaviors: talk of fears; feeling scared, tense, nervous, upset, stressed, fretful, restless; inability to think clearly.

Other social behaviors: appearing clingy, needy, dependent, and/or shy; being withdrawn; uneasiness in social situations.

Children and adolescents might show a generalized feeling of anxiety. They have excessive and unrealistic worries about competence, approval, appropriateness of past behavior, and the future. Others might show a *specific* feeling of anxiety. They might have a separation anxiety, feeling anticipatory uneasiness about separating from parents or other loved ones. Or they might develop a phobia, a specific fear that results in avoidance behaviors and functional and social impairment. Common phobias seen with children and adolescents include fear of animals in general, cats, dogs, blood, fire, germs, dirt, height, insects, small or closed spaces, snakes, spiders, strangers, and thunder.

There are other types of anxiety disorders seen in young people. Some may develop a social phobia, showing significant anxiety provoked by exposure to certain types of social or performance situations, often leading to avoidance behavior. Following a traumatic experience, a child or adolescent might develop a post-traumatic stress disorder. The individual is anxious and overly cautious, and often reexperiences an extremely traumatic event accompanied by symptoms of increased arousal and by avoidance of stimuli associated with the trauma.

For some, the anxiety level gets so high that a fight-or-flight response is triggered off. This is called a panic attack and is seen with panic disorders. The individual experiences a sudden onset of intense apprehension, fearfulness, or terror, often associated with feelings of impending doom. During these attacks, the body responds with such symptoms as shortness of breath, palpitations of the heart, chest pain or discomfort, choking or smothering sensations, and fear of "going crazy" or of losing control.

If a child or adolescent develops a high level of anxiety or one of these anxiety disorders at a specific time in her or his life, it is important to explore the cause. The anxiety might be understandable. For example, many children with learning disabilities begin to show anxiety in late August as they realize school is about to start again. The anxiety might relate to family stress such as the illness or death of a close relative or tension between parents. Sometimes the cause is not readily apparent.

The difference between these children who suddenly develop anxiety and individuals who have a modulating disorder manifested by anxiety or panic attacks lies in their personal history. These are children who are described in early childhood as more tense and anxious. They have always been more fearful. The current set of problems is only the current example of a long-term problem. At an earlier age, they were afraid to be separated from mother or afraid to go to sleep alone. Later, they had frequent nightmares, woke up, and needed to sleep with parents. Now they might be afraid to be in a part of the house (another floor) if no one else is there or might be afraid to play outside because there are bees. Or, now they are afraid to be around crowds or noisy places or to play sports.

If your son or daughter shows evidence of generalized or specific anxiety, it is important to speak with your family doctor or to a mental health professional. Reflective therapy, behavioral therapy, and/or family therapy might be very helpful. However, if you are aware that the current problem with anxiety is a chronic pattern for your child or adolescent, stress this theme to the professional. A modulating disorder related to anxiety is often treated in a different way. I will discuss these treatment approaches later in this chapter.

Problems Modulating Anger

Anger, like anxiety, is a normal feeling to have. What is important is how the child or adolescent handles or shows this anger. Parents usually model acceptable ways of showing anger. Thus, some youths will show anger by being negative, walking off stomping their feet, yelling, or slamming doors. Others may throw a pillow or bang their fists. Some learn that in their family there is no acceptable way to show anger as a child or adolescent. They may go to their room and beat up their pillow or stuffed animal.

Youths with a problem modulating anger show a very different picture. They explode. As with the other modulating disorders, they have a chronic history of difficulty regulating anger. Parents might note that this child had terrible temper tantrums as an infant, had violent tantrums lasting a long time as a younger child, and now has explosive behaviors.

These explosive behaviors are called *intermittent explosive disorder*. They are manifested by a sudden onset of explosive behavior. The threshold point for controlling anger appears to be so low that often it may not be possible to figure out what caused the explosion. Once the child or adolescent explodes there is no reasoning or control. He or she will scream, yell, curse, throw things, hit, break things. During the episode he or she may sound paranoid: "Everyone hates me" or "You're trying to hurt me" or "Don't hit me." The episode lasts from three to five to twenty minutes or more with most children and adolescents. Then it stops as quickly as it started. Once it is over the person may be so tired, he or she wants to rest or sleep. There might be some show of remorse for what happened. More often, the child or adolescent doesn't want to talk about it. He or she just wants to watch TV or do something similarly bland or neutral.

These explosive outbursts are frightening and difficult to handle or tolerate. When they occur each day or several times a day, everyone becomes overwhelmed and nonfunctional. Parents feel helpless. Siblings are afraid and avoid their brother or sister.

Usually, children and adolescents with anger regulation problems explode only at home with parents or with other significant adults. It is not clear whether they know they have to "hold it in" at school or over at a friend's house or whether the stresses that cause the anger are more associated with family issues. Occasionally, these explosions may be seen with peers. Less so, they may be seen at school.

The treatment for intermittent explosive disorder goes beyond talking or behavioral therapy. The specific treatment approaches will be discussed later in this chapter.

Problems Modulating Mood

Depression also is a normal feeling. Each major growth step experienced by a child is associated with some anxiety and depression. The toddler learns to walk and can get about without help: There is the anxiety of moving out alone, and there is the sadness or depression of leaving behind a special kind of closeness and dependency that will no longer exist. Adolescents can feel the same. They are anxious about growing up and becoming an adult, and they feel the sadness or depression of giving up the special experiences and safety of childhood.

A child or adolescent who is depressed might show one or more of the behaviors listed here.

BEHAVIORS ASSOCIATED WITH DEPRESSION

Depressed or irritable mood
Diminished interest or loss of pleasure in almost all activities
Sleep disturbance
Weight change or appetite disturbance
Decreased concentration or indecisiveness
Suicidal thoughts or thoughts of death
Agitation or slowness of thinking
Fatigue or loss of energy
Feelings of worthlessness or inappropriate guilt
With children, irritability and increased anger

So that you can be familiar with terms used by psychiatrists and other mental health professionals, I need to mention two specific types of depressive disorders. When the child or adolescent shows a depressed or irritable mood that lasts a year or longer and the individual is never symptom-free for more than two months, the depression is called dysthymia. He or she may show appetite changes, sleep changes, decreased energy, low self-esteem, difficulty making decisions or poor concentration, and/or feelings of hopelessness. If the individual shows a depressed mood or loss of interest or pleasure; evidence of changes in appetite or weight, sleep patterns, or clearness of thinking; decreased energy; feelings of worthlessness or guilt; problems with concentrating or making decisions; or recurrent thoughts of death or suicidal thoughts for a period of at least two weeks, it is called a major depressive episode.

An individual who has a depression might have difficulty modulating the "upswing" as well. The person might go into a euphoric and excited (hypomanic) state manifested by an abnormal and persistently elevated, expansive, or irritable mood. He or she might have an inflated self-esteem or grandiosity (unrealistic views of self), decreased need for sleep, rapid speech, racing thoughts, distractibility, increased involvement in goal-directed activities, or muscle restlessness. This hypomanic state might last a day or a week or more, if not treated. A person who experiences both major periods of depression and hypomania has a bipolar disorder (formerly called a manic-depressive disorder). A person who experiences only periods of normality and depression has a unipolar disorder.

We do not yet know the exact clinical picture of these depressive disorders in young children. Often what we see is irritability and anger. The mood swings might go less from normalcy to sadness and more from pleasantness to anger. Thus, the younger the child is, the harder it is to make the diagnosis of a depressive disorder (dysthymia or major depressive episode) or a mood disorder (unipolar or bipolar).

Children or adolescents can become depressed at a certain age. The cause might be apparent or unclear. Parents of a youth with a modulating disorder report that this child is always moody or sad or unhappy. He or she rarely shows happiness or enjoyment in relationships or activities. The current problem is only the most recent manifestation of this chronic problem. Treatment for these depressive disorders will be discussed later in this chapter.

Obsessive-Compulsive Disorder

Obsessions are unwanted thoughts, images, or impulses that the individual realizes are senseless or unnecessary, intrude into his or her consciousness involuntarily, and cause functional impairment and distress. Despite this lact of control, the sufferer still recognizes that these thoughts originate in his or her own mental process. Since they arise in the mind, obsessions can take the form of any mental event—simple repetitive words, thoughts, fears, memories, pictures, or elaborate dramatic scenes.

Compulsions are actions that are responses to a perceived internal obligation to follow certain rituals or rules. They also cause functional impairment. Compulsions may be motivated directly by obsessions or efforts to ward off certain thoughts, impulses, or fears. Occasionally, children report compulsions without the perception of a mental component. Like obsessions, compulsions are often viewed as being unnecessary, excessive or senseless, and involuntary or forced. Individuals suffering from compulsions will often elaborate a variety of precise rules for the chronology, rate, order, duration, and number of repetitions of their acts.

A person with obsessive-compulsive disorder may have obsessions or compulsions, or both. These behaviors result in difficulty functioning. He or she feels forced or invaded by the symptoms and perceives the senselessness or excessiveness of these thoughts or acts. The person might try to ignore or suppress these thoughts or actions; however, the anxiety builds and the behaviors break through.

Common behaviors seen with individuals who have obsessive-compulsive disorder are listed here.

BEHAVIORS SEEN WITH OBSESSIVE-COMPULSIVE DISORDER

Counting or repeating behavior: the need to touch something a certain number of times or an even (odd) number of times; the need to repeat a specific behavior or pattern of behaviors; the need to count certain things until finished.

Checking or questioning behavior: the need to check and recheck something (front door is locked, stove is off, car keys were brought in, closet light is off); the need to ask a question a specific number of times or until the respondent answers in an exact, particular way.

Collecting or hoarding behavior: the collecting of matches, rocks, pieces of glass, pieces of paper; the hoarding of newspapers or other items. The person becomes upset if these are thrown away.

Arranging and organizing behavior: the need to tie shoes or to dress or undress in a certain sequence or certain way; the need to organize toys or dolls or other items in a certain way. The person becomes upset if anything is changed.

Cleaning and/or washing behavior: the need to lather and rinse an exact number of times while showering or to brush the hair a certain number of times in a certain pattern; the need to wash the hands repeatedly.

These obsessions and/or compulsions may begin to appear at age six or seven. A person who has obsessive-compulsive disorder clearly reports that the behaviors were causing frustration and difficulty by early adolescence.

Treatment for these Modulating Disorders

The research of the mid- and late 1990s has begun to clarify these modulating disorders. The common theme appears to be that the areas of the brain involved use the same neurotransmitter, serotonin. The modulating disorders appear to be due to a deficiency of this neurotransmitter. This possibility had already been observed with the depressions and with obsessive-compulsive disorder, and medications that increase the level of serotonin in these areas of the brain have already been established as the best treatment. Recently, these same medications have been used for children and adolescents with a chronic pattern of anxiety- and/or anger-regulation problems. Current studies strongly suggest that they help. As the level of serotonin goes up, the anxiety and the angry outbursts decrease or stop. Much more research is needed in these areas. But, for now, the clinical treatment for each of these modulating disorders is to use medications that increase the level of serotonin in these areas of the brain. In addition to the medications, behavioral therapy is important. In some situations, verbal therapy or family therapy will be recommended as well.

The medications used are called selective serotonin reuptake inhibitors (SSRIs) because they appear to increase the level of serotonin by decreasing the reuptake of this neurotransmitter at the nerve ending. At this time there are four SSRIs available, as shown in Table 7-1.

Table 7-1 The SSRIs

Trade Name	Chemical (Generic) Name
Luvox	Fluvoxamine
Paxil	Paroxetine
Prozac	Fluoxetine
Zoloft	Sertraline

The current availability of information on using the SSRIs with children and adolescents does not show clear guidelines for choosing one over the other. Each clinician might prefer to start with one and then, if needed, move on to another.

This book focuses on learning disabilities and ADHD. It is important to understand that these modulating disorders might exist along with these two disabilities. However, it is beyond the scope of this book to go into more detail about the medications and treatments for the modulating disorders. If you have made the decision to place your son or daughter on one of the medications discussed, the prescribing physician should explain the actions, the potential side effects, and other important information.

The Tic Disorders

A tic disorder is not a modulating disorder. However, tic disorders are frequently found as part of the neurological continuum discussed in Chapter 1. Most of the studies showing that these disorders are frequently seen together focus on one type of tic disorder, Tourette's disorder. Of all children and adolescents with Tourette's disorder, about 50 percent will have ADHD. About 60 percent of individuals with this disorder will have a learning disability, and 50 percent will have obsessive-compulsive disorder.

A tic is a sudden, repetitive movement, gesture, or utterance that typically mimics some aspect of normal behavior. Usually of brief duration, individual tics rarely last more than a second. They tend to occur in bouts and at times have a convulsion-like character. Individual tics can occur singly or together in an orchestrated pattern. They can vary in their frequency and forcefulness. Although many tics can be temporarily suppressed, they are often experienced as being involuntary.

Muscle, or motor, tics vary from simple, abrupt movements, such as eye blinking, head jerks, or shoulder shrugs, to more complex, purposeful-appearing behaviors, such as facial expressions or gestures of the arms or head. In extreme cases, these movements can be obscene or self-injurious (hitting or biting). Vocal tics can range from simple throat-clearing sounds to more complex vocalizations and speech.

Types of Tic Disorders

It is important for parents to know the types of tic disorders and the terms used for each. If the motor or vocal tics begin before age eighteen and last for more than a month but less than a year, the disorder is called a transient tic disorder. This problem is not uncommon with young children. If left alone, the tics go away and never are seen again. If the motor or vocal tics begin before age eighteen and last for more than a year, the disorder is called a chronic motor or vocal tic disorder. If the person has a chronic motor or vocal tic disorder where the tics occur many times a day nearly every day or intermittently throughout a period of more than one year with never a tic-free period of more than three consecutive months and where the disturbance causes marked distress or significant impairment in social, occupational, or other important areas of function, the disorder is called Tourette's disorder. Individuals with Tourette's disorder frequently have a family history of close relatives with this disorder.

Most individuals with either a chronic motor or vocal tic disorder or Tourette's disorder will first begin to have tics between the ages of seven and twelve. Most adults with these disorders report that their tics began during this time.

Treatment for the Tic Disorders

Tic disorders are not treated unless the motor and/or vocal tics create a psychological or social problem for the child or adolescent or these tics are so severe as to cause muscle soreness. If it is necessary to treat the tic disorder, certain medications can decrease or stop the tics. The most frequently used medications today are listed in Table 7-2.

Table 7-2 Medications for Tic Disorders

Trade Name	Chemical (Generic) Name
Catapres	Clonidine
Haldol	Haloperidol
Orap	Pimozide
Tenex	Guanfacine

As I mentioned with the modulating disorders, it is beyond the scope of this book to go into detail on the medication treatment of the tic disorders. If your son or daughter receives treatment for a tic disorder, the physician prescribing the medication should inform you of the actions, effects, and side effects.

THREE

Emotional, Social, and Family Problems

Normal Development

A mother called me about her child. Her son refused to leave her and began clinging and crying if she tried to walk away. If she left him with someone else, he threw a tantrum. What should she do with him? I couldn't say anything until I found out her son's age. If he were one year old, this behavior could be quite normal. If he were two, I would be slightly worried. If he were four or eight, I would be very concerned. If he were fifteen, I would be alarmed. Normal behavior has a great deal to do with your son's or daughter's age and the stage of development that the child is in at the time.

All children go through stages of psychological and social development, and most do so with minimal difficulty. They may occasionally face a stressful situation—being in the hospital, getting used to a new baby brother or sister, or coping with their parents' divorce—and briefly retreat to earlier behaviors. But ordinarily, they soon rally and move ahead again. Growth means many steps forward with occasional steps backward.

Much of this psychological and social—psychosocial—growth interweaves with stages in physical growth. As the brain and body mature, the child develops new abilities with which to handle problems. This same growth, however, also introduces new problems.

Most children go through the various stages of development noticeably, but without serious problems, while some progress with few obvious difficulties. Some children and families find certain stages of growth more difficult than others. The child with a learning disability, however, may have trouble with some or all stages of psychosocial development. First, I'll review what we understand to be normal development. This knowledge will help you see the ways in which learning disabilities inhibit or alter this development.

Normal Child Development

The newborn infant functions initially as a physiological being—the brain receives messages from the body and environment and responds. During the early weeks and months, the baby begins to recognize sounds and some visual inputs. He begins to become aware of certain significant people, recognizing, for example, mother's or father's voice, image, or smell. As the infant begins to relate to his world, he is unaware of any distinction between his body and objects in the environment—he has no sense of any boundaries. People, pets, food, furniture, toys—all outside objects appear to the child merely to be extensions of himself. For now, the infant and his world are one. Since the infant does not yet distinguish between people, all significant adults are referred to in the literature as parenting objects. This stage of development is depicted in Fig. 8-1.

Basic Trust

Gradually the infant begins to discover that objects have extensions and limits to them as well. The child discovers her fingers, hands, toes, and feet, and finds that these objects belong to the same body that she has begun to experience. By about three months, the infant can recognize certain pieces of the external world and relates to these "part objects" in special ways that acknowledge their importance. Now, for the first time, the "social smile" can be seen. The child looks at the face and smiles. This social smile is an early psychological landmark of normal development.

By about nine months, an infant has completed the process of discovering where she leaves off and the world begins. Having learned to associate pleasurable experiences with certain human objects, the baby begins to comprehend that these specific human objects are very important—that they are, indeed, absolutely necessary. Thus,

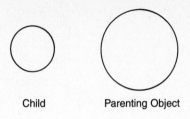

Child   Parenting Object

FIGURE 8-1

the baby learns to place basic trust in these key people and becomes totally dependent on them.

With the establishment of basic trust, the infant masters the first major step in psychosocial development. But, now the baby becomes upset if he or she is left alone. The child fears separation and strangers. Before this stage, anyone could pick up the baby and get a smile. Now if someone the baby doesn't know very well picks her up, she starts to cry. This fear, which normally appears at around nine months, is another psychosocial landmark. This stage of total dependence, manifested by separation anxiety, is depicted in Fig. 8-2.

Separation

The next task in psychosocial development is mastering separation. The infant must realize that he can separate from these significant people and still survive, and then learn how to do that. Mastery of this stage of development involves several steps that start at about nine months and usually finish at around three to three and a half years. (Today many children who are placed in day care during the early months seem to master separation much earlier.) Until mastered, separation from the significant people in his life results in anxiety—separation anxiety. This accomplishment of separation, which leads to a sense of an autonomous self, is illustrated in Fig. 8-3.

Initially (see *a* in Fig. 8-3), the infant must have some form of sensory connection with the significant person. The baby cries, hears a parent's footsteps in the hall, and stops crying. This auditory linkage is enough. Or the infant crawls behind a chair, loses sight of a parent, and cries. When the parent moves into view, the child stops crying.

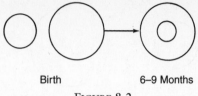

Birth   6–9 Months

FIGURE 8-2

This visual link, the sight of the parent, reestablishes the necessary contact. Or the baby cries at night. When the mother or father picks him up in the dark and holds him, the crying stops. The touch, smell, and voice of the parent reassure the infant that the intimate connection is not broken.

Beginning at about eighteen months, the child slowly learns to separate for longer and longer periods of time (see *b* in Fig. 8-3). However, the toddler still must frequently return to the parent to "refuel" or "tag up." A hug or a kiss or a cookie will do, and the child is off again. Some children find these early efforts at separating easier if they can take something that reminds them of a parent along with them. Children usually select these favorite items, which are commonly known as security blankets but more properly called transitional objects, because they have a familiar smell, soft touch, or the cuddly feel that they have learned to associate with the parent.

By about three, the child can usually separate from his parents with no discomfort (see *c* in Fig. 8-3). Again, children who are placed in day care settings early in life might master separation earlier than age three. This full mastery of separation is yet another landmark in psychosocial development.

Two major psychological events take place during this stage of mastering separation; one is internally motivated, and the other externally caused. Each aids in mastering separation and in establishing autonomy, and each has a major influence on personality development. The internal event, negativism, begins about age two. During the "terrible twos," the child responds to most requests or comments with "No" or "No, I do myself." The child is beginning to separate and to show that he has a mind of his own. Although exasperating to parents, this healthy step toward separation and autonomy is a very necessary one.

The other event, which occurs between ages two and three, is toi-

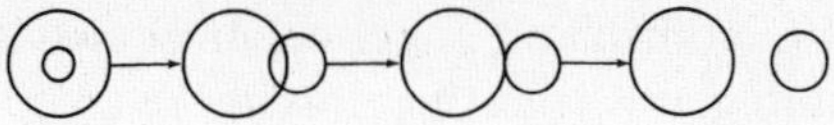

(a)   (b)   (c)

9 Months   3½ Years

FIGURE 8-3

let training. In learning to accede to this requirement of the outside world, the child confronts two new tasks that have to be mastered. First, the child must alter his concept of love and relationships. Until now, the child has perceived the whole world as being there to take care of him. Love and caring were automatic and free. Suddenly, the child faces a situation in which love appears no longer to be free and available on demand. Now, in the child's perception, if the child wants love, he must do something to get it. Loving relationships no longer center totally around his wishes and needs; now the child must learn to participate in a give-and-take process. Urinate in the potty and mommy loves you; urinate in your pants and mommy frowns. Getting love sometimes requires doing what the other person wants. To receive pleasure requires pleasing. This forces the child to make a revolutionary shift in his concepts of the world, people, and relationships. He must move from a self-centered world (primary narcissism) to a world where he is aware of his own needs as well as those of others.

Toilet training introduces a second new concept that provides the child with a new way to handle angry feelings. For the first time, the child has an active weapon in the battle to get what he wants. Prior to this, the child could cry or have a tantrum, but the parents could choose to ignore it. Prior to this, the child experienced anger and expressed it openly by crying, screaming, kicking, or hitting. Now the child begins to realize that there are different ways to express anger, and that the way one does express anger has a great deal to do with getting and keeping love. Direct expressions of anger don't work. The price one has to pay may be too great. A child now learns that more indirect expressions of anger work somewhat better than hitting and yelling. Now, when angry with a parent, the child can squat right in front of the parent, preferably when company is around, and, with a big smile, "make" in his pants. If he is pleased with mommy and daddy, he will "make" on the potty. The child begins to learn the importance of controlling anger or, more precisely, of acquiring subtler, more ambiguous, and therefore more acceptable ways to express anger.

These issues—the reciprocal nature of loving and being loved and pleased, and the handling of angry feelings—are struggled with individually and together. The two themes often interrelate. At this age, one can readily love and hate the same person at the same time or hurt and care for the same person at the same time.

Individuation

When the child has mastered the first major task of development—establishing basic trust—and the second major task—handling separation—she is ready for the third task, individuation. This task involves asking and trying to answer the question "Who am I?" Now that the child knows that she is a separate person who can survive without being totally dependent on important people, she wonders what kind of person she is. The struggle to answer these questions usually takes place between the ages of three and six.

At this age, the brain is still immature, and not all thinking is based on reality. Fantasy, which seems as real as what is real, forms one basis for a lot of the child's thinking. If the child thinks something is so, it may as well be. A child at this age, then, can have opposite beliefs and feelings simultaneously, with no notion that a contradiction exists or that only one or two or more different possibilities can come true. For example, loving and hating, wanting and not wanting, going to a movie and at the same time going on a picnic—the child excludes nothing and sees no problem with believing in all possibilities coming true at the same time.

The child also tries out many roles. If she pretends to be Superman, she is Superman. What is it like to be big? little? aggressive? submissive? a boy? a girl? Children play house, school, or doctor, exploring various roles and different situations. One day a little girl may act like a boy; the next day, like a girl, or a mommy, a daddy, a teacher, a cartoon hero. The child tries to learn about people and how to do activities, and attempts to master those concerns through repetition in play. For example, children must learn to listen to adults other than their parents. When they play school, they take turns being the teacher who gives instructions and orders, and then the pupil who must listen and obey. When they play doctor, they take turns being the doctor who explores and the patient who is explored.

Whenever a child tries to "be" someone else in the family—for instance, mother or father—she may feel the need to compete with siblings who may also want to be that parent. The child also has to try to attract the attention of the other parent. So another characteristic of this age period is the child's tendency to cause splitting and tension between parents as well as among siblings. Children learn with remarkable aptitude how to divide parents, getting one closer to them and pushing the other away. Thus, on one day a child may seem close and loving, yet on another day she is irritating and hostile.

For the first time, in Fig. 8-4, the diagram of the child's relationships must include both parents.

If the boy or girl wants to play "being mother," then mother must be pushed away, along with any siblings who might compete for her role, as in Fig. 8-5.

If the child wants to play "being father," then father has to be pushed away, along with any siblings who might want that role, as in Fig. 8-6.

Because both splits occur from time to time, the diagram of the child's relationships looks like that depicted in Fig. 8-7.

A child's thoughts at this age are magical—that is, they are not reality-based—and the child often has trouble distinguishing among her actual feelings, thoughts, and actions. The child's thoughts, especially her angry thoughts, scare her. Nightmares are common. A child worries that others, like her parents, know what she is thinking and that they will retaliate. This magical fear of retaliation causes the

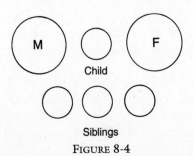

Figure 8-4

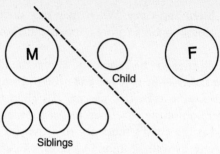

FIGURE 8-5

child to worry excessively about body integrity and body damage. Any cut or scratch is a disaster. This is why this age is often called the Band-Aid stage.

During these frustrating fours and fives, most children and their parents do have a lot of fun. The child is animated, uninhibited, and imaginative and enjoys interacting and playing. However, the child can cause stress between parents and among siblings and have trouble sleeping, have nightmares, or want to sleep with parents. One minute you love and cuddle the child, the next you feel like giving her away to one of your neighbors. All of this is normal.

By about age six, most children begin to find preliminary answers to the question "Who am I?" Little girls begin to learn that they are to become "just like mommy" and enjoy playing this role. They give up wanting daddy all to themselves and look forward to some day having someone just like their father. Little boys begin to learn that they are to become "just like daddy." They give up wanting mommy

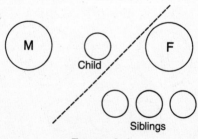

FIGURE 8-6

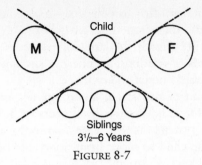

Figure 8-7

all to themselves and settle for the idea of having someone just like their mother some day. Although some of these self-assessments may later change, it is through this process of identification that children learn to become more or less like the parent of the same sex. (The child in a single-parent family may have more difficulty working through this stage of development. Most make it through, but if you think that consulting a mental health professional would help, don't hesitate to get advice yourself and perhaps for your child.)

During this time, between about three and six, most children are struggling to establish basic assumptions about themselves. It is during this time that parents and other significant adults introduce concepts of stereotypical sex-role behaviors. If a boy reaches for a doll to play with, he may be told that boys play with trucks or guns, not with dolls. Cultural clichés like this always amaze me—adult males must know how to relate lovingly to their children, among other people, not how to use guns, and men know that. Adult females must know how to express themselves productively, not just how to use eye makeup, and women know that. Still, many adults continue to teach little girls that they play with dolls and do tasks in the kitchen, they do not work with tools or excel in sports. Girls are taught that it is acceptable to express love and sadness, but not self-assertion or anger. Boys often learn that it is acceptable to express anger, but that "big boys don't cry."

Fortunately, the consciousness-raising efforts of the women's movement have helped to free more and more families from the need to pass along these stereotypes. Children must feel free to explore and to learn many roles to become fully developed males or females. They must learn that true maleness and femaleness has nothing to do with the things one does or how one expresses different emotions, but instead with the kinds of resources and experiences one has, the kinds of relationships one can sustain, and the respect one develops toward oneself and others.

Toward the end of this stage, about age six, two changes take place that help the child master the process of individuation. The central nervous system takes a large maturational leap forward, and this helps the child to move from nonreality-based thinking to reality-based thinking. Contradictory feelings and thoughts can no longer coexist with equal power. The child begins to understand that feeling or thinking one thing means that she cannot believe in its opposite at the same time with equal conviction; for example, she cannot love and hate the same person at the same time. In other words, the realization dawns that one cannot do or be two (or more) things at the same time. The child can now distinguish between reality and fantasy. For example, the child might pretend to be Superwoman, but she now knows it is only pretend.

The other change during this stage involves the child's emerging awareness of the various accumulated values and value judgments that she has learned. At this age, the child fuses these beliefs into an established conscience called the superego. This "voice," or conscience, stays with one throughout life and becomes increasingly significant. It "tells" the child which thoughts, feelings, and actions are acceptable and which are not. Initially, the parents teach these values, and the child usually adopts them fairly automatically. The child may rebel, but this is more because she wants her own way, not because any serious questions about moral or intellectual validity come up. In adolescence, as we shall see, these parent-taught values are routinely reviewed and reconsidered.

Latency

Once the child has mastered the third task of development, individuation, he moves into a period of consolidation. Sometime around age six, the child becomes free to move out of the family and into the community. With the major psychological work of childhood done, the child's energy is freed to range more widely, in school and other learning activities, and in expanding relationships. This period, which lasts about six years, is called the latency period, illustrated in Fig. 8-8.

During the latency period, a child learns to relate to adults other than his parents and to children other than his siblings. The child begins to focus on relationships with children of the same sex, and may ignore or move away from peer activities that include children of the opposite sex. Boys prefer boys and often don't like girls. Girls prefer girls and may avoid boys. Very intimate "chum" or "best friend" relationships develop, and the behavior that you got used to during the individuation stage changes completely. A boy will shrug and push mother away if she tries to hold or kiss him. Two boys or two girls may walk down the street arm in arm. During this period, children explore and learn the ability to relate to people of the same sex and form both intimate and casual friendships with them.

The latency period usually covers grades one through six. Massive knowledge must be learned and mastered, from reading, writing, and arithmetic to subject information and study skills. A child who does not resolve or master each stage of psychosocial development before entering these grades can have difficulty functioning in school or mastering the required tasks.

By the age of twelve to fourteen, this period of consolidation ends. Adolescence arrives and, with it, new tasks to master. Everything is about to change—possibly for the worse, but eventually for the better. Each stage of psychosocial development for the child must be mastered, and he must feel comfortable entering adolescence. If any previous developmental stage was not resolved, the child might have more difficulty with adolescence.

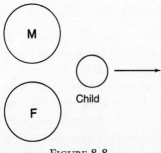

FIGURE 8-8

Normal Adolescent Development

Adolescence is a difficult time for almost everyone and for almost all parents. The period of adolescence prepares a person to move out of childhood and into adulthood. This transition has to be unique for each generation. Parents often rely on their own models and experiences, responding to their teenage children as their parents did to them or as they think they should have been responded to. The difficulty is that these role models and experiences more or less successfully prepared today's parents for the last third of the twentieth century. Today's adolescents have to learn to live in the twenty-first century. You will have to speculate right along with your teenage child on the strengths, attitudes, and skills needed for adulthood. Your own life experiences will be out of date and probably too restrictive.

As parents of an adolescent, you must teach your youth the values that you believe are important, but you must also take into account the unique issues that your teenager struggles with in the world as it is now and it will be for him or her. You have to give your teenager roots and wings at the same time. The adolescent will need the roots—the security that comes with a solid foundation—in order to spread his or her wings and fly.

The adolescent must rework most of the psychosocial tasks of childhood. Physical growth still plays a major role in the stages of psychological growth. Some adolescents go through these stages with little or no difficulty; other have problems with a stage, then regroup and move forward.

Problems with Physical Changes

It is useful to distinguish between puberty—the period of physical changes—and adolescence—the period of psychosocial changes. Ideally, the two occur hand in hand. However, with some teenagers, these processes get way out of sync. When one is out of phase with the other, the person has to cope with even more stress than usual.

Think of a girl who, at ten or eleven, is taller than all of the other girls, full-breasted, and already menstruating, or the seventeen-year-old boy who is five feet tall, with peach fuzz and a high voice. Both are physically normal, but each is at a different end of the normal growth curve. And each has additional stresses with which to cope. The reverse can be equally stressful. For example, the boy in sixth grade who is already almost six feet tall and growing a beard, or the short, flat-chested young woman who still looks like "a little girl" as she graduates from high school. Each must cope with more than his or her share of the stress that adolescence normally brings.

Just as children do, adolescents have feelings and thoughts that cause conflicts and tension. However, their physical growth gives them capacities for action and reaction that no child has. When a six-year-old boy cuddles with his mother, he feels pleasant sensations; when a fourteen- or fifteen-year-old boy does so, he may be embarrassed when he has an erection. A little girl can thoroughly enjoy sitting on her father's lap, but a thirteen-year-old girl who does so may have physical sensations that worry her. Wrestling with or tickling a sibling of the opposite sex can become both sexually stimulating and distressing. These new reactions that come with physical maturation may be so upsetting that the adolescent feels forced to transfer the relationships that cause these feelings to "safer" people outside of the family.

The same is true for angry feelings. For example, it is one thing for a little boy to feel rage at his mother when his eyes are at the level of her kneecaps. However, it is another situation when the angry adolescent realizes that he is taller and bigger than his mother and that he could really hurt her.

The distress and loss of confidence caused by these physical and emotional changes encourage the early adolescent to become more dependent on home and parents. But, the same newly discovered emotions and physical reactions make it more difficult to explore and work out relationships and problems with parents and siblings. Thus, there is conflict—within the adolescent and eventually within the family. The adolescent pushes to become more dependent and childlike while, at the same time, pulling to become more independent and adultlike.

Initially, the early adolescent may attempt to cope with all this by using fantasy, choosing to relate to people who are unavailable and therefore safe. For example, boys and girls have "mad crushes" on movie stars, rock musicians, and sports heroes. The probability that a rock music star will suddenly knock on the door of an adolescent girl

and ask her for a date is remote enough to allow her to safely fanta-
size a relationship with him. Gradually, however, the young adolescent will begin to explore relationships with real, potentially available
people. At first, these interactions are likely to occur within groups,
then within smaller groups, and finally with individual people. Very
early dating is usually narcissistically motivated: The adolescent
wants to date someone who makes him or her *look* good—the cheer-
leader, the football hero, someone whom everyone thinks is desirable. Often a boy behaves toward his date much as he would toward
a male friend, clowning around, showing off, or hitting. Later on,
both adolescent girls and boys will date people who makes them *feel*
good. Looks are still important, but less important than personality.

Issues of Psychological Changes

The psychological phases adolescents go through as they move toward adulthood can be seen as occurring in three stages:

Independence
Identity
Intimacy

INDEPENDENCE.   The first task of adolescence is to move from
being a dependent person to being an independent person. The initial struggle often revolves around the concepts of sex roles and
identification. The old techniques that the child used to master separation at age two may turn up again.

Negativism reappears—"No, I can do it myself" or "Don't tell me
how long my hair can be" or "Don't tell me how short my skirt can
be." This negativism is the young person's renewed attempt to tell
first you and then the world that he has a mind of his own. And
again, it becomes an active verbal way of expressing anger. An adolescent seizes almost any opportunity to exploit an issue that shows
that he has a mind separate from his parents'. Parents and an adolescent may argue about the choice of friends and peer groups; school
plans and courses; points of philosophy, religion, and etiquette.
Clothing, hair styles, and jewelry have always been favorite issues
with which to prove one's independence. The casual or unisex theme
of today resembles the "cause" of every other generation—the flap-

pers, the zoot-suiters, the rockers, the hippies, and so on. Remember how you showed your parents that you had a mind of your own? Each generation can recall how they used clothes, hairstyles, and other external badges (e.g., earrings for boys; multiple earrings for girls; piercings in different parts of the body)—the more shocking the better—to show their parents that they had minds of their own.

All the old struggles over expressing love and anger reappear as new issues. For example: What do you have to do to be loved? to keep love? to show love? What do you do with angry feelings? All of these questions have to be worked through with family and friends. In the process, the adolescent begins to develop more consistent concepts of relationships and styles of expressing feelings. Thus, the adult personality is beginning to form and emerge.

In the process of gaining independence, the adolescent often feels a need to reject the parents' values and to reformulate his own value system. Unless this happens, the adolescent's parents remain with him forever in the form of the conscience programmed in during childhood. A teenager may need to rework these previously accepted values to fit with the values he wishes to adopt for today and tomorrow. The adolescent will probably reject his former values at first, pointing out contradictions in the parents' values. He may feel that "no one over thirty can be trusted." The adolescent may challenge his parents for giving conflicting messages: "What do you mean, all people are created equal? You get mad at me if I date someone who's Jewish [Protestant, Catholic, black, white, Hispanic, Asian]" or "Why should I be honest? You cheat on your income tax" or "Why shouldn't I drink [smoke]? You do."

This interim vacuum, when old values are rejected and new ones have not been established, can be upsetting. Some adolescents temporarily seek a preset package of values such as those of the Boy or Girl Scouts with specific oaths and laws. For others, the peer group provides this interim system. Closed cliques (the "in" groups) often set rules about all kinds of behavior—how to dress, whom to talk to, who is "in," and who is "out."

Slowly, the adolescent begins to blend many different values from all kinds of sources into his own existing values. By young adulthood, a new conscience, or superego, is established. The compatibility and flexibility of this new superego strengthens his ability to handle and express feelings and emotions in relationships. All through life, his superego will have to be able to change and grow in order to accomodate new life situations.

As the adolescent begins to feel independent of his family, and as the family supports and encourages this emerging maturity, the question of the three- to six-year-old is heard once again—"Who am I?" The answer, of course, can no longer be "just like Mommy (or Daddy)."

IDENTITY.   The second developmental task of adolescence, establishing one's identity, begins at this point. Becoming a "chip off the old block" isn't enough and can be too restrictive. Unlike the child, the older adolescent will select characteristics from many people—religious leaders, teachers, neighbors, relatives, parents, friends, maybe even famous people—blending certain of their features with her own to become a unique new person. This new person, or identity, is not her final self, but it forms the basis of what she will become. Her identity must be reworked throughout life as roles change. She must adjust to becoming a graduate, a spouse, a worker, a parent, a grandparent, or a retiree.

Each generation and each culture exerts different social and cultural pressures on human beings. The child growing up in the Victorian era heard very different messages from the outside world than did the child growing up in the "wild" decade of the post–World War I twenties. The adolescent growing up in the post–Vietnam War world of the eighties and nineties experienced different social and cultural standards than her parents did. So, too, adolescents of today struggle with different issues of relationships, careers, and the future than did the adolescents of even twenty years ago. Let me note again that it is crucial for parents to understand and accept that their adolescent lives in a different world than they did as adolescents, and their child's adulthood will be different from theirs.

The total developmental process that begins at birth culminates in an identity for each person. If your child successfully masters all of these tasks, she will have a successfully functional identity with healthy and positive feelings about herself. If any tasks are not successfully mastered, this identity can be restrictive or dysfunctional.

INTIMACY.   The adolescent has one remaining task to master. Until this time, relationships have been primarily based on a child-

adult model. Now the adolescent or young adult has to learn to relate successfully to other people, and eventually to one other person,
as an equal, on a one-to-one basis. This kind of relationship is often
referred to as intimacy. This task starts in late adolescence, but it is
not complete until young adulthood.

When people relate in a dependent-independent mode, they need
and depend on significant and more powerful people, like parents.
When you are young, you may very well feel as if you and your
parents are one. This is intimacy, but not a workable kind of intimacy in an adult world. In an intimate adult relationship, in the
independent-independent mode, each person depends on the other.
However, even though each loves, leans on, and needs the other for
his or her emotional well-being, neither loses his or her boundaries.
At all times, each can still function well independently. This is a goal
that most of us work on all of our lives and few of us achieve with
total success. But, because it represents the best that human beings
can make of their adult relationships, it makes a fitting close for the
discussion of normal development from childhood to adulthood.

9

Psychosocial Problems Seen with the Child Who Has Learning Disabilities

Children or adolescents with learning disabilities plus possible attention deficit hyperactivity disorder (ADHD) have more than school and classroom problems—they have problems with all aspects of life. As discussed earlier in this book, the same disabilities that interfere with reading, writing, and arithmetic also interfere with emotional and social development or cause emotional and social problems. Some infants may have difficulties from the earliest stages of development. Some children may struggle, unable to move forward through critical stages of development. Still others may develop within normal expectations, showing adequate progress at first, and then be set back by the stress of entering school or reaching a grade in school where they cannot succeed.

Problems in Early Stages of Development

Infancy may be very difficult for the child who will have learning disabilities. Although these disabilities will not be apparent until later in life, some of these problem areas can affect the child from birth. Remember the road map in Chapter 1. A child with ADHD might be hyperactive, inattentive, and impulsive from earliest childhood. So, too, a child with one of the modulating problems might show difficulty regulating anxiety, or anger, or mood from early life.

Basic Trust

It is not uncommon for parents to report that their child has been irritable since birth. This child never slept or slept for brief periods of
time only. She was colicky, and feeding was a chore. She was difficult
to calm or comfort. For some parents, these behaviors did not improve until age three or four; and for others, these behaviors remain
in modified form throughout childhood.

These subtle, invisible, neurologically based problems might have
a significant impact on the earliest parent-child bonding and interactions. (One mother's experiences with such a child will be described
in Chapter 11.) Babies with motor problems might be floppy and
poorly coordinated. Poorly coordinated infants also may have difficulty sucking and eating. Infants who are hyperactive might thrash
about, their constant activity creating constant problems with
care.

We do not know what the full impact of perceptual disabilities may
be during the early months of life. Could visual or auditory perception problems be present during the early months and years? Could
such disabilities interfere with critical visual and auditory inputs that
are needed to orient the child to the world or to bond with a parent?
Might some also have difficulty with smell or taste? If so, how might
this affect the child's early development? Parents who had irritable
and difficult babies would say yes, there were problems.

Earlier in the book I discussed sensory integration disorder. Infants with this disorder might be sensitive to touch. They might not
like to be held and might often cry and thrash. The more the parent
cuddles to comfort, the more they cry and push away. Soon, some
parents learn to place the baby on a pillow and to hold the pillow, or
to lay the baby in the crib and prop up the bottle. Since most physicians do not know about tactile sensitivity, they don't believe the
parents and tell them that they are too anxious and must learn to
relax. Fathers, who often come home late or who may be too uncomfortable to hold or play with the baby, may not experience the
same reactions and may reinforce the physician's beliefs. All of this
leaves the mother confused, deprived of the desired interactions with
her baby, and feeling inadequate.

If these invisible neurological difficulties affect the infant, what
about the parent? Mothers and fathers often feel helpless and inade-

quate. They try hard to comfort and please their infant, but nothing seems to work. They get little sleep and may become frustrated and irritable with the infant. Neither the infant's nor the parents' state of functioning helps the parents to bond with and enjoy their baby.

Separation

Children with learning disabilities plus possibly ADHD or another of the related problems often have difficulty with separation. Mastering separation requires at least two things. First, the child must feel secure enough to venture out and explore the world. Second, the world must be attractive and fun enough to make the child want to stay out there and engage with the people in it. The child may have difficulty interacting, communicating, or doing what other children are doing. He may find the outside world stressful and retreat back to the inside world. Parents sense this discomfort and lack of success and intuitively reach out to comfort. If either or both situations occur, the mastery of separation will be delayed.

The result may be a child who prefers to stay at home. When things don't work out in day care or nursery school, the child resists going or, if forced to go, avoids the other children or interacts poorly with them. As these children struggle to master separation, you may see the negativism, the power struggles, the need to control, and the difficulties with relationships that were normal for age two persisting into ages three, four, and beyond.

Individuation

What about the next stage, individuation? If the child is having difficulty with other children, with play activities, and with preschool situations, the steps in development that are normal for individuation will start late and may last long after the appropriate age. Other children will have long since outstripped the child in their emotional maturity. Even after age six, the child may continue to be fearful or may try to divide adults and other children or may avoid certain activities for fear of being hurt—problems that normally occur between three and six. When these immature behaviors still take place in kindergarten or in the first and second grades, teachers quite understandably become annoyed with the behaviors. Classmates, too, tend to tease and fight with this child.

Unless the disabilities have been recognized and helped, boys may have a special problem becoming "just like daddy." For example, the son who does poorly in games and sports may become insecure and prefer staying home with his mother. Father may be disappointed that his son is not doing what boys are supposed to do and lets his son know this verbally or nonverbally. The son senses the message and feels that he cannot be what his father wants. Father may get angry at the mother, blaming her for making his son a "sissy." Father is angry and disappointed; mother is angry and hurt; and the child struggles to find a way to master individuation. He often cannot fully succeed and feels less confident in himself.

Latency

Some children master each stage of development more slowly than most. They may enter the latency period and grade school with some weaknesses in their psychological foundation. Each new task causes stress, which in turn causes a temporary retreat to earlier behaviors. The child with problems may now consistently lag behind. A break in development or a retreat to an earlier behavior can happen at any stage along the way, even into adolescence. Some children will have so much difficulty reaching these landmarks in psychosocial growth that they need professional help. It is critical, should this be necessary, that the mental health professional recognize the child's underlying neurological difficulties and the effects these have had on parenting and on the child's development.

Let me illustrate these difficulties with growing up by sharing an interview with an eleven-year-old boy. The session was taped. His words are noted; mine are in parentheses.

I'm smart but in an L.D. program because I'm socially disturbed. I don't like to be around other people—only my parents. Maybe I'll be a bachelor. I pretend the kids are not there—only the teacher. Why can't I just be with my parents and never marry? Just stay with them. Why would any girl want to marry me? I'm not strong. I don't like myself. I'm always sad and depressed. I'm different from everyone else. I don't like sports but

I'm curious about science, but I don't learn. I don't like getting into trouble like they do.

(You say you are smart.) No. I got a D; therefore, I'm not smart. (What is the solution?) Suicide, but I don't want to kill myself. I just don't like me and people don't like me.

I'm always depressed. I stay by myself and ignore others. My mother and father think I'm exaggerating. I try to get them to understand. (Whom do you turn to?) Nobody. I think my parents like me but no one else likes me. (Who loves you?) No one loves me. (And you?) I don't like me. I think the world would be better off without me. (Therefore, you want to die?) If I did not wake up one day, people would be happy. My class would have a party.

(How long have you felt this way?) Since a baby. I was never sure that my parents liked me or loved me. Why should they love me? I'm not special. I'm just a normal dumb sixth grader. (You are their son.) I think that they wanted someone different. (Who?) One who is smart; who listens and does not talk back. I'm the opposite.

(What makes you happy?) I never accomplish anything to be happy about. I'm nobody special. I'm not the Prince of England. I would like to stay home and have a private tutor.

I don't care what happens to myself. If I get sick, no one cares or if I get hurt. (Wouldn't your mother?) Maybe about the doctor's bills.

(Life appears to be so miserable for you.) No one ever liked me.

This child is depressed with low self-esteem and a poor self-image. He shows difficulty with basic trust, separation, and individuation. The full evaluation provided probable reasons for his current emotional status. He had gross and fine motor difficulties, resulting in doing poorly in sports. He was ignored at recess. His learning disabilities were not identified until age nine, in fourth grade. By then he had experienced failure and embarrassment at school. His parents, not understanding the reasons, were angry with his difficulties at school. Following the suggestions of his teachers, they treated him like a child who just "was not trying hard enough." This child's feelings about himself and about his perception of how other children saw him and how his parents felt about him were based, in his world, on the realities he lived with.

Emotional Problems

Parents might find it helpful in understanding children and adolescents with learning disabilities plus possible ADHD to realize that their children have had only one brain all of their lives. They don't know that it is different from anybody else's brain. Nor do parents, teachers, and other meaningful adults in their lives. These youngsters look normal and appear to be bright. Their problems can be invisible to the outside world. People yell at them, telling them to sit still, to pay attention, to keep quiet, and to speak up. They cannot understand, either, why they are more active or distractible than others or why they have more difficulty with the schoolwork. They try just as hard to learn. Why don't they succeed? Their experiences confuse and frustrate them. Why do they constantly seem to fail? Why are they constantly embarrassed? Is it any wonder that they develop emotional and social difficulties?

The special education team points out that Billy has visual perception or visual motor problems. These learning disabilities interfere with his mastery of reading and written language skills, they say. The special education team is used to focusing on problems such as this. But, what about Billy on the playground who misses the ball because his eyes can't tell his hands what to do quickly enough? How do the other kids react to Billy's clumsiness and poor performance? How does Billy feel when he is the last one to be chosen when the kids pick sides? And what about the physical education teacher? She or he may not have been part of the school meetings about Billy's learning disabilities or may not understand the effect of these disabilities on his ability to perform in sports and other physical education activities. This teacher might yell at Billy or tease him in front of his classmates.

So it is with Allison. Educational and language evaluations identified her as having auditory perception and expressive language problems. Based on this information, the school professionals developed a specific educational and language therapy program for her. But is that enough? What happens to Allison when she is with her friends? She misunderstands what they say and responds wrongly. Her friends think she is not paying attention or is dumb. They may exclude her from their games. Furthermore, although someone explained her auditory and language difficulties to her regular education teacher, no one ever explained them to her lunchroom monitor or her art or music teacher. These key people in Allison's school life might become upset with her ability to comprehend and communicate. And no one explained them to her parents and siblings. They, too, get angry with her for "not paying attention" or "not following instructions." What does this do to Allison? How does this shape her friends' reactions to her? How must she feel in the family? What does she begin to think about herself?

All too often such problems are not correctly diagnosed. Even more often, they are not communicated to all of the people who must know. The child goes on experiencing repeated frustrations and failures. Finally, he or she develops emotional problems and is referred to a child and adolescent psychiatrist such as myself or to other mental health professionals for an evaluation. It is essential to distinguish between a child whose emotional problems are *causing* the school and academic difficulties and a child whose emotional problems are the *consequence* of these school and academic difficulties. I cannot stress this point too much. Painfully too often, mental health professionals see the smoke and miss the fire. They see the surface behaviors but do not see the underlying learning disabilities and possible ADHD that are causing the behaviors. The child is seen as primarily emotionally disturbed, and the parents are often seen as dysfunctional. Both may be true; however, the causes of this end result are not purely psychological.

Let me illustrate this important point by describing an all-too-common situation that results in a referral to a mental health professional. A child starts school. He begins to fall behind and to struggle. The school professionals decide to handle the problems by keeping the child back. This approach is used too often despite research that shows that repeating a year (except for the preschooler or kindergartner who is not yet ready to go on) usually accomplishes little and causes damage to the child's self-esteem.

Now, he is a head taller and a year older than classmates. His friends have moved on to the next grade. The child feels different, dumb, and embarrassed. Much of what is taught that year was material the child learned the previous year, and the child is bored. The material not mastered the previous year may not be learned any better this time since the same teaching techniques are in place that were not successful the previous year. The child begins to feel frustrated and angry. Soon, he may begin to act out in school and/or at home.

Throughout this time, two things are one hundred percent predictable. One occurs in the home and one in the school. At home, both parents become frustrated with their child's difficulties. If there are two parents in the family, one parent will believe that the best way to help this child is to be firm and strict while the other believes that the best way to help is to be understanding and permissive. Thus, the parents begin to clash with each other. This parenting difference might result in marital stress.

At school, the classroom teacher becomes frustrated. The teacher is doing everything possible to teach this child without success. Further, the child's behavior is now disrupting the class and making it difficult for the teacher to teach the other children. This teacher often foists this frustration onto the parents. Parents begin to get calls from the teacher: "Please be sure that Billy does his homework each night." "Ask Mary to write more neatly. I can't read her writing. And practice her spelling so she can spell better." "Tell your son to quit calling out in class." "You have got to read more to him so that he understands how important it is to be able to read."

The parents are frustrated. If they could have changed anything, they would have done it already. Finally, the principal calls the parents in and says, "Your child is not learning. It is clear that he has an emotional problem, probably because of your marital problems. Get him to a mental health professional."

If you are smiling as you read this because you have been there, don't let the school professionals do this to you. At the risk of being accused of being repetitive, it is critical to clarify whether your son's or daughter's emotional, social, and family problems are *causing* the school and academic difficulties or whether these emotional, social, and family problems are a *consequence* of the school and academic difficulties and the frustration experienced by the child, by the parents, and by the teacher. Each is a totally different situation and requires a different approach to help.

It is critical that the mental health professional who sees that child referred by the principal looks at the total child in his total world. To address the acting-out behavior in school or in the family or to address the couple's stress without understanding the role of the academic frustrations and failures is to misdiagnose and mistreat. How can I change the self-image of this child with one or two hours a week of psychotherapy when he experiences twenty or more hours a week of frustration and failure? This child's self-image is accurate and based on life experiences. I cannot talk this child into having a better self-image. Only interventions that result in academic success can accomplish this.

As you read about the kinds of emotional problems children with learning disabilities and/or ADHD can develop, think of your daughter or son. If you recognize any of these symptoms or behaviors and you have not already asked for help, discuss the situation with your family doctor, the school counselor, or with a mental health professional.

Problems of the School-Age Child

When children experience stress, they usually react with anxiety and/or depression. This stress could be a normal developmental stress. For example, the two-year-old begins to master separation. As she moves out into "the world" there is anxiety about this unknown experience. There is also sadness about leaving the comfort of a closer, more consistent attachment to mother or father. So, too, the kindergartner who starts school. There is the excitement and anxiety about this new adventure, and sadness at not being home or in a known and comfortable preschool program.

The child with learning disabilities begins to feel the stress of school and of less or little success with learning. This child will react

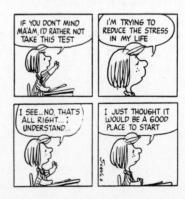

PEANUTS reprinted by permission of United Feature Syndicate, Inc.

with anxiety and depression. The anxiety is that she cannot perform as expected. The depression is the sadness of not being able to please the teacher and parents by doing what is expected.

When the stresses a child experiences become too great, she must do something to cope. In general, we see children doing one of four possible approaches to coping:

Internalizing the stress
Externalizing the stress
Somatizing the stress
Using other approaches to cope with stress

Internalizing the Stress

Some children become very aware of the problems and feel the anxiety or depression or both. These feelings are seen at school and at home. They often lift and lessen or disappear during the summer and school vacations.

ANXIETY. They might focus their anxiety on school, showing a fear of going to school (school avoidance) or a fear of doing school work. This anxiety might expand into a generalized anxiety disorder. They might become afraid of sleeping alone or of being in part of the house alone. They might be afraid to ride on the school bus. Some become so upset when doing homework that they will not start, or they become upset as soon as they have any difficulty doing the work. Others might become fearful in the classroom

PEANUTS reprinted by permission of United Feature Syndicate, Inc.

and appear to withdraw from any potentially frustrating or uncertain situations by getting upset and resisting the work or by pulling back and becoming passive, thus becoming unavailable for learning.

Eight-year-old Bobbie had these problems. She was of superior intelligence; however, because no one identified her learning disabilities, she had failed often and was currently starting second grade for the second time. When I asked her what she did in school when she couldn't do her work, she replied, "When I was younger I used to crumble up my paper and cry . . . then they teased me and called me a cry baby. So, I decided that school was no fun. Since I couldn't leave, I sat and pretended that I was home in my room with my dolls . . . I made up stories and had a good time." Bobbie's teacher complained that she would "daydream the day away if I let her."

DEPRESSION.   Some children with learning disabilities plus possible ADHD do not develop the ability to cope with the pain of frustration and failure experienced at school and experience a true sense of depression. Failures, inadequacies, and poor interactions with peers and significant adults leave the child feeling angry and devalued. Younger children, who are often unable to experience the depression internally, may express their feelings by being irritable and aggressive toward everyone. Older children may exhibit classic symptoms of depression. They appear to be sad, cry easily, and may have trouble sleeping and eating. Sometimes the child turns so much of his anger inward that he becomes self-destructive or speaks of "life not being worth living" or of committing suicide.

David, an eleven-year-old boy with learning disabilities and a long history of failures, was referred for evaluation because of his overly polite, passive manner. During the evaluation he described himself as a "bad troublemaker." He went on to say "I'm stupid and I can't do anything right." This, of course, was in marked contrast to his usually overly serene behavior. He added, "I get so mad with myself when I make a mistake, I send myself to my room. Sometimes I punish myself by making myself go to bed early or by finding my favorite TV show and not letting myself see it. Sometimes I get so mad I slap or pinch myself."

Some depressed children feel so bad about themselves that they cannot accept praise. They feel that they are too bad to deserve such praise. If a teacher compliments a piece of work, the child may feel compelled to destroy it. If a parent compliments the child, he might act terrible until the parent yells or enacts a punishment.

After repeated lack of success in school, some children develop a feeling of worthlessness, resulting in a poor self-image and low self-esteem. These children see themselves as inadequate, bad, worthless people who can't do anything right. Feedback from the outside world often encourages this self-image and, at the very least, does nothing to help correct it. Ronnie, a markedly depressed ten-year-old boy with such feelings, had been hyperactive since birth. Ronnie was always all over the place. His mother reported, "All he ever heard from me was 'no' or 'don't' or 'bad boy.'" Ronnie was kicked out of nursery school for being a "monster." He grew even wilder in kindergarten and was no better in first and second grade. Still undiagnosed, he repeated second grade, started third, and was then suspended from school. He had never known himself to be anything but bad, dislikable, inadequate, and stupid. The fact that he was finally found to be very bright and to have learning disabilities and ADHD didn't change his self-image.

No one can talk these children out of their self-assessments because the self-image results from a collection of real experiences. They can improve, however, when they begin to see the changes that come with appropriate help and when they begin to master learning and behavioral tasks.

Arthur is another example of a child with a poor self-image and depression. Now twelve, Arthur had been diagnosed at age five as having learning disabilities and ADHD. He was placed on medication and received several years of intensive special educational therapy as well as psychotherapy. When Arthur eventually went back to a regular sixth-grade class and did well, he reminisced with me:

Remember when I was at the special school and you kept telling me how smart I was? Well, I thought you just wanted to make me feel good because I couldn't read or do anything . . . I almost gave up and felt that I would just never make it. Then one day something clicked and I started to read. I *really read*. Then I started to do math. Boy, I could really learn just like you told me. I must have grown five years that first week I started to read.

Depression with the resulting poor self-image or low self-esteem might be apparent in the child's comments. One hears the child say that he is "stupid" or "dumb" or "not as smart as the other kids." Class and homework challenges are met with "I can't do that. It is too hard." There is a sense of sadness about this child. Not infrequently, he will say that he feels sad and unhappy.

The depression might lead to regression. The child retreats to an earlier stage of psychological or social development. Earlier behaviors or immature, infantile interactions, things you think the child has completely outgrown, recur. For example, the parents of seven-and-a-half-year-old Debbie complained that their daughter had been happy and "normal" until she entered kindergarten. As her mother explained it, at this point "she had a change of personality. She had trouble keeping up with the other children. In first grade she just didn't learn much so now she's repeating first." The father added, "Home life is terrible. We yell at her all of the time. Since school began this year, she's gone backwards, acting like a baby and talking like a baby. She's impossible. She won't listen and tunes me out. She's begun to wet her bed for the first time since she was three. She even eats with her fingers." At a therapy session, Debbie talked about school. "I have trouble because I don't understand the work, especially reading and math. It's hard and I can't do it. The teacher yells at me all the time. Maybe I'm just not as smart as the other kids."

Externalizing the Stress

Some children find the discomfort and pain of stress with the resulting anxiety and depression too much to cope with. They decide not to cope with the stress by "getting rid of it." They externalize the anxiety and depression. To do this, they project all of their problems to others. Suddenly the behavioral or academic problems are because this kid did this and that kid did that. They get into three fights at school in one week and insist that each was the result of someone else's behavior: "Billy started the fight by . . ." or "Don't blame me. I didn't do it. Mary made a face at me and got me mad." So, too, it becomes the teacher's fault or a parent's fault.

By projecting all of the blame onto others, this child does not have to accept responsibility for any problems. The child is in the principal's office because of getting into trouble twice in the same day. The child is sitting back not upset. "I didn't cause the problems. The first time my teacher didn't listen to me and then got angry. It was her fault." The other time "the teacher didn't see that John kicked me under the table. I just told him to stop, and the teacher accused me of talking. John should be in here, not me."

The characteristic of children who externalize their stress, then, is that they accept no responsibility and appear not to be anxious or depressed. All of the meaningful adults in such a child's life—parents, teachers—feel anxious and depressed about the child. This is a difficult child to help. Since she accepts no responsibility for her behaviors, the child doesn't see a need to be in therapy and insists there is nothing to talk about.

Under the current mental health guidelines (listed in the *Diagnostic and Statistical Manual for Mental Disorders*, Fourth Edition, or DSM IV), children who externalize, are seen as one of two types. If they externalize primarily within the family—challenging rules, getting into difficulty and then blaming others, being oppositional and defiant—we label the child as having oppositional defiant disorder (see Table 9-1).

If the behaviors expand beyond the family, leading to challenging school and societal rules, fighting, stealing, breaking rules, we label the child as having a conduct disorder (see Table 9-2). In reality, these are ways of describing the areas in which the child externalizes stress.

It is not uncommon for a child to be initially described as anxious or depressed, later to be seen as having oppositional defiant disorder, and still later to begin to get into the types of problems that lead to being seen as having a conduct disorder. It is important to understand that these diagnostic categories for externalizing behaviors do not explain the *cause* for the behaviors, only the style the child uses to cope. For the children we are discussing, the most frequent problem is that the frustrations and failures experienced in school, in the family, and with peers lead to significant stress. It is this stress that might be externalized as an oppositional defiant disorder or a conduct disorder. Children with failing experiences in school often develop one of these disorders. It is critical to understand the relationship of the learning disability or ADHD.

Table 9-1 Diagnostic Criteria: Oppositional Defiant Disorder

1. The child shows a pattern of negativistic, hostile, and defiant behavior lasting at least six months, during which four (or more) of the following are present:

   Often loses temper.
   Often argues with adults.
   Often actively defies or refuses to comply with adults' requests or rules.
   Often deliberately annoys people.
   Often blames others for his or her mistakes or misbehaviors.
   Is often touchy or easily annoyed by others.
   Is often angry and resentful.
   Is often spiteful or vindictive.

2. The disturbance in behavior causes clinically significant impairment in social, academic, or occupational functioning.

Table 9-2 Diagnostic Criteria: Conduct Disorder

1. The child shows a repetitive and persistent pattern of behavior in which the basic rights of others or major age-appropriate societal norms or rules are violated, as manifested by the presence of three (or more) of the following criteria in the past twelve months, with at least one criterion present in the past six months:

   a. Aggression toward people and animals
      Often bullies, threatens, or intimidates others.
      Often initiates physical fights.
      Has used a weapon that can cause serious physical harm to others (e.g., a bat, brick, broken bottle, knife, gun).
      Has been physically cruel to people.
      Has been physically cruel to animals.
      Has stolen while confronting a victim (e.g., mugging, purse snatching, extortion, armed robbery).
      Has forced someone into sexual activity.

   b. Destruction of property
      Has deliberately engaged in fire setting with the intent of causing serious damage.

Has deliberately destroyed others' property (other than
fire setting).

c. Deceitfulness or theft
Has broken into someone else's house, building, or car.
Often lies to obtain goods or favors or to avoid obligations (i.e.,
"cons" others).
Has stolen items of nontrivial value without confronting a victim
(e.g., shoplifting, but without breaking and entering; forgery).

d. Serious violations of rules
Often stays out at night despite parental prohibitions, beginning
before age thirteen years.
Has run away from home overnight at least twice while living in
parental or parental surrogate home (or once without
returning for a lengthy period).
Is often truant from school (beginning before age thirteen years).

2. The disturbance in behavior causes clinically significant impairment in
social, academic, or occupational functioning.

Somatizing the Stress

Some children focus their anxiety on bodily functions. A child may
develop stomachaches, lower abdominal cramps, headaches, diar-
rhea, or frequency of urination or bowel movements. These complaints often occur only in the morning of a school day and rarely on
weekends, holidays, or during the summer. The child often has to
leave class to go to the school nurse or to go home. As with any
physical symptoms, the discomfort is real. The pain goes away when
the child is allowed to stay home, not because she or he is faking, but
because the stress of going to school is reduced when the child is
able to stay home.

Katie, who was around seven at the time, once explained, "Sometimes I get into trouble because I forgot to do what the teacher said
or I erase too much . . . The teacher yells at me and I get scared . . .
Then my stomach starts to hurt and I have to go to the nurse." Similarly, Franklin woke up each school day with severe stomach cramps
and vomiting. His mother kept him home from school, and the
pains usually disappeared by noon. A complete medical workup

found Franklin perfectly normal. He must have guessed why he was brought to see me. His first words were "I know my stomach trouble is because I'm afraid of school. Only it really does hurt, no kidding!"

Other children may explain their anxiety by focusing on their increasing awareness that something must be wrong with their bodies. They have heard parents, teachers, and doctors talking about their brain or their "nervous system," and they have been through countless examinations and tests, so they express their worries by being hypochondriacal: "My back hurts" or "My head aches" or "My knee feels funny." Sometimes this concern with their bodies extends into a general concern with body image or body damage. At times these complaints become a complete rationalization for failure: "I can't help it if I made a mistake. My arm hurts today."

Other Approaches Used to Cope with Stress

Some children use their behaviors to handle difficult situations. These behaviors are often disruptive to others.

THE CLASS CLOWN.   Some children cope with the stresses of school by being the class clown. Clowning can be very successful. The child learns what to do to the wrong person at the wrong time to disrupt the lesson plan or to be kicked out of class. Clowning serves several functions. It can be a way of controlling feelings of inadequacy—the child clowns around to cover up feelings of worthlessness and depression. By playing the clown or freak, the child seems to be saying "They call me a clown, but that's only because I choose to be one. I really can turn it off if I want to, but it's too much fun this way." If the child succeeds in this behavior, he or she disrupts the lesson plan or is told to leave the group, thus avoiding the academic work and therefore the potential failure. Clowning behavior may win a certain measure of peer acceptance. Suddenly, the child everyone teases becomes the class hero because of what he or she did. The clowning behaviors are reinforced.

In some schools, the "punishment" for being sent to the principal's office is well worth the effort—not doing schoolwork; talking to the secretary; delivering messages; or playing with the computer. After four years of special education and psychotherapy,

Jack returned to regular classes and was doing well. He saw me, and I asked him to describe what he remembered about his previous experiences in regular classes. "Boy, were those teachers stupid. Anytime it was my turn to read or to do anything I had trouble with, I would tease another boy or joke around. It worked great. I got sent out of the room." Then he added, "Only you got me to see that I was the stupid one. . . . You can't get help if you're not in class and I sure didn't want to spend the rest of my life in a special class."

HANDLING ANGER.   When some children have difficulty dealing with anger, they may choose an indirect way of showing it. One such style is called passive-aggressive. The child's behavior is not actively aggressive in and of itself, yet the child seems to make everybody angry with him or her much of the time. While supposedly getting dressed, for instance, the child may play with her clothes or with toys until the parent becomes furious. The child then looks up in bewilderment and says, "Why are you so mad at me? I didn't do anything." A special education teacher once said to me of such a child, "He was so cooperative and helpful and sweet that I felt like hitting him."

Other children become passive-dependent. Initially, the child avoids failure and unpleasant feelings by staying out of the situations that could result in failure. But this passivity can expand into a veritable lifestyle. He or she avoids taking any initiative in anything and minimizes getting involved in everything. A truly helpless child arouses sympathy in adults. The passive-dependent child's behavior often makes people angry because the helplessness appears to be deliberate and contrived.

Occasionally, children appear to act in an overly mature way. Faced with feelings of being different, inadequate, and fearful that no one will like them or take care of them, these children decide to grow up quickly. They also sense that they are not succeeding as a child with other children and guess that it would be safer to be an adult. Often they have a compelling need to be in control and they become upset if they cannot control every situation. This controlling behavior might be their way of coping with a world that they experience as out of control. It might be a way of becoming an adultlike person and taking control of the world. They look, act, and relate to others like serious adults. This behavior may pay off. Adults compliment them and spend more time with them. Chuck is an example of over-maturity. His parents described this seven-year-old boy as not needing anyone to take care of him. Chuck was totally independent; in fact, he took care of everyone else in the family and in his school class. He enjoyed most having discussions with the teacher. He had no sense of humor and was described as a "perfect little man," completely self-sufficient. In a psychiatric diagnostic session, Chuck's fantasy and play reflected great concern about dependency needs and a fear that no one would meet them. So he had to take care of himself. Chuck denied his anger and his wish to be taken care of. He used all of his emotional energies to maintain his protective facade.

Social Problems

Studies show that for children, self-esteem is based on two experiences—academic success and peer acceptance. Children with learning disabilities often do not experience academic success. They often have social problems and are not successful with peer interactions.

All of the emotional problems discussed to this point profoundly affect a child's social relationships. A few other special types of social problems also deserve mention.

As discussed throughout this book, some children have difficulty because their learning disabilities interfere with peer activities. Visual-motor problems that affect certain sports and language problems that interfere with communications are examples. One result of such problems is avoidance of peer interactions and activities.

Some children will prefer to play with younger children because they cannot handle the interactions or participate in the activities of their own age group. They intuitively seek out an age group whose skills they can manage. A boy of nine might have visual perception, fine motor, and visual-motor disabilities, but good strengths in auditory perception, language, and gross motor areas. He goes out with his classmates but finds he cannot play baseball or basketball well enough to keep up. Then he learns that five- and six-year-olds do a lot of calling to each other and prefer running, climbing, and riding bikes. These gross motor activities and interactions he can handle. In addition, the younger children look up to him while his peers avoid or tease him. Thus, he spends more time with the younger children.

Another special social problem relates to the child's difficulty in reading social cues or learning social skills. It is not understood why these problems exist; however, they are very common. Most children learn very early in life to "read" body language—facial expressions or tone of voice or body tension—and adjust their behaviors accordingly. For example, a child of three knows that when he is outside playing and mother yells to come in, the tone of her voice means either you can ignore her for a little longer or you had better come in quickly. Children can sense a parent's emotional status by body language and know whether to approach or avoid this parent when he or she comes home from work. Many children with learning disabilities do not pick up the subtle and not-so-subtle messages that suggest that they need to react differently or change their behavior. They don't back off. The joking around goes too far. Feelings get hurt and tempers may flare. They miss the nonverbal cues that say "Enough!"

In Closing

The pain that children can experience because of their frustrations and failures is real. Unattended to, it can have a major impact on personality development. Without help, these feelings and thoughts can shape behavior both for the present and the future. I will illustrate with another clinical example.

Bob's parents were concerned. He was eight years old and had just completed second grade. He had done poorly in first grade, not learning to read or print well. During second grade he made some progress in reading but was not yet up to grade level.

"He seems intelligent," his mother reported. "But Bob's so angry and unhappy. He's a perfectionist and gets upset if he can't do his schoolwork." The consultation with me followed a conference required by the principal. The principal spoke of Bob's high anxiety level in school and his poor self-image. The principal thought that he had an emotional problem and needed psychotherapy.

Bob's father said that Bob set very high standards for himself. "If he cannot do things, he says he is no good or stupid. Now he's so afraid that he won't do well that he avoids trying any new activities."

When I went out to the waiting room to greet Bob, he stood up and shook hands. He was a very serious and tense child who behaved more like an adult than an eight-year-old. As we entered my office, I tried to help him relax by encouraging him to choose a toy or game to play with and by chatting with him about general things. He went through the motions of setting up some toys but preferred to sit on the floor with me and talk.

The following is an excerpt from a tape recording of this session. Throughout this session Bob was verbal and serious and showed signs of being tense (e.g., twisting his fingers, frowning). His comments are presented. My comments are in parentheses.

(Tell me about school.) I don't like to make mistakes. (Oh.) I get angry and frustrated. (What do you do?) Sometimes I feel like crying but I toughed it out. (You can't cry?) The kids would think I was a baby. (What else do you feel?) I get angry with myself. I say I'm dumb or stupid or can't learn. (How do you feel when you say these things?) Bad. I'm just a jerk. (What do you do with these feelings?) I distract myself until they go away.

(Bob, why do you think you feel this way?) I don't know. (Could it have something to do with school?) I don't read or do math too good. (And the other kids . . . ?) They do it easier. (When you say that you look upset.) Yeah.

(What else happens in school?) I get scared sometimes that the teacher will be angry with me. (I see.) If she doesn't like my work, she sends me back to do it again. I get mad because I did my best. (What do you do?) I distract myself and push it out of my mind. Then I do the work. (How do you push away such angry feelings?) I get busy with the work. (Don't you feel like yelling or throwing something or . . . ?) No, that would be bad.

(You know, Bob, I get the feeling that you don't like yourself too much.) There's nothing to like. (You mean you cannot think of anything about yourself that is good?) I guess. (You guess?) Well, sometimes I think that Mommy wanted a girl because they don't cause so much trouble as boys. But, they may want a boy to carry on the family name. (So, you may not like yourself, and now I hear you say that maybe your parents don't like you either.) Sometimes I think that.

(You know, Bob, I think the real problem is that you don't like yourself.) Yeah. (And you look so sad right now. How long have you had such feelings and thoughts?) I think they started in the first grade. (Tell me about it.) I couldn't do some of the work. The teacher used to make me do it again. The other kids got smiles from the teacher. I just got disappointed looks.

(What do you think was the problem in first grade?) I don't know. (You seemed to have trouble doing the school work.) Yeah. (You know, Bob, I've worked with other boys and girls with problems like yours. Sometimes they worry that their problems are because they are bad and being punished or because there's something wrong with their head or maybe because they're dumb or retarded. I wonder what kind of thoughts you have.) I do think about these things. (You look so sad when you think about these things.) Maybe. Sometimes I think that maybe I'm retarded. (Retarded?) Yeah. (That would be pretty upsetting to think that you were retarded.) Yeah. (Maybe we had better find out what the problems are so that you won't have to worry about things that may not be true.) I'm just too dumb to learn anything. (I can see why you might think that way. I'd like to find out what it is so that we can do something about it.) I can't do anything right.

Last year at the pool I hit my head a couple of times. (And maybe that caused the problems?) Maybe that's why I'm so dumb. (I don't think that's the reason you're having trouble in school. But, then, it's hard for you to believe me.) There's no hope for me.

At this point in the session I put Bob on my lap and held him. He finally began to cry. I reassured him that I would help him and his parents to solve his problems in school so that he could like himself again. I told him that I thought he was a pretty nice kid and that it hurt me to see him in such pain.

Formal testing identified Bob's visual perception, sequencing, visual memory, and fine motor disabilities. There was a wide inconsistency on the subtests of the IQ test. Bob was of high average to superior intellectual potential. Special education interventions were developed for third grade; his teacher would be briefed.

But the damage to Bob's self-image and psychological development had already been done. He was sad, hurting, and in need of help. Psychotherapy was begun, but not for the reasons given by his principal. He was not primarily emotionally disturbed and therefore having trouble in school. He had learning disabilities, and his trouble in school caused him to be emotionally disturbed.

This therapy, however, would not be successful without the special education interventions in school. How could I help him rethink his self-image and feelings about himself if he continued to have failing experiences in school?

10

Psychosocial Problems Seen with the Adolescent Who Has Learning Disabilities

If your son's or daughter's learning disabilities were first recognized in childhood and he or she received the help that was necessary, you are ahead of the game. Adolescence is a stressful time, but it is less so if the basic educational, social, and family supports are in place and you can build on them. If your child's difficulties were not recognized until a major behavior problem surfaced in middle school or junior high school or high school, your task will be much more difficult. With the adolescent's problems compounded by late diagnosis and by the physical changes of puberty itself, it is even more critical to move in with a full team evaluation and a comprehensive intervention program that addresses each area of identified difficulty.

During adolescence, the fact that a learning disability is a total life disability takes on even greater meaning. It affects every kind of life involvement and interaction. Adolescents whose problems were recognized and treated during childhood must now handle new challenges. Those youngsters whose problems went unrecognized until adolescence have a double problem—they must deal with their existing disabilities while trying to compensate for the academic and emotional price they have already paid.

The adolescent with learning disabilities has special problems. Early adolescence is characterized by a strong need not to be different. The person who, as a child, cooperated peacefully with a special education routine may, as an adolescent, suddenly refuse to continue to take part in the special classes or tutoring and insist on being in regular classes. He may refuse to continue taking medication. You may have to come up with some creative compromises: switching special tutoring or other remedial help to an out-of-school, and therefore less public, setting or allowing the youngster to administer his own medication rather than having him go to the school nurse.

Adolescence is a time of rebelling against rules and authority figures. It is an especially difficult period of time for an adolescent with learning disabilities. As parents, you will often be in no-win situations. If you insist that your daughter act her age, your adolescent suddenly acts like a five-year-old. If you baby her, your adolescent suddenly erupts in anger, complaining that you are treating her like a child. If you back off and leave her alone, your adolescent accuses you of not caring. If you give your child adultlike freedom or responsibilities, she abuses these privileges and then gets angry if you take them away. My best advice is to accept the idea that you cannot win. Talk through this whole matter frankly with your adolescent, and try to communicate about and struggle through the issues together. If the rebelliousness gets out of hand, you may need to seek professional guidance.

Normal Developmental Stages

Emotional stress is to be expected during adolescence. The adolescent with learning disabilities has even more emotional problems than the normal adolescent. I have already emphasized the importance of distinguishing between emotional, social, and family problems that are *causing* the academic difficulties and those that are the *consequence* of academic difficulties. The learning disabilities have resulted earlier in frustration, failure, and behavioral problems. Now the behavior problems that resulted may have taken on a life of their own, growing to such proportions that they have made the adolescent unavailable to school participation and learning. Both areas of difficulty—the learning disabilities and the emotional problems— must now be resolved.

In addition, leftover problems from infancy or childhood may resurface. We reviewed the normal developmental tasks of adolescence: moving from dependency to independency, establishing one's identity, learning intimacy. Adolescents with learning disabilities are more likely than most to have trouble in each of these areas. We will discuss each task, focusing on normal adolescent issues as well as the special problems of the adolescent who has learning disabilities.

Independence

Becoming independent, or separating, means going out from the family and realizing successes and positive experiences on one's own. Adolescents who are insecure, have a poor self-image, and do poorly with their peers may not be able to move away from their family comfortably. Instead, some adolescents simply embrace their dependency, turning away from outside companions, staying in the home, and putting on an appearance of being content, even preferring, to be alone or to watch television. Others find these excessive feelings of dependence upsetting and fight them, internally or by lashing out at others. Negativism, power struggles with adults, and unacceptable clothing, hairstyles, and choice of friends are often ways of expressing one's fear of and discomfort with dependency. Although you may find all of these behaviors irritating, don't be completely turned off. It is extremely important that you understand, maintain communication with, and try to help your adolescent.

As you try to help your adolescent through this struggle for independence, keep in mind his specific strengths and weaknesses. For your youngster to find out that he can and must succeed on his own, you must work together to maximize successes and growth-producing experiences. You may have to rethink chores. You will also want to work with your adolescent in selecting after-school activities, sports, or jobs very carefully.

Adolescents with learning disabilities face special problems with their friends. If your teen understands what she or he can and cannot do well and feels comfortable talking with you about these things, you can work together to map out special strategies that will increase the probability of success.

For example, Cathy, who was fifteen, would not go out with her friends to get a snack after school or out to a restaurant on the weekends because she had difficulty reading the menu and was embarrassed. We discussed this problem in family sessions. Cathy's sister suggested that she pretend she didn't know what she wanted and wait until last to order. This would enable her to listen to the others' orders and to pick from among their choices. Her father suggested that he could copy the menu from the local fast-food places and other possible restaurants so that she could practice reading them at home. She tried both approaches right away, and they proved help-ful. Later, as she became more comfortable with her friends, she shared her problem with one friend to whom she felt particularly close. This friend understood and began to help too. When the group was at a restaurant, her friend would turn to Cathy and say "Gee, I can't decide if I want a pizza, a meatball sub, or spaghetti. What do you think?" Ideally, Cathy would feel comfortable sharing her problem with all of her close friends. Thus, each would under-stand and help her.

You probably never stop to think how many situations call for quick facility in reading, but they are everywhere: One must be able to read street signs or maps, bus stops, TV listings, the movie guide, or a movie marquee. If your adolescent has a reading problem, it is essential that you all come up with imaginative suggestions for han-dling it.

Understanding and acting on spoken instructions is another skill that everyone must have to get along in daily life. If you can't com-prehend what you are told, your opportunities for action and for learning are limited. Here again, if the adolescent has this problem, some creative solutions are in order.

Rico, who is seventeen years old, had auditory perception and au-ditory short-term memory problems. He went for his driver's license test. He knew how to drive, drove well, and passed his written test with ease. There he sat behind the wheel waiting for the road test to begin. His father got out of the car. Rico slid behind the wheel, and the examiner got in beside him. This examiner said, "Okay, son, lis-ten to me. See that white line? Pull out from the curb. Then bring the car to a complete stop at the white line. Then turn left and go to the stop sign. Let's see you do it." Rico misunderstood some of the directions and could not remember all of them. He failed the test, not because he was a poor driver but because he had learning disabilities.

Rico's father suggested that he speak to the examiner and tell him about his learning disabilities. He thought that perhaps the examiner would give Rico written instructions or break down the instructions to shorter steps. Rico, however, refused to be treated differently. That night he and his father worked out a compromise. They went back to the test site, talked with several people after they completed the test, and learned the routine. Rico's father wrote it out, step by step, and Rico memorized it. He reapplied for an appointment and took the test again. The examiner could have been talking in a foreign language. It did not matter. Rico knew the demands and successfully passed the test.

Whether the task is using public transportation, learning to shop, cooking, handling money or a checkbook, driving a car, or interacting with friends in everyday activities, work with your adolescent to develop strategies for coping with the tasks that he or she finds difficult. Building on strengths and compensating for weaknesses is critical because self-confidence, self-image, and finally, a sense of independence are all based on these small and large successes. No one can write an instruction booklet for *your* family. Indeed, no one really can tell your son or daughter the best way to do activities—the disabilities to be overcome are theirs as are the tasks to be accomplished. But, you can help in every way possible as they "write their own book."

Before leaving the stage of moving from dependency toward independence, let me discuss one other concern. Your son or daughter should be receiving special education help. This help might be provided by each teacher, by resource room professionals, and/or by private tutors. All too often, these professionals contribute to the adolescent's feelings of dependency. They don't mean to do so, but they teach "learned helplessness." They are given exercises or assignments and asked to do them. They are asked to show their homework and then helped with the areas of difficulty. When they have a pending exam, they study with the tutor. They are passive, and the special education professional tells them what to do. Not uncommonly, the reasons for the help are not discussed. What a difference there is between a tutor's saying "I want you to do these worksheets for me today" and a tutor's saying "Look, we know you have difficulty with visual figure-ground and that when you read, you often skip words or lines or read the same line twice. I want you to work on these exercises, which will help you learn to minimize this problem." The first statement is an adult-to-child, let-me-tell-you-what-to-do, situation. The second statement is a colleague-to-colleague statement that respects the individual and facilitates self-understanding and self-help.

This understanding of self is critical. Unless your daughter understands her areas of disability and ability, she is unable to take an active role in problem solving. As she moves through high school and beyond, it is essential that she understand her brain and how it works. She must know her strengths and weaknesses so that problem areas can be clarified and creative approaches to problem solving developed. What a difference between a teenager who walks into the tutor's office and sits down, waiting for instructions, and a teenager who walks in and says "My science teacher lectures all of the time, and I can't get everything down fast enough. Can you help me solve this problem?"

Another theme is equally important. We often want our adolescents to feel good and not be overwhelmed by their learning disabilities. So, professionals and parents make comments like "You just learn differently, and we will help you learn how to learn in this different way." Or "Since the teachers are making adjustments and you are getting tutoring, you will do as well as your friends and only have to work as hard as they are." No. Don't mislead your child. Having a learning disability is a disability. The only way to prevent it from becoming a handicap is by hard work. Thus, this hard work will take more time. You can offer empathy and hugs. You can be supportive and be sure he gets the right help. But the bottom line is that your adolescent will have to understand and accept that he will have to work harder and longer to be successful. He will have to see work as acceptable and, maybe, pleasant. The pay-off is that he will succeed or that he can be in regular classes rather than special classes.

To illustrate this important concept of self-knowledge leading to self-advocacy, I would like to tell you about seventeen-year-old Jimmy, a high school junior. I had worked with Jimmy and his family since the third grade, primarily helping them learn the concepts in this book. Jimmy understood himself and what he had to do to succeed. He had accepted his responsibilities. He requested a meeting with his new English teacher during the first days before school started in the fall. At the meeting Jimmy started by saying that he had personally selected him as his English teacher. He did not do this to impress the teacher or to win favors. Jimmy had learned how he learned best. He knew that he did best with teachers who were organized and who taught by active discussion in class more than by using worksheets and books. At the end of the tenth grade he had asked all of his friends in eleventh grade to describe each English teacher. He picked the one who was best for him. His parents made sure he got that teacher.

Next, Jimmy said, "You may not remember, but I got the reading list from you last June. I have a reading problem and cannot read very fast. But don't worry. Over the summer I read the first four books on the list so that I won't fall behind. Also, one of the books is by Shakespeare, and I know it will be hard for me to understand; so, I've ordered it through the books-on-tape service. One favor, though: When I read out loud, I sometimes mispronounce words or skip words. Would you please not call on me to read in class unless you tell me the day before so I can practice?" He went on to say, "One other favor: I have a written language problem. At home I use a word processor. But in class I need more time on tests. Could I have untimed tests? I am willing to come in early or return after school to finish, and I promise not to cheat."

What tremendous understanding Jimmy has of himself! What awareness of what it will take for him to do well! He has learned what he must do to succeed, and he is motivated to do all that it takes. But, there is another advantage to Jimmy being his own advocate rather than a parent taking that role. It would take a hard-hearted teacher to say no to Jimmy's needs. What would have happened if Jimmy's mother had come in to ask the same requests? The teacher might have said, "Look, I have twenty-five students in each of five classes a day. I can't do all these things. Either your son will have to make it like the other kids, or he needs to be in a special class" or "Jimmy is in eleventh grade. You have got to get off of his back, and let him grow up."

When they are children, they need parents to be assertive advocates. As these children move into adolescence, parents must help them learn to be their own advocates. Without this ability, this adolescent will have difficulty moving into adult life, whether it is in college, on the job, in the military, in a trade training program, or in a relationship.

Identity

Once some beginning sense of independence has been achieved, the great task of adolescence is that of finding one's identity. This is difficult at best in a world where value systems change, career opportunities vary, and options unpredictably expand and diminish. The adolescent of today—as of any day, for that matter—questions some of the current "adult values," wonders what you have done to make the world the mess it is in, and shares in rather more than less uncertainty about the future.

Much of this is just like what you experienced when you were an adolescent. But, in some ways, the world that today's adolescents face is quite different from that which you encountered. Sexual values and the importance of relationships have changed. College no longer guarantees the opportunity for social and economic advancement. Family life has become and will continue to become more mobile. Almost 50 percent of children and adolescents today live in single-parent or remarriage families. In terms of future jobs, productivity may be much harder to identify with a person's individual effort and input. More and more, education, computer skills, and technical knowledge are essential for success.

Under these uncertain circumstances, what kind of identity can adolescents establish if they feel like a failure at school, with friends, or within the family? Any learning disability only exacerbates the problem. Such adolescents can hardly be blamed if they remain immature and childlike in their behavior. They may be bland and passive, showing no personality, or they may be quite unstable, constantly changing their minds, not knowing what or who they want to be. But if they cannot be blamed, they cannot be excused. With the proper help in school, and understanding, support, and help at home, they can workout these problems. If not, professional help will be needed.

Adolescence is a time when being different is not tolerated. Being just like everyone else in the peer group is a criterion that must be met before a sense of difference and a pride in individual differences can emerge. This emerging sense of identity as a person, of course, is a big step toward growing up. However, youngsters who have learning disabilities are already different, and their social problems are innumerable, especially where their peers are concerned. They may have difficulty taking part in sports, dancing, and most other activities in which their peers are involved. They often lack social skills. Making small talk, maintaining eye contact, listening to others, waiting for someone to finish talking before they speak—all of these abilities are critical to social acceptance. Your adolescent may have mastered none of them. Your son may misunderstand what is said, make inappropriate remarks, or forget what a conversation is about. Your daughter may be bossy, aggressive, and belligerent, or so quiet, shy, and passive that she fades away in any group.

None of these behaviors leads to easy peer acceptance, and instead of pushing in the right directions, some adolescents withdraw into the house, content with watching television, listening to the stereo, or reading. Others will be so desperate for social acceptance that they may be vulnerable to peer pressure and act inappropriately, getting into trouble. Some may move into using alcohol or drugs because their friends do. Girls may become sexually active in an effort to get attention and "love." Boys may try acting tough, hanging out on the fringes of a gang, or become a follower, getting involved in petty crime.

None of these problems are easy to solve. Fortunately, most children cope with adolescence well enough to make it through. Some, however, remain misfits until, and even after, they become adults. Often, situations improve as adults. The stress of school may be past history. The pressures and demands on adults are different. The nonathlete or the quiet person may be more valued, or valued for different qualities.

As parents, the best you can do is understand that your adolescent is going through his or her first identity crisis. If you try to understand the problem, it may lead to an understanding of the behavior. Help your daughter or son seek out activities, sports, and other programs that offer the best chances of success. Keep communication open and set up some systematic way that you can work together on solving problems.

Many adolescents, in fact, will find techniques that they can use to help themselves. They can be very creative in finding activities at which they can succeed or ways of relating to classmates or friends. Encourage their explorations and growth.

I cannot think of a better example than Ron. He had just about every type of visual perception, organization, sequencing, and gross and fine motor problem possible. In addition, his reading comprehension was slow and difficult as was his written language ability. He had been in a self-contained special education school since his early grade-school years. In tenth grade, he started in a small private regular high school. His family and I worked together during this year. Ron was determined to succeed. He negotiated with each teacher to get the accommodations he needed. He worked three to four hours each night to accomplish work that most of his classmates did in only two hours. Every assignment was carefully organized. If he had a report to do, he would block out specific time, often weeks earlier, for library work, reading time, outlining time, writing and rewriting time. For lengthy reports he dictated to his mother who then typed the material.

Ron was succeeding. He was bright and got good grades. Toward the end of the tenth-grade year, his English teacher asked each student to write an autobiography that could be given to the eleventh-grade English teacher as an introduction. Let Ron tell his own story. Note his self-confidence and learned ability to problem solve, compensate, and cope.

I look at Ron and I see a young man with a great deal of willpower. One can see this in my drive to overcome the limitations that impede my learning. This is also seen in my capabilities and successes. I am what is frequently referred to as learning disabled.

The first thing one sees about me are my many limitations. One of my learning disabilities is that I cannot spell. Although I have tried for many years to learn, through memorization, key words, phonetics, and other teaching devices, I cannot spell. I remember taking a spelling achievement test year after year and staying at the same grade level.

The next limitation I have is that I cannot write legibly, even to myself. For instance, I remember taking a biology test, putting down what I knew were the right answers, and getting the paper back marked 10 of 25 and "can't read." Another limitation that affects my schoolwork is that I cannot calculate quickly, even illegibly.

Some of my limitations have nothing to do with school, but concern my athletic ability. I cannot hold a canoe paddle correctly and coordinate the movements of my arm so that the canoe does not go in circles. I cannot coordinate between the sight of the incoming ball with my eyes, the level of the bat, and the swing of my arm. Consequently, 9 times out of 10, I miss the ball completely. This problem manifests itself on the other side of the batter's box as well. I can keep my eye on the ball, follow the ball, see the ball come to me, put out my glove, and miss the ball from 3 to 9 feet.

I try to overcome my limitations through coping with them. With spelling, as previously described, I cannot learn how to spell. Even using a dictionary is hard for me because I cannot figure out the first two letters of a word. I find that the best way to cope with the problem is to inform teachers of it and whenever possible, have someone who knows how to spell around. As for handwriting, although I have tried to produce a form of legible script, under the careful and patient tutoring of many, I found that this is next to impossible and my writing looks like a cross between chicken scratch and arabic. Therefore, whenever possible, I type my papers, thus eliminating the necessity for legible handwriting. To cope with my problem in calculating, I use a calculator, thus eliminating any careless errors or c.a.e.'s as they are called. I remember going to my math teacher after class one day and saying, "I can do the work; I understand the concepts; but, I just cannot physically do the computations."

As for my athletic coordination, I try the best I can. I remember being out on the lake one day, alone in a canoe. A brisk wind arose and I was trying to go from one side of the lake to the other in a perpendicular line to this wind. This situation was made doubly frustrating because I knew I should point the canoe upwind of where I wanted to go, but could not manage to keep it pointed in that direction. I try to cope with my problems playing baseball by going out to the field when no one is there, tossing the ball as high as I can and trying to catch it.

Despite my limitations, I have many capabilities and have had several successes. I have an ability to grasp the general concepts which a teacher is trying to explain. I have been able to write essays and papers that are clear and concise. I can learn from my mistakes and from constructive criticism of my work. And, if genuinely interested in a subject, I will try to find the most information I can about it. I also have a good memory and retain factual information. I am highly motivated to get things done not only on time, but early, if possible, and am equally highly motivated to learn.

My successes are many. These include my schoolwork, where I usually get either A's or B's, of which I am very proud, and fighting my own battles with teachers to make them understand my limitations. I have some sports-related successes, also. These include my sailing ability, which enabled me to pass the sailing requirements for a patch at a summer camp I attended. At the same camp, I learned to become a fair shot and passed the four lowest shooting levels in a relatively short time. And if I couldn't paddle a canoe, I developed an ability to row, a simpler and more enjoyable form of human-powered water activity.

My most recent success at school includes surviving, if just barely, a rather confusing three days with a science teacher, thanks to the help of an English teacher, and surviving by not going crazy at the thought of what I cannot do.

Recognition of my capabilities has led to an urge to overcome my limitations and has produced many successes. I admit, however, that I could not have succeeded without the encouragement of many people.

Let me amplify Ron's next-to-last paragraph, the one about surviving. His science class went on a one-week trip to a nature facility. Each day the staff lectured on different topics. Ron wanted to learn, but he could not write as fast as the speaker spoke. Soon, he was lost and couldn't understand the demonstrations or the assigned projects. For example, "Now go out into the woods and look for examples of the symbiotic relationship I just described." He asked his biology teacher for help. She sent him to the instructor. The instructor seemed puzzled and didn't know what Ron wanted. No, he could not provide notes of his talks. They were not written down.

By the third day Ron was so frustrated that he stormed out of the class, muttering to himself about the stupid teacher. He walked off into the woods, angry at himself for being so unable to handle the situation. Why hadn't he explained his needs to the instructor? What would he do if he didn't learn everything? How would he ever make it in college with all that lecturing? All of his old doubts and fears resurfaced. After a time he decided he needed help. He went to his English teacher, who was also on the trip and was someone Ron felt close to and trusted. He explained his problem. His teacher went with him to the instructor and discussed the problem. The English teacher agreed to take notes for Ron who was then freed up to listen. The rest of the week went well.

Ron finished high school and went to an excellent college that understood people with special needs and provided the necessary services. Ron began to take his laptop computer to class to take notes. He graduated with honors and went to an excellent law school. He graduated, passed the bar examination, and is now practicing law.

As you watch your adolescent grow up, talk to other parents whose children have had similar problems, to your family doctor, and to the special education professionals at your school. If your adolescent is having more trouble than you can manage, don't hesitate to seek professional help.

Intimacy

Most adolescents slowly work on and through the tasks of moving toward independence and developing a beginning identity. The task of intimacy begins in late adolescence, but is really worked on more in early young adulthood. The high school senior may begin to experience being in love with someone who makes him or her feel good and may begin to learn the sharing and interdependency of intimacy.

If your son, say, has a poor self-image or low self-esteem, dating and close relationships may be very difficult. If he has poor social skills and difficulty making or keeping friendships, dating and close relationships may also not be a possibility. The longer the limited successes or isolation exists, the greater the problems become. First, class friendships develop and reputations are established. Even if your child changes classrooms or schools, it is hard for him to undo his reputation or to break into the peer system. Second, with each month the social problems exist, he loses that much more experience. Thus, he falls even further behind in social comfort or in mastering social skills.

There are no simple answers. One approach, however, is to seek opportunities for social contact for your child that have a potential of being successful. Initially, try finding for your son activities that are centered around a topic or task rather than on social interactions, maybe a computer club, nature club, or volunteer work group sponsored by the school or your religious organization. The focus will be on what is learned or done rather than on talking or interacting. Ideally, this activity should be adult supervised rather than peer supervised. Your son will begin to be part of a group activity without having to be accepted or successful with group interactions. By using the adult leader plus problem solving, your son might begin to feel more comfortable and successful around peers. Encourage him to go and to practice relating to the others in the group. At a minimum, he will have a positive group experience. All the better if he gains some confidence and social abilities. At the best, your child might start a friendship with someone not from the school where his role and reputation are known.

Special Problems Seen with Adolescents

If learning disabilities have gone unrecognized and untreated or if they were addressed in grade school but not in middle or high school, the adolescent is likely to develop psychological difficulties.

Resistance to School and Learning

Some adolescents begin to resist their education and fight being in school, doing class work, or doing homework. They lie about and avoid homework. Some will try to convince you (and themselves) that they could be successful but that they just don't care about school. You hear that "school is stupid" or "who needs to learn that subject" or "the teacher is terrible." Some will act out in school, cutting classes, or getting into trouble with school rules. Some of these young people who need special help, sadly, resist getting the help or going to the tutor or special education room.

Some get the message that the school does not really want them and drop out of school. I call this "school pushout" rather than school dropout. Current statistics show that 50 percent of students identified by the school as having a learning disability quit high school. How could this happen? The teen is known to have a learning disability. He or she could be provided such minimal services that the teen gets the message: School is not for me. Once out from under the pressures of school, he or she may settle down, get a job, work toward a high school equivalency, and move on with life. Many, though, without professional help, will carry their problems and difficulties into adulthood.

Acting-Out Behaviors

Refer to Chapter 8, the section on normal adolescence. The adolescent who is insecure with limited academic and peer successes may have to struggle with becoming independent more than the average adolescent. As this teen struggles to resist the wish to remain safely dependent and with becoming independent, all of the normal adolescent rebellious behaviors may become worse. More negativism and power struggles arise in an effort to deny dependency needs. Conflicts around clothing, hairstyle, jewelry, and peer groups may be significant.

What happens if even these efforts fail to help the struggling adolescent survive and cope? Some may need to move to a greater level of acting out. The goal here appears to be to numb or deny the anxiety and depression they are struggling with. These behaviors can be serious, destructive, and possibly life-threatening. Sadly, some of the more common of these extreme efforts to deny or numb the pain are:

1. Alcohol use, misuse, or abuse.
2. Drug use, misuse, or abuse.
3. Running away from home.
4. Cutting classes or skipping school.
5. Delinquent behaviors.
6. Apathy—a state of being where the only motivation is to not feel any emotional pain for the next hour or so. The teen is self-destructive but unable to see that what she or he is doing needs to stop.
7. Suicide gestures or suicide.
8. Increased sexual behavior—for boys as a means of control and power, for girls as a means of getting attention and acceptance.

If your adolescent is moving into these more destructive levels of defending against pain or is already there, you must seek professional help immediately.

Attention Deficit Hyperactivity Disorder (ADHD)

About 50 percent of children with ADHD will continue to have this disability as adolescents. The same treatment approaches will be needed. Medications will still be part of the treatment plan. School understanding and accommodations will still be necessary.

It is critical that medication be considered for every aspect of the adolescent's life when the hyperactivity, distractibility, and/or impulsivity interfere with success. These problems are apparent in school. They might interfere with family relationships, peer interactions and activities, and sports or other activities. (The issue of medication management will be discussed in Chapter 16.)

Girls who are distractible might not be recognized as such until high school. They are quiet and do not usually get into trouble. They are seen as average students. Their friends call them "airheads" or "space cadets" but accept them. No one observes the distractibility and short attention span. Once such a girl is diagnosed and treated, she improves remarkably. She becomes more organized and capable in school. She talks in a more sophisticated way. She relates better with everyone. If your daughter has learning disabilities and has struggled each year, or if teachers still complain that she does not pay attention or does not complete work, consider the possibility of distractibility. Remember, you do not have to be hyperactive to have ADHD.

In Closing

I can't emphasize it enough: Learning disabilities are life disabilities. They will continue into adolescence. Thus, it is critical that you continue to work with your school for the necessary services. Don't let the school offer a watered-down approach. One period a day of resource room time with fifteen to twenty-five other students may not be enough. It is very easy for the school to give up on continued remedial and compensatory efforts and to shift totally into accommodations. The students are then given less demanding classes. Teachers work around the reading, writing, math, or other disabilities. Your daughter or son might graduate, but he or she will not have the necessary skills and education needed for life.

If you live in an area where the school system puts its emphasis on grade school and provides minimal services by high school, you may need to seek private help. Even if you choose this route, become an advocate for the programs that your adolescent needs. If *your* son or daughter needs such classes, doubtless others do as well. Even if you can afford the private help that is necessary to supplement the deficiencies in your high school program, don't be content just to continue that way. Get together with other parents or parent groups and try to push your school to develop appropriate programs within the school.

If your teen's learning disabilities were not diagnosed until high school, he or she will need intensive special education interventions. In addition to needing remedial, compensatory, and accommodation programs, your child may need help in filling in deficiencies from the past. He or she probably has major gaps or holes in basic knowledge that have to be addressed. If your adolescent did not learn basic multiplication, division, fractions, or decimal facts in grade school, she or he will have great difficulty with algebra. The same may be true in English if your child didn't learn basic grammar and punctuation rules.

In Chapter 21, I will discuss issues relating to educational services to be provided by your school system. The plan designed by your school system is called an individualized education plan, or IEP. Education law specifies that school systems must add an individualized transitional plan (ITP) to the IEP during the high school years. Realistic expectations at the time of graduation must be addressed. The focus might shift toward vocational training, social skills training, or work-related skills training. If your son or daughter is not going to college, be sure to stress the need for programs that maximize the ability to be independent and capable of working after high school. Start looking into the many postsecondary options other than college that are available.

If he or she is going to college, start to plan early for the type of college program needed. What services will be needed? Will a community college be best as a first step? Will accommodations be needed for the various college admission tests, like the SAT? Some colleges are well prepared to help the student with learning disabilities. Tutoring, advisors, liaison with faculty, and resource rooms are available. Other colleges might have fewer services. And some colleges, despite the statements in their catalogs, offer nothing. Seek advice from the high school college counselor or others in selecting the right college.

It all boils down to this. As your son or daughter gets older, he or she must begin to accept some and later most of the responsibility for his or her own life and well-being. As self-image and identity emerge, that advocacy becomes inescapable. No one else is on the front line, and no one else knows better what your child needs. You must help your adolescent to learn to speak for her- or himself and to fight for what is necessary. You cannot do your adolescent's job for him or her any longer, and high school is a good time to face this and to help with the transition toward adulthood. You cannot move into the dormitory with your college student, nor can you go on the job or to military basic training with your teen. Teens must be prepared to handle themselves after high school.

Earlier I gave an example of a high school student who learned to cope. Let me share another story.

At seventeen, John was a senior in regular classes, but taking two hours a week of private special education tutoring. John had been in special programs since the fifth grade. He was a bright young man with learning disabilities. He had difficulty with reading comprehension, organization, and written langauge. However, he had learned the necessary study skills and strategies to succeed if he received the appropriate classroom accommodations.

When he began his senior year English class, he met with his teacher and explained what he could and could not do. He requested permission to have more time when taking written tests in class. He explained that he would get his homework in on time because he would take the extra time at home and would use the computer. He did not, he said, want to turn in unfinished tests in class, however, and he volunteered to come in early or come back during lunch or after school to finish them. He asked to be trusted not to cheat or pass the questions on to others. He also requested that he not be called on to read out loud in class and explained why.

As the semester progressed, the teacher allowed for the accommodations, except for one. The teacher had the students read literature assignments and write reports on these assignments. John did his assignments and did each well. Each week, however, the students had to take turns reading their reports out loud in class. John was not excused. At first, he memorized his reports. In class he pretended to be reading as he recited his material. As you can imagine, this soon became a major time drain, and it seemed counterproductive to John. So he stopped memorizing his written work and approached his teacher again to explain his wish to avoid reading in class. The teacher insisted that John read, and John politely but firmly refused.

He worked hard and got an A on each report and on each examination. In spite of this, he received a B at the end of the first marking period. At this point, he called me for advice and we worked out a strategy. He asked if I could come with him when he went to implement our plan. I told him that I would role-play the situation with him and help him in any other way I could, but that it was time for him to fight his own battles. I assured him that he could do it.

John requested a conference with the teacher and the principal. Prior to this meeting, he made sure the principal had a copy of his special education file and a copy of the IEP that listed the necessary accommodations. He started the meeting by telling the principal that he had received a B in English. Then he asked the teacher what grades he had gotten on each report and test. The teacher acknowledged the As. John opened a folder and showed the principal these reports and exams. Then he asked the teacher why he had received a B rather than an A as an overall grade. The teacher replied that the grade was also based on class participation. When John asked for clarification, the teacher admitted that John participated in class discussions but that he refused to read his reports in class.

Calmly—we had rehearsed this before—John asked the teacher if he was aware that he had learning disabilities, specifically, a reading disability. The teacher said that he knew of this but thought that if John wanted to be in a regular class, he had to be able to be like all of the other students. John took a deep breath and said, "I wish to advise you that if you do not change the B to an A, I will file a legal suit against you for discriminating against the handicapped based on Section 504 of the Rehabilitation Act of 1973 and the Americans with Disabilities Act of 1990."

That night John called to brag. He got his A. He was pleased with his grade and with himself. I was delighted with the confidence he had gained and the growth that his behavior reflected. Yes, his parents could have done it, maybe better, certainly in a more indirect style, but John needed the experience of fighting for what was right for him and he got it.

11

Family Reactions to the Child or Adolescent with Learning Disabilities

We discussed the problems that children and adolescents with learning disabilities and/or attention deficit hyperactivity disorder (ADHD) have in their relationships with people both outside and inside the home. The emotional and social problems of family members who not only want to, but have to, deal productively with their daughters and sons with these disabilities also deserve special attention. Let's start by discussing the normal reactions of parents and siblings to having a family member with these problems. Then let's look at the larger problems that arise when perfectly normal reactions and feelings linger too long or become too extreme.

When one member of a family suffers, everyone in the family feels the pain and reacts to it, sometimes with nearly equal distress. Parents, brothers, sisters, grandparents—all are part of this human system within which the child or adolescent with learning disabilities lives and grows. Everyone in the family needs to understand the full range of problems this family member has if anyone is to be of help. Everyone needs to understand her or his own reactions as well. Sometimes this is a painful and difficult process.

After your child or adolescent has been through an evaluation, someone on the evaluation team should explain the findings to you. The child, too, should know and understand, to the degree possible, the results of the findings. Sometimes the evaluator routinely takes care of this. Rarely, however, does anyone, including the parents, explain the findings to sisters, brothers, and other family members. Yet, it is imperative that everyone connected with the child know about and understand the problems.

Some parents sense a feeling of relief and comfort when they learn of their child's or adolescent's disabilities. They knew something was wrong. Now there is an answer and a plan for helping. Other parents may have difficulty accepting that their son or daughter is different, that something is wrong. They may have experienced, or may yet experience, a series of reactions not too different from the grief reaction that people have when someone dear to them dies, although this grief is of lesser intensity. In a way, this reaction is very valid. Initially, the parents might fear that they have to "give up" a part of their child, or at least their ambitions for the child that the parents fear may never be realized. As we talk about these reactions, don't become distressed. These feelings are not only normal, they are to be expected.

Later, I will discuss the many problems that increase the stress that the family already feels about the situation. If you recognize what I discuss later as problems in your family, you would do well to consult your family physician or a mental health professional. Above all, don't feel ashamed to discuss feelings that may seem "selfish" or "unworthy" to you. These problems are real and your feelings are genuine. You must look at them squarely and deal with them. Keeping a stiff upper lip or denying that they exist only makes things worse for you and for your family.

I remember talking to the parents of a ten-year-old boy I evaluated who had major behavioral problems within the family. When I met with the parents to review my impressions and recommendations for help, I started by saying, "You know, I hate to say this, but now that I have gotten to know your son, I must tell you that if he were my son, I would have killed him by now." The mother began to cry. She was so relieved to hear that someone else could be as angry at this child as she was.

Normal Reactions of Parents

It should not surprise you that in addition to being mothers and fathers, parents are also human beings. They have their own feelings and thoughts. They usually have mates with whom they enjoy special relationships, relationships that are often hard enough to manage successfully without additional family stresses. Having a child with a disability stirs up feelings and thoughts, fears and hopes for which most people are unprepared. These reactions affect the parents both as individual people and as a part of a couple.

At no point is the stress greater than when the diagnosis is finalized: This is the moment when parents feel the first rush of anguish, fear, helplessness, anger, guilt, shame—all at once. Nothing can describe the thoughts going through a parent's head as he or she rides home from the school or the professional's office after the first conference. Even if a parent has suspected a problem for years, there is something so final about someone's saying "Yes, you are right. There really is a problem."

No sensitive professional should ever describe a child's problems to a parent without acknowledging these feelings and ending with a positive course of action with words such as "and this is what we will do about it." Unfortunately, not all professionals are this sensitive. Some play what I call the "Ha-ha, you have leprosy" game. They throw out a lot of labels, banging a parent over the head with "Your child is disabled or . . ." and then say good-bye. Out the parents go, overwhelmed, with little understanding, hope, or direction to take.

When people experience a loss, in this case that their child has a disability, the reality can be more than difficult to accept and handle. The initial response may be denial. The reality is so difficult to accept that the mind cannot process it. You know it happened, but you just can't believe it. Often what follows is a feeling of helplessness. How could this have happened to me? How can I make sure nothing like this happens again? To take control, people usually try to find a cause. "It was my fault. I caused it." This reaction results in guilt, but it at least makes you feel that you can prevent future disasters by not causing them. Another effort to find a cause is to blame others. "It was so-and-so's fault. He caused the problem." This reaction results in anger but, again, provides the assurance that you can control the future by handling this person. These reactions of denial, guilt, and anger may last for months or longer. Gradually, you work through this grief and begin the long mourning process. This is the process of slowly accepting the loss and moving on with life and with the challenges of helping your child or adolescent. Let me illustrate in detail these *normal* reactions as they might relate to a parent with a child or adolescent with learning disabilities and/or ADHD.

Denial

Denial is often the first reaction. "It can't be true. The professional must be mistaken." Or "She only saw him for an hour; I don't believe it." You may doubt the competence of the bearer of such news and may criticize this professional. Frequently, parents seek other opinions. Getting other evaluations can be useful. Unfortunately, "doctor shopping" for someone who will tell you what you want to hear does not do anything productive for your child.

Another form of denial is the "cover-up" reaction. One parent, usually the mother, wants to "protect" the other parent by not sharing the results of the studies or school conference or by minimizing the problems. The parent may successfully cover up for years the fact that a daughter, say, is getting special help in school. Sadly, the parent who remains uninformed about the child's true abilities and disabilities often continues to build up unrealistic expectations and may demand results from the child that she may not be able to produce. The child, seeing through this cover-up, perceives the true reason for it: "They can't accept me as I am; they have to pretend that I'm different than I really am." This reaction often makes the child understandably angry or sad and may result in her having difficulty accepting herself as well.

Anger

It is common for a period of anger to follow the initial denial, especially as the ability to accept increases. Parents may direct this anger inward, against themselves, or project it outward, blaming the other parent or any other outside source. Upon learning of a child's disabilities, it is normal to feel anger. Other sentiments, such as "Why me?" or "How could God do this to me?" or "We never should have had children!" are often expressed. This anger might be projected to family members or to people outside the family.

Guilt

Parents may turn their anger inward, attacking themselves rather than others or the problems. The result is that they do not feel good about themselves. Some may feel depressed. Associated with this reaction may be feelings of guilt. It is a very short step from "How could I have done this?" to "It's all my fault." Parents may berate themselves with statements such as "God is punishing me because . . ." or "I didn't follow my doctor's advice" or "I've been given this extra burden to prove my worthiness."

Feeling guilty and/or depressed represents an attempt to establish control over a situation perceived as basically hopeless and out of control. Parents who can lay the blame on or attribute the cause to themselves then conquer the situation by explaining it, however erroneously. Their logic is that if this happened for a reason—on account of something they did—and if they do not practice this transgression again, then nothing like what has happened will happen again.

Just as a child who feels depressed tends to become quiet and to pull away from people, so the depressed parent becomes isolated. If this depression is allowed to continue, the parent may withdraw from the child or the other parent at just the time when one or the other, as well as the other members of the family, need the person the most.

If initial anger has been displaced outward, the parent enters into a pattern of blaming some outside experience or agent. Like the guilt reaction, blaming an outside agent at least places responsibility "somewhere," and this too protects the parent from feelings of helplessness. The father may blame the physician because "he didn't get to the hospital fast enough." Or the mother may say "I told the doctor I was in labor, but she wouldn't believe me; and I almost delivered in the car" or "If the pediatrician had come out to see him rather than prescribing over the phone, he wouldn't have had that high fever." A person may generalize this reaction to all professionals, who then become bunglers, incompetents, and charlatans. Statements such as "It's the school's fault" or "She's just a young, inexperienced teacher" or "He's just a rigid old teacher" are common. The teacher or doctor who is the butt of the anger probably never hears these complaints. But the parent may never allow the child to forget them. Reactions such as these undermine the child's faith in and respect for the very people he or she must turn to for help and hope.

Some parents attempt to suppress their guilt or their need to place blame somewhere else by overprotecting the child. The most normal, human thing to do when your son is hurting is to reach out and try to protect him. This is necessary and helpful. But your goal must be to protect your child only when he needs protecting and to encourage him to grow when he does not need protecting. A blanket of overprotection covers the child's weaknesses but also smothers the child's strengths. Not only will overprotectiveness keep your child immature and delay growth in areas where that is possible, it will also make your child feel inadequate. He knows what's happening. For example, when everyone else has a chore to do but he does not, when everyone takes turns clearing the table but he never has to, your son will very probably conclude "See, they agree with me—I am inadequate."

Most parents work through these normal phases of denial, anger, and guilt. When they do, they gradually can process the problems. Often this parent requests another meeting, wanting to go over again the test results or to hear again what is wrong. With acceptance and understanding, parents can become strong advocates for their children, mobilizing their energy in constructive ways.

Pathological Reactions of Parents

Some parents just cannot accept that their son or daughter could have anything wrong. They struggle but do not get through the normal reactions described above. These parents move into a chronic life pattern of denial, anger, and/or guilt. It is important to recognize that if a parent has moved into one of these chronic phases, she or he will need help.

Chronic Denial

Some parents cannot give up their denial. They continue to doctor-shop in a relentless search for the doctor with the magic answer or magic cure or for someone who will say that nothing is wrong with their child. Such parents greet the newest professional on the block with flattery and praise, criticizing the many professionals whose opinions they have rejected. Ultimately, the new "hero" too is rejected and then attacked. As their frustration grows, they hop from one promised cure to another, often becoming the victims of those who capitalize on people in distress. This hopeless shopping, of course, deprives the child of time that should be spent in constructive programs and the valuable interventions that he or she needs.

This chronic denial reaction has other potentially serious consequences. Because each authority fails, she or he must be downgraded when the parents move on to the next one. The child picks up the message not to have faith in anybody in any professional capacity. This faith and trust is absolutely necessary in order to have hope, and hope is absolutely necessary if one is to work toward overcoming the handicaps. And, as I commented before, the child also picks up that subtle but clear message "We can't accept you as you are. We must find someone who will tell us that you are not the way you are." The child hears, knows, and reacts with anger, shame, and a conviction of inadequacy.

Chronic Anger

If parents do not resolve the initial anger and learn to handle it, they may continue to project it. With this attitude, nothing can go right. Someone is always perceived as wrong. "After all this time and money, you haven't helped my child. Why?" Or, to the child, "After all of my efforts, why can't you do your homework better?" Some parents, miserable themselves, are almost impossible to live with.

Professionals may find it difficult to work with this parent as well. When this mother walks into the school, every teacher hides. The principal quickly tells the secretary to say he is in an important conference and cannot be disturbed. No one wants to interact with her; no one wants to experience the anger. Unfortunately, this anger chases away the people the child or adolescent needs.

Chronic Guilt

When parents handle their unresolved guilt by becoming overly dedicated to the child, they are apt to be covertly furious about it. What comes across in public is the dedication: "No task, no trip, no expense is too great to help my child." What comes across behind the scenes is the anger at having to do all of this and at having to give up things. Some parents become professional martyrs. They never let anyone forget how great the effort, how selfless the sacrifice. The surface behavior may be sweet and admirable, but somehow the child picks up the bitter parallel message: "Look how much I do for you, you ungrateful child. You're a burden on me, and you show no appreciation for what I do for you."

Parents may handle unresolved guilt by withdrawing from other social and/or family contacts and totally dedicating themselves to the child. Some carry this to the point where they have almost no energy left for relationships with the other children in the family or with their spouse. Taking care of the one child's needs becomes so demanding that they are too worn out and weary to meet the needs of the other children, to participate in social activities, or to continue meaningful relations with the spouse. The result is a dysfunctional family and, probably, a strained marriage. Sometimes the anger at this state of affairs is not openly discussed between the parents but displaced onto the child, who is seen as the cause of it all.

For other parents, the normal initial reaction of overprotecting the child might become a lifestyle, one which both prevents growth for the child and the parent and increases the child's feelings of worthlessness. Under these circumstances, the child can easily become infantilized. Occasionally, overprotective behaviors may stem from a parent's attempt to cover up feelings of his or her own inadequacy as a person or a parent. People with low self-esteem and feelings of worthlessness may achieve feelings of being wanted and needed by deluding themselves that they are "all the child has in the world." When the child's immaturity and feelings of incompetence lead to failure, the child naturally retreats back into the home. The overprotecting parent sees this and feels even more justified in moving in and protecting some more. A self-defeating cycle begins to repeat itself. The child increasingly realizes that she or he is helpless without the parent. This response confirms the parent's fear that the child is incompetent. This parent then acts in a way that reinforces the notion that the child cannot survive without him or her.

In Summary

It is expected that parents will experience the normal denial, guilt, and anger following the confirmation of their child's or adolescent's disabilities. It is not expected that these difficulties will continue and become a chronic pattern of functioning. If you see yourself or your spouse in these more chronic descriptions, consider getting help so that the difficulties can be handled. This assistance will make you, as well as your child or adolescent, feel and function better.

The Reactions of the Other Children in the Family

As discussed earlier, when parents suspect a learning disability and/or ADHD and become concerned, they usually agree to have an evaluation done by the school professionals or they take their son or daughter to one or more specialists. Finally, someone explains to them what the problems are and what needs to be done about them. At some point, someone probably sits down with the parents and interprets the findings. Occasionally, but not often enough, someone sits down with the child or adolescent and explains to him or her what the problems are, what the treatment will be, and why. Almost never does anyone explain any of this to the child's brothers and sisters—yet, as part of the family, they need to know. Remember: *When one member of a family hurts, everyone feels the pain* and hurts and reacts. When the siblings are left in the dark, what are they supposed to do? How might they react?

The reactions of your other children may be made worse because you expect more of them than you expect of yourselves. The child or adolescent with these disabilities is very good at getting parents frustrated and angry. One parent may yell or hit. Another parent might cry, withdraw, or pout. Your other children get just as frustrated and angry living with this person. They are human too. Yet, if they yell, hit, cry, withdraw, or pout, they are often punished or told that they may not act that way. Or they are told they must be more understanding. You cannot tell your other children to be more human than you are. You cannot model one set of behaviors as parents, and then get upset if your children do the same. You must acknowledge that they experience the same frustration and anger that you experience. They have normal and expected feelings, and may need help in learning what to do with them. If they cannot act as their parents do, teach them an acceptable way of expressing their feelings.

If the two parents disagree on parenting styles or discipline methods, the stress and conflicts between the other children and the child with the disabilities can cause major stress between the parents. This problem can be even worse if there is a divorce and the children spend time in two different families, each with a different style of responding.

Your other children and adolescents might struggle with many different feelings as they live with and try to cope with their sibling who has the problems. Let me review some of these reactions.

Anxiety

Some siblings become very worried and feel anxious. This is especially true in families where the cover-up is on and little, if anything, is said. For example, a sibling might ask "What's wrong with Jim?" to which a parent says "Oh, nothing special . . . It's okay." Yet, the sibling sees the parents taking Jim from one place to another and knows they go to special meetings at school. Or the sibling hears "Where are we going to get the money for all of this?" The brother or sister sees mother or father upset, maybe in tears, maybe angry. Aware that something is wrong but not knowing what it is, the sibling's imagination may take over. Frequently, the brother or sister fantasizes worse problems than those that are real. Then he or she worries. I have heard siblings say "Will he live? Is he going to die?" or "Will it happen to me?" or "If it's not important, why all the whispers and hush-hush?" Your other children must have clear information at a level that each can understand. They need to understand what is happening and why.

Anger

Brothers and sisters may become angry, fighting with the child who has the problems or with their parents. If double standards are in effect, you can be sure that they will notice them and become angry. For example, "How come I've got to make my bed and she doesn't?" or "He broke my toy and you didn't do anything" or

"Why is it that when I do something I get punished and when he does the same thing I am told that I have to be more understanding?" The most famous statement by a sibling is "It's not fair!"

The time and energy that parents spend with the child who has the disabilities may make the other children very jealous. Taking the one child to special tutoring, special programs, and professionals leaves little time or energy available for the others. This child demands most of the spare time to be spent on his or her homework, leaving little time for the parents to help the others. So much money may be spent on this child or adolescent that everyone else has to do without or vacations have to be compromised. One can't really blame the siblings for complaining.

Siblings may have to take some teasing at school. "Hey, how's your dummy brother?" or "Your sister sure acts funny. She's so weird. Is she retarded?" Anyone, and especially a child, is embarrassed by such comments and gets angry. Even at home, a sibling may not feel comfortable. Parents insist that a brother let the child with problems who has no friends play with his friends when they come over. The child acts immature or silly or is aggressive, embarrassing the brother. Then the brother stops bringing his friends home for fear of being embarrassed. He may even do everything he can to be at a friend's house after school as much as possible.

Guilt

Siblings may feel guilty too, particularly about their anger. The verbal or nonverbal message from their parents is "He can't help it" or "It's not her fault." This is a hard message to swallow for someone who has not yet gained a lot of perspective on life. Or a brother or sister may secretly think "I'm glad it's not me" and then feel guilt or shame for thinking such thoughts.

Acting Out

Because of feelings of anger or guilt, siblings might act out against the child with disabilities. They may tease and provoke the child to encourage misbehavior, or they may do something themselves, and then set up the child as a scapegoat. They are so frustrated and angry; yet they are told that they cannot show their feelings. So, they get even, often in subtle ways. As the parents punish the child with problems, the sibling feels revenged. Sometimes normal siblings set up the child with disabilities to look or act bad simply because they think that the worse their sister or brother looks, the better they look.

Whenever a child in a family misbehaves or shows anger, it is helpful to think of both aspects of "exploding." I like to think of the analogy of dynamite blowing up. You have the sticks of dynamite that explode and you have wires going from the dynamite to a plunger box. When the plunger is pushed down, the dynamite blows up. In families we know who the "exploders" are. It is important to look for the "plungers" as well. This may be the sweet, innocent child who does just the wrong thing at just the right time to set another child off. Sometimes the only way a sibling can get even with the sibling with disabilities is to be the plunger.

I'm reminded of a family I worked with. The ten-year-old son was a terror, especially to his eight-year-old sister. He often got in trouble for hitting her. In one family session the sister admitted what she was doing. She was smaller and weaker than her brother; thus, she could not get even with his abuse by hitting back. She had a way of getting even, though. When she and her brother were upstairs, she would tease him with "special words" until he began to be angry. She knew exactly when he was about to blow. At this time she would run downstairs and into the kitchen. He would run after her and hit her. As she planned it, he hit her when mother was looking. He got punished and she smiled. The parents were surprised to hear her describe her role as a plunger. I pointed out that before she could change, the parents would have to find another way of protecting her from her brother.

Covering Up Success

A normal sibling can also negatively affect the child with disabilities. It seems to be the plight of children with learning disabilities and/or ADHD to have a younger brother or sister who is not only super-normal and delightful but precocious, quickly passing him or her academically and socially. This hurts. Yet, in all fairness, the other children must be encouraged to live up to their potential. They deserve encouragement and praise. Do not hold back or minimize praise for fear of hurting your son or daughter who has the disabilities. Do not ask them not to discuss their report card if their brother or sister is around. Children and adults with disabilities have to learn to cope with reality.

In Summary

There is no way that you can prevent some or all of these feelings from surfacing in your family. None of your children were born self-denying, altruistic models of charity. Besides, all of these feelings, provided they are kept within limits, are normal and can be handled. The more you are aware of your behavior and the more you try not to have double standards or to expect more from your children than they are capable of doing, the less there will be difficulties. The only way to forestall the worst of this anger among your children is by (1) giving them all the facts, (2) letting them know that it is safe and acceptable to discuss with you what they are thinking and feeling, and (3) answering their questions rationally and honestly.

Help each member of the family understand the true concept of fairness. Fairness does not mean that each child gets an equal amount of whatever (food, toys, attention). Fairness means that each child gets what he or she needs at that time. Therefore, each child will get different amounts of different things at different times depending on the child's needs at that time. Love is unconditional and equal with all. Time and energy are given fairly, based on what each child needs at any one time.

It is not always easy to be a parent or a sibling of a child or adolescent with learning disabilities and/or ADHD. In a later chapter I will suggest ways of handling unacceptable behaviors within the family. If you feel that you need help in explaining to your child's siblings or if you feel that your family is not functioning well, don't hesitate to ask someone for help.

An Example of Normal Family Reactions—Danny

I first met Danny for an evaluation at age three. I followed his progress and worked with the family off and on for the next ten years. I still keep in touch with the parents. Danny is now an adult.

Shortly after the initial evaluation, his mother began a diary. Initially, she tried to reconstruct her experiences with Danny from the time of his birth. I have interwoven Danny's clinical picture with excerpts from that diary. His mother writes exceptionally well, often eloquently, but don't mistake this for a fictional account. Her words suggest that she read this chapter before she started her diary. In reality, this chapter and this book had not been written when she wrote her diary. As she confronts and finally begins to bring the various stages of her despair under control, you will be struck by the truth and validity of her account. Perhaps you will share her tears and pain because you are there in your own life or you have been there.

Pregnancy and Birth

Mrs. S's third pregnancy and birth, after two sons (one four years old, the other two), went without complication. Her comments reflect the anticipation with which both parents greeted this child.

A third son? What a joy, what a delight, such pride for the father—what pleasure for the only woman—the queen in a household of adoring men. The other two are dark-haired and dark-eyed like mom and dad. The third is a unique one with his blue eyes and strawberry blond hair. Grandma says he was meant to be a girl. Everyone agrees, "Well, if you had to have a third son, at least he's different." We didn't realize at that time just how different he was.

Danny had the advantage of being the third child. By the time a third is born, all of the anxieties implicit in the care and handling of a normal infant have vanished. No more fits of panic when the baby cries unexpectedly. No more wringing of hands at the first sign of a sniffle or loose bowel movements . . . just a placid, cool, nonchalant parent juggling baby on one arm, holding middle brother with the right hand, pulling the wagon laden with sandbox toys with the other, calling to the older son to look both ways while crossing the street on his bike. The combination of self-confident mother and animated, stimulating surroundings is calculated to make this third baby so happy, so comfortable, with none of the pressures or tensions that the other two had to endure. "They bring themselves up, these third children do. He'll be your easiest," assured our pediatrician.

Delivery and the First Year of Life

Danny's delivery was normal, with no reported difficulties, and his physical examination prior to discharge from the hospital was also normal. Mrs. S quickly noticed, however, that he was different from the other children—irritable, overactive, unable to focus. Feeding him was a problem, and was often accompanied by his vomiting. The pediatrician treated him for colic. Danny also had trouble getting to sleep, and he often slept only three to four hours at a time. Sometimes he cried and thrashed about for thirty minutes to an hour. Holding him did nothing to comfort him. Several other early suggestions of neurological difficulties were present. Danny's skin was overly sensitive to the touch, and he responded to being held by pushing mother away.

Mrs. S reported that from the start, Danny didn't like her. When she picked him up, he cried; the more she cuddled him, the more he cried (the tactile sensitivity). When she turned his head toward her nipple, he pushed her away (probably a reflex called a tonic-neck reflex, which should have stopped by this age). She felt helpless, inadequate, angry, and guilty. She did not yet understand, so she blamed herself.

> Well, then, why did he cry so much? Why did he squirm in your arms as if pleading to be released to the security of his crib? Why the endless bouts of vomiting before, after, during his meals? Why not the same show of pleasure at being rocked and played with like his brothers? Why no "coos" or "goos" or babbles or giggles? Where was this joyous, relaxed, happy third baby syndrome?

> By the end of Danny's first year of life, I attempted to review all of these statements regarding the easy routine with third baby—the enjoyment I was supposed to be savoring through him—the idea that "he's your last, so lap it up" sort of notion. All I could come up with was a dull ache in the pit of my stomach. Why isn't he fun for me? Why doesn't he return my love? Why no give-and-take between baby and anyone? His constant crying and whining, his discontent and apparent discomfort, convinced me that he must be in some physical distress. That question, along with his persistent vomiting, brought me to the pediatrician, who assured me that he was fine. I must relax and learn to loosen up. That along with a little sympathetic support was supposed to reassure me.

But the dull ache in head, heart, and stomach persisted. Why the relief for me at Danny's bedtime? Why the feeling of incompleteness when he was around and the feeling of solidarity and wholeness without him?

My growing conclusion was that there must be something wrong with me to result in this personality conflict. I was perplexed by my feelings of guilt in relation to this child, because if that were my pattern, why wasn't I feeling guilty in relation to my other children? I realized later that my guilt originated from ambivalent feelings toward him—feelings of love and hate, of sympathy and anger, of concern and fear. The insecurity that my relationship to him created inside of me resulted in feelings of self-doubt about my capacity as Mother and in regard to my own emotional stability, which had never been in question.

My loneliness while submerged in these feelings was intense. In spite of a good marriage and a loving husband, I was alone. Many of these feelings and observations were not shared by my husband, who wasn't with Danny as much as I, who never saw him vis-à-vis his age peers, and who by virtue of a very placid, calm nature had a greater capacity to accept a wide diversity of behaviors. Every attempt I made to acquaint him with my concerns was met with assurance that Danny was fine—perhaps a little immature, but fine. The family reminded me that I was older when I had him—perhaps two kids had been enough, all of this being after the fact. All I was left with were doubts, fear, and anger directed toward myself and toward this creature who was the source of all of my problems.

In looking back over Danny's first year of life, as well as those of others like him, it is difficult to pinpoint just what impact his neurological disabilities had. Auditory perception disabilities were later diagnosed. What effect did they have on his orienting to sound or on his learning to relate to or becoming attached to his mother? What effect did his auditory figure-ground disability have? Could Danny orient himself at all to his mother's voice? How must he have perceived the world if he experienced being held as uncomfortable or painful? Mrs. S describes her frustrations, confusions, and ambivalent feelings toward the developing relationship with her infant son. Could Danny's feelings have been any less troubled?

Years One and Two

Danny's language development was delayed. On top of everything else, he now became frustrated by his inability to communicate his needs. His gross motor development was delayed also, resulting in very slow mastery of sitting, standing, walking, and running. He was hyperactive and distractible. He did not outgrow his tactile sensitivity and became defensive to touch, avoiding too much body contact. Possibly because of these neurological problems, he had trouble dealing with separation. Both parents found handling Danny overwhelmingly difficult. With no information and no reassurance from her pediatrician, Mrs. S continued to search within herself for an explanation.

By thirteen months of age, a lock on his bedroom door was required to keep Danny protected from his own enormous fund of aimless energy which was consistently directed toward destructive pursuits. Perhaps his resentment at being locked in or an increasing hyperactivity was the cause of the extreme havoc he wreaked on his surroundings. Linoleum was lifted up off the floor of his room. Pictures in their frames were torn down from the walls; window shades were replaced because they were ripped up. A rocking chair was used to bang against the wall, thus creating dents in the plasterboard. A harness held him down in his high chair and one was used in the stroller when he was reluctantly wheeled away from his exhausted mother by an equally reluctant baby-sitter. And all the time I'm thinking what is wrong with me that I have created this child who I wish I never had.

The more I disliked him, the more he clung to me, the less able he was to let me go, thus causing horrendous scenes at my departures, serving to increase my guilt and self-blame. "When I leave he gets so scared. Therefore, I shouldn't leave. But, if I don't I'll go mad. So, I'll leave but he'll scream and I'll feel so awful." This internal dialogue characterized every separation we were ever to endure.

His constant aimless running resulted in many falls and bruises, the worst of which was a collision with Danny's nose and the dining room table. Sutures were required for that accident, which was followed by several other close calls, all a result of his hyperactivity and poor coordination. Along with this went the assaults by Danny upon anyone who dared get physically close. Once he was seated on my lap, I would in a five-minute period of time receive several blows to my jaw from the unpredictable banging of his head. His frantic squirming discouraged me from holding him or cuddling him. Kicks on knees and in stomach, little hands pushing my face away from his—so many efforts to keep me away—all added up to one conclusion. He doesn't love me and I don't love him, and it's my fault and it's unnatural and wrong, and I wish I didn't have him and I've ruined my life forever. And yet, there he sat with his sad blue eyes and his confused forlornness. He was as unhappy as I was and I had to find out why.

Year Three

Danny's gross motor problems persisted. He showed difficulty with fine motor control of his hand activities. He began to develop language, but he often appeared to misunderstand or to respond in ways that made little sense. His parents felt that his thinking was more concrete than his brothers' had been at the same age. He developed fears of unknown places and of new objects. His separation problems persisted. Although toilet trained for bowel functioning by age two and a half, he still wet the bed at night. Danny started nursery school.

> At last Danny was three. A new era was ushered in by his enrollment in a nursery school—relief for mommy and some friends (please, God, some playmates) for Danny. But more important, at last some objective feedback from emotionally uninvolved teachers who see normal three-year-old kids all the time. No more would I have to rely on dad's calm assurances, upon grandmother's accusations, upon my own frantic self-inquiry.

> Several months passed before the teachers decided that it was time to confront me with reality. Danny was not involved with the other children, they reported. Furthermore, he was tense, frightened, highly distractible, and, most of all, very unhappy. It was with mixed feelings that I received this news. On the one hand I was very upset to hear my worst suspicions confirmed. On the other hand I was relieved to hear that someone else saw the same thing—that my sanity and clear vision need not be held in doubt any longer. Most of all, I was grateful for the sense of purpose and motivation that this shared awareness endowed me with.

It was at this point that the parents brought Danny in for consultation. In the course of the evaluation, his pediatrician and a pediatric neurologist, as well as a special education professional, occupational therapist, and a speech-language therapist saw him. I did the child psychiatric and the family evaluations. The concluding diagnoses included:

1. Specific learning disabilities, manifested by auditory perception, sequencing, abstraction, auditory memory, gross motor, fine motor, and demand language disabilities.
2. *Hyperkinetic reaction of childhood* (the term in use then for what would now be called ADHD), manifested by hyperactivity, distractibility, and impulsivity.
3. Sensory integration disorder, manifested by tactile sensitivity and defensiveness, gross and fine motor planning difficulties, and vestibular confusion.
4. Emotional problems, manifested by separation anxiety, fears, and poor peer relationships.
5. Family problems, manifested by overwhelmed, frustrated, helpless-feeling parents.

Also noted was Danny's difficulty stopping certain behaviors once started and his bedwetting. These were seen as another reflection of his dysfunctional nervous system.

The following treatment plan was recommended and implemented:

1. Special education, speech-language, and occupational therapy as part of a therapeutic nursery school for children with learning and language disabilities.
2. A trial on medication to minimize the hyperactivity, distractibility, and impulsivity.
3. Preventive family counseling focused on educating the parents about their child's disabilities and their role in helping.

The medication, Ritalin, significantly decreased Danny's hyperactivity, distractibility, and impulsivity. The bedwetting stopped, possibly because of the decrease in impulsivity. His parents learned to use deep touch stimulation when holding Danny, lessening his tactile sensitivity and thus his tactile defensiveness. He adapted to the new therapeutic nursery, and slowly his language improved. The long process of special education therapy began.

Mrs. S describes the evaluation and its impact. Her awareness of her feelings and the shift in her ways of handling them reflect the counseling she began to receive.

It was these feelings that enabled me to have Danny evaluated. He was seen by many specialists, each seeming to focus on one part of his problem. By the end, all the parts came together and presto—a diagnosis—something to grab hold of—something to explain it all, and most of all a means, a method, a way to help.

Danny's neurological impairment caused perceptual problems which resulted in learning difficulties, we were told. His restlessness, his dislike for being touched and touching, his chronic unhappiness and frustration all could be explained. The cause of it was unknown. So who could be blamed? There was a way to help him . . . please tell us how? There is a way to handle him at home that will make him feel good and happy and worthwhile . . . please tell me and I'll try. It will take time but he'll get better . . . or will he??? How great!

So, with all this, I gazed upon my neurologically impaired Danny, lifted my eyes to the heavens and whispered, "Thank you. It's not as serious as I thought. Thank you. There is help available. Thank you. He will in time get better. Thank you, again. You are not a crazy, unlovable, unnatural mother. Thank you; thank you; thank you!"

But if that's the case, why didn't anyone believe or support me? Why was I kept in this state of anxiety and fear all these years? Where were the experts or even the loved ones? Why didn't they trust me? Why didn't they hear? And so once again I was angry—a state that was becoming second nature to me—descriptive of my mood and personality.

The anger directed itself inward; then because it was futile and uneconomical to express it, I became sad, depressed, forlorn. In short, I felt pity for myself. Why did it have to happen to me? What did I do to deserve this? How will I ever find the strength to endure? How can I be a mother to this poor, defenseless child? Days of brooding were to follow. I was caught up in a grief reaction that was all-consuming. I accused everyone of being unable to understand what I was going through. In a way I was trying to say, "Look how I am hurting. Won't someone take care of me and see how much I am caring?" The only problem with this behavior, I soon determined for myself, was that it accomplished nothing positive nor worthwhile, and, furthermore, it led me to feel unattractive and selfish.

As soon as this awareness surfaced, a new era dawned. Self-indulgence, once completed, paved the way for the realization that Danny and I were going to be involved with one another for many years to come and that I'd better come to terms with the problems and begin to work on it with him so that both of us could be happier than we were. Thus, I allowed myself to become informed by the professionals, comprehending the "whys" and learning the "how-tos." With this knowledge came understanding, and with this understanding came coping, and with this coping came a growing sensitivity toward his positive changes and progress. This encouraged me to continue with renewed courage and with expectations for Danny, based on the reality of the situation.

No longer was there room in my rationale for unproductive self-pity, brooding, or accusations. I realized that the effects of this attitude would result in more problems. Let's then acknowledge that we have a problem. Let's not be afraid to label it, to explore it, to learn about it, and to accept it.

Years Three Through Twelve

Although Danny remained in special education programs through the fifth grade, by the fourth grade he was in a regular education program, receiving special education and language therapy one hour a week each. He remained on Ritalin. His parents worked closely with his school programs and his teachers throughout the years. They carefully selected those peer activities and sports that tended to build on his strengths rather than to magnify his weaknesses. Each year brought successes and new challenges. Mrs. S reflected on these experiences:

But, does acceptance defend a mother against uncomfortable feelings? Does she ever adjust to the situation and simply continue her day-to-day existence, giving minimal thought or worry to this part of her life? The answer for this mother is a resounding *no!*

The process of adjustment is an ongoing one. On his bad days I feel bad. Back creeps the old sense of fear and foreboding. On good days I feel hopeful and perhaps a trifle excited at the glimpse of health and wholeness I see under the surface. On most days I feel the responsibility of another day. I decided that I will try to begin at his beginnings—to love him, to accept him right where he's at. I realize I must plan according to his needs at that moment and with this comes the task of ignoring some of my own. No one can do that without feeling some anger.

And what about the feelings of deprivation when you see how poorly he measures up to his age group, and, as he grows older, how poorly he stands in relation to children even younger than him? What of the feelings you get when you see him rejected by children and adults alike because he can't relate in the expected, conformist manner? What of the embarrassment you feel when his problems result in antisocial behavior in public? What kind of excuses do you force yourself to fabricate to ease your self-consciousness? What do you say to family when they assure you that all he needs is some discipline and he'll fall into line? The disruption he causes in the tempo of family life—the interference with certain pleasures arouses anger, deprivation, and guilt. And how about the emptiness in your gut when you catch a glimpse of his inner world of confusion and loneliness? How does that make you feel?

With all of these feelings resurfacing with every new situation, how can one ever expect to be adjusted? The only answer I have found is to make room for the feelings, to accept them—not to luxuriate in them, but not to deny them . . . to say them out loud to yourself or to whoever is unafraid to hear them. This paves the way for a stronger, more positive relationship with Danny.

The way I relate to Danny becomes reflected in the way he sees himself. If I allow his problems to scare me, he too becomes scared. Communicating to him that he is worthwhile and lovable and that I have hopes for him enables him to face his future with hope and courage. This places a great responsibility on me, but it is the only chance any of us have for a good life. If we have hope for Danny, he will have hope for himself.

I still wish I had three perfect sons. I occasionally indulge in that "Wouldn't it be lovely" fantasy. I have come to treasure in the other two what many people take for granted. I have a great investment in them but I do in Danny, too. It is an investment imbued by the implicit faith I have encouraged myself to have in him and in me. It will take a long time and it will be difficult, but I have hope that it will work.

Follow-Up on Danny

Mrs. S stopped writing her diary when Danny was in the fifth grade. With her permission, I included her diary and my comments in the first edition of this book. At that time, Danny was in the eighth grade. Academically he was doing well. His peer relationships were limited and best handled one at a time. He related well to his parents and brothers but was described as a "little aloof" with others. He continued to need the medication. Danny had no apparent psychiatric problems.

As I prepared the second edition, I called Danny's mother. He was about to enter his senior year at an excellent college. Academically he was doing very well, and he had a B-plus average. He had learned to be very organized and efficient. His major was music. Danny's mother reflected that music had always been his "salvation." He was good, and he could escape into playing for hours at a time. He played the keyboard, and composed and recorded his own music. He was well respected as a musician.

He still had social difficulties. He had friends, but no special friend. He still did not have a sense of humor, and although much improved, he did not pick up many social cues. Yet, he had completed three years of college and was comfortable.

She ended this conversation by saying, "He's a real sweetheart, a lovely person. Yet, he is never going to be perfect . . . I hope he will not be a lonely person." Although she agreed that he had accomplished far more than any of us dared to wish for when he was three, four, or five, the worry about his future never ended.

As I prepared to write the third edition of this book, I again called Danny's mother. He had graduated from college and was living on his own in the Midwest. He held a job and also worked as a musician. He had a small group of friends and appeared to be happy. Danny and his brothers had a good relationship with one another and kept in touch. She added, "I wish he would meet a nice girl who would understand and take care of him, but I don't think this will happen. He is on his own, supporting himself, happy, and comfortable with his small group of friends. What more can I ask for?"

FOUR

Diagnosis

12

Learning Disabilities:
The Evaluation Process

As I have stressed throughout this book, the child or adolescent with learning disabilities often has other related neurologically based disorders—attention deficit hyperactivity disorder (ADHD), the modulating disorders, the tic disorders. In addition, most have secondary emotional, social, and/or family problems. This awareness is critical when planning an evaluation. To evaluate this person fully, a team effort is required. This team might work in a medical setting, in a mental health facility, as part of your school system, or in a private practice model where each professional might have an independent practice but the various professionals interact with one another. Your family physician might be part of the team, might be the one who requests the evaluation, or might have nothing to do with the evaluation.

It is difficult for one person to evaluate your son or daughter and clarify the many possible areas of difficulty. Before you initiate an evaluation or agree that your school professionals may do the studies, you need to know at least two things: (1) who will see my child or adolescent, and what will she or he do; and (2) who will coordinate the evaluation, integrate the findings, and present them to me?

Most often, the classroom teacher or another school professional becomes concerned and initiates an evaluation. Ideally, the school special education team will collect information from parents, the family physician, and anyone else who has worked with or who knows your child. Be forewarned that you may have to push assertively for the necessary studies and then work hard to be sure that each person involved communicates with the others. Don't let each person send you a report, expecting you to understand the results and to integrate the information from each professional. One hopes that all will interact. If they do not, however, you must insist that they come together to form a working team.

I wish we were past the time when children who do not succeed in school are routinely kept back, but we are not. As I've said, repeating a grade may be appropriate for some children, especially less mature preschoolers or kindergartners. But, for most kids, repeating a grade only results in a loss of self-esteem. A child with learning disabilities who is kept back, but who gets no additional help the second time through the grade, may do no better during the repeated year. Further, he or she will be bored with the work already learned. Don't let the authorities at your school force your child to repeat a grade unless they have done an evaluation to show why the difficulties have occurred and how a repeated year will help. Don't casually accept such comments as "immature" or "needs another year to grow." The questions to be asked are "Why is the child less mature?" and "Why would another year of the same program be of help?" Unless you can be told why your child did so poorly and can be presented with a specific rationale for such an action, think before you respond. If your child is immature and underachieving and you agree to repeat the year, press for him or her to receive special education services during the repeated year.

I will discuss first where to go to get an evaluation, then who should be involved in doing it and what you should expect from it. Such efforts might be with your public school, a private organization, or a group of private practitioners. I shall also suggest ways to prepare your child or adolescent for such an evaluation. In the next chapter I will go into more detail about the specific studies done by each evaluator and show you how to understand the findings.

Where to Go to Get the Evaluation

Your first option should be your public school system. If you are in the public school, you are entitled to a free assessment. If you are in a private school, your public school is required under law to provide a free assessment. Your first step is to talk to the principal. If you are in a private school, talk to the principal of the neighborhood school your child would have attended. In most public schools, the principal initiates bringing in the special education diagnostic team to evaluate students in need. If the principal disagrees or refuses to forward your request, seek guidance from a consultant, perhaps a special education person in private practice. You can appeal above the principal, but you will need to know how to do this within your school system.

If you want to have a private evaluation, find out who to contact by discussing your concerns with your family doctor, with other parents, or with members of parent organizations (see the appendix for a list of organizations). In many communities, there are private diagnostic services that have the full complement of professionals needed to do the evaluation.

The Evaluation Process

An evaluation should have three parts: the planning, the assessment (that is, the testing, observing, interviewing), and the interpretation of the findings. First, of course, parents should know who will see their child or adolescent and why. The child must also know why he or she is being evaluated and what to expect during the testing. When the planning phase begins, the team members or primary coordinator should decide what questions need to be asked and who should try to answer them. For example, why is this child not mastering reading? Why is she or he so distractible with a short attention span? Why does he or she get into so much trouble in school?

During the evaluating phase, several different people see your child or adolescent to conduct formal studies. One person may observe him or her in school and/or get information from the classroom teachers. Someone will meet with the parents to inquire into past medical, developmental, educational, and psychosocial information and to explore the current problems in school and at home. Other specialists will also observe and test the individual. Finally, the information and impressions that result from these multiple studies must be pulled together and synthesized. The questions prompting the evaluation must be answered. One person may share these conclusions and recommendations in an "interpretive session" with the parents, or each specialist may summarize his or her findings. Later, in Chapter 17, I will describe the way I prefer these interpretive sessions to be conducted.

Several professionals are involved in the team evaluation. An educator with special training and/or with a graduate degree in special education—the special education diagnostician—will evaluate your daughter or son to determine if he or she has learning disabilities and, if so, in what areas. In many states only a doctorate-level psychologist can administer these educational diagnostic tests or supervise the educational diagnostician. This person also explores areas of learning strengths and approaches for intervention in problem areas. These studies determine your child's or adolescent's level in certain skill and performance areas.

If these studies show difficulties in the receptive and expressive language areas, a speech-language therapist may do additional studies to clarify these difficulties and to explore possible treatment approaches. If the basic studies show difficulties in the gross motor and/or fine motor areas, an occupational therapist may do further studies to clarify further these problems and to identify types of intervention.

A doctorate-level psychologist, often a clinical psychologist or a school psychologist, will evaluate and study the child or adolescent to clarify several issues. This evaluation is usually called a psychoeducational evaluation. Does the child show evidence of an emotional problem? If so, what is it? What is the child's level of intellectual functioning? What are her or his approaches to organizing, thinking, and problem solving? Are there test findings suggestive of an attentional problem and/or impulsivity?

Sometimes a neuropsychologist will do the psychological assessment. The studies are now called a neuropsychological assessment. For this assessment, the neuropsychologist performs most of the tests done as part of a psychoeducational evaluation plus other tests that assess for specific areas of brain function.

The family physician should do a complete physical examination. In some instances other physicians might be asked to see the child. A neurologist or pediatric neurologist may examine the individual if a seizure disorder or other neurological disorder is suspected. This physician might do a brain-wave test (electroencephalogram, or EEG) or other diagnostic studies. These studies should not be done routinely but only when necessary. If a hearing problem is suspected, an audiologist and/or a physician specializing in ear, nose, and throat disorders (an ENT specialist, or otolaryngologist) will see the individual. If a vision or visual problem is suspected, an optometrist or a physician specializing in eye diseases (an ophthalmologist) may participate.

The mental health professional who sees your child or adolescent may be determined by who is available within the school system or by the questions asked. Thus, your son or daughter might be seen by a school counselor, social worker, psychologist, psychiatric nurse, general psychiatrist, or a child and adolescent psychiatrist. These professionals assess for the level of psychological and social functioning and explore for evidence of emotional conflicts, stresses, or disorders.

The special additional issues involved in evaluating for ADHD will be discussed in detail in Chapter 14. The broad evaluation might provide strong clues that the child or adolescent has ADHD, but further assessments are needed to confirm this diagnosis.

Ideally, the team members then meet to discuss their findings, to establish a clinical impression or diagnosis, and to develop a treatment plan. One or more members of this team should meet with the parents to share the findings. Later, someone should meet with the child or adolescent. Ideally, someone should meet with the full family to explain the findings and recommendations.

As parents, you must be sure that you understand all of the findings and that you are comfortable with the recommendations. At a minimum you should have a clear answer to the following questions:

1. Does my child have learning disabilities? If yes,
   What are his or her learning disabilities?
   What are his or her learning strengths?
   How far behind is he or she and in which areas?
   What plans do you have for helping?

2. Does my child have a language disability or motor disability? If yes,
   What are his or her areas of disability?
   What are his or her areas of strengths?
   What plans do you have for helping?

3. Does my child have ADHD? If yes,
   Why do you feel he or she has this disability?
   Is he or she hyperactive? distractible? impulsive?
   Who will direct the treatment?
   If medications are recommended, who will work with us to help us understand this treatment approach? Who will monitor progress?

4. Does my child have evidence of other related neurologically based disorders? If yes,
   Do you find evidence of an anxiety disorder, a depressive disorder, or problems managing anger? Do you find evidence of obsessive-compulsive disorder or a tic disorder?
   If so, who will coordinate the treatment for this problem?

5. Does my child or adolescent have emotional or social problems? If yes,
   What are they?
   Why do you think they exist? Do you see them as primary or secondary?
   What do you recommend we do?

6. Do we have family problems? If yes,
   What are they?
   What do you suggest we do? (If no one sees the effect of the problems on the marriage, siblings, or general family functioning, mention these issues now and ask for help. If doing this would be uncomfortable in front of the people present, seek out someone later and discuss these concerns.)

7. Who will coordinate all of these recommended actions and who will be sure that all involved communicate with one another? (If no one is named, pick someone yourself and ask if she or he will accept this role.)

8. How will we assess progress and when should we meet again to look at the progress and to plan ahead? (Don't leave with a vague answer. Try to set a general time; for example, "We will meet again in sixty days.")

Preparing Your Child or Adolescent for the Evaluation

When an evaluation is in order, your daughter or son must know why it is being conducted, whom she or he will see, and what will be done. Be as honest and direct as possible. You might say, "You have been struggling in school. I know you want to do well. We are having these tests done to try to understand why you are having so much difficulty and what we can do to help." By doing this, you are saying that you understand your child's frustration and unhappiness, that you share these feelings, that you want to understand why the problems exist, and that something can be done to correct the problems and to make things better. The words you choose to get this across will depend on your son's or daughter's age and your style of relating to this child, but the message should not vary: We care about you. You are hurting. We must do something to help. There is help and hope.

If possible, make a list of each person who will see your child or adolescent. Identify who each is and what each will do. If you do not know these answers, find out. You might explain the assessments in this way.

Educational testing: "This is not like a school test. There may not be right or wrong answers. The test will help us understand how you learn best and where you have trouble learning. The results will help us plan a way to help you if you do have problems." There is a characteristic of these studies that needs to be explained. In order to find out where your son is performing in different skill areas, it is necessary to present successively more difficult tasks until he fails three or more consecutive questions or tasks. Explain this concept and stress that he should not get upset or discouraged if it appears that he is making lots of errors. Explain that the tests are designed to have this happen.

Psychological testing: "The psychologists will talk with you and do different tests. These tests will help us understand how you learn and how you solve learning and life problems. Yes, an IQ test may be done to help us understand why you might be having difficulties." Stress that no one thinks the child is dumb or mentally retarded. "We know you're smart. The test will help us learn how you learn."

Mental health evaluation: "No formal tests will be done. A person will talk with you." If your daughter or son is young, you might add "You might play with toys or games while talking." "This person knows about learning difficulties and about the worries and problems people can have when they are not doing well in school." Tell your child that you do not think she or he is crazy. However, you see that she or he is frustrated and unhappy. This specialist can help the family learn what can be done to help. If the professional is a physician—for example, a child and adolescent psychiatrist—and your child is young, you might want to reassure her that unlike the family doctor, this doctor will not give shots.

Special studies or tests: If special studies or tests are to be done, like brain-wave studies, ask the person who will be doing them to help you explain what will happen and why the studies are to be done.

Never surprise your son by keeping him in the dark or by tricking him into seeing someone. Don't lie and say that the person is just a "nice person who wants to meet you" or by avoiding the title of doctor. Your youngster has a right to know what is going on and why. If he refuses to participate in any part of the evaluation, ask a member of the team or the person he is upset about seeing how to handle this resistance.

I remember arranging for an evaluation for a sixteen-year-old girl who had struggled in school all of her life. She was sent to see me because of behavioral problems. I suspected she had learning disabilities. She refused to take the tests. Finally, she agreed to do all of the studies except the IQ test. It took several sessions of discussion before she was able to put into words her fears. "All of my life I have feared that I was retarded. I believe my parents kept telling me I'm smart because what kind of parents would tell their child the truth if she was retarded? Now I feel almost safe because I know it is just a fear. If I take *that* test and find out that I *really* am retarded, I could not live with myself. I would kill myself." She was finally able to handle her fears and take the test. I made special arrangements. She could not tolerate waiting weeks to get the results. What we worked out was that she came to my office first. I walked her to her car so that she could drive to the psychologist. We planned in advance for her to return to my office as soon as the testing was done. The psychologist agreed to score the test immediately and to call me. By the time she got to my office, I was able to give her the results. I was prepared to support her whatever the results. In this young lady's case, she was of superior intelligence but with significant evidence suggestive of learning disabilities.

After the Evaluation

Once you, the parents, understand the results and recommendations, you should see to it that your child also knows what they are. If you feel capable of sharing this information yourself, you might try it. Preferably, however, one of the professionals who participated in the evaluation should meet with your child or adolescent and review the findings and recommendations. I have made this point so many times in this book that you might accuse me of being redundant. But I cannot stress too much how critical it is for the person with the disability to understand himself or herself.

At some point the rest of the family should be fully informed. Sisters and brothers need to know. Grandparents or special aunts and uncles may need to know what the results show and what will be done to help.

The evaluation is only the start. You must follow up on every recommendation to make sure that everything agreed upon continues to be done. Even when the school has done the evaluation and started a program, you must monitor it to see that everything that was agreed upon is offered and conducted. Frequent contact is needed, and usually you must initiate it.

You must also be sure that everyone involved in the treatment process communicates with everyone else. The regular classroom teacher must know what the special education teacher is doing. The physician prescribing medication for ADHD must get feedback from you and from the classroom teachers. And, don't forget to talk about all of this with your son or daughter. How does he or she feel things are going? Is the help useful? Is the medication helping? Your child's opinions are critical, and he or she must feel respected and part of the process.

If things don't get better or if they get worse, talk to the teacher or special education teacher. When a school year comes to an end, request a meeting to review progress and to make plans for the next year. I suggest that parents think in six-month units of time. Each spring they meet with the team to summarize progress and to plan for the next school year. Each fall they meet to see how the new school year is going and to make any changes in what was planned last spring.

Being a constant advocate is hard work. You cannot rest. No one can be as motivated and concerned as you, the parents. Your task is not only essential, it is unavoidable.

13

Learning Disabilities:
The Evaluation Procedures

Now that you understand the process for evaluating a child or adolescent for a possible learning disability, I want to review the specific procedures and tests involved. The more you know about these procedures, the more intelligent a consumer you can become. You cannot afford to sit through meetings with professionals and be lost while they speak in their professional tongue. You must know the information that allows you to understand and be an informed consumer.

This knowledge will help you better understand your son or daughter and how to help. At times, your having this knowledge might prevent a professional from misdiagnosing your child, or, at the least, will send the message that you will not accept everything said just because it is said. You do not have to become a professional; however, you can learn enough to be intelligent about that profession.

School professionals are competent people. They score the studies they do in the same way as a private professional would. However, some school systems have created guidelines for their professionals that might place barriers or exclude some children from services. The professionals try to base their conclusions on the test data. However, their supervisor might create exclusionary factors such as how far behind the child has to be or the minimal age to qualify for services. These factors, in my view, are based on one issue only—balancing the school budget. Thus, when you meet with your school team, you must be prepared. If possible, get copies of the studies in advance and go over them with a consultant or advocate.

Let me illustrate. A psychologist reports to you, "Your son has an IQ of 106, and he is about at grade level. I do not know what you are so concerned about. He's working at his potential." Having read the reports, you reply, "Could you give me his verbal IQ and his performance IQ scores?" The psychologist then must inform you that his verbal IQ is 128 and his performance IQ is 95. You then ask for the subtest scatter and are told that the scatter was from 7 to 15. (I'll explain these terms shortly.) You comment, "How do you explain the verbal-performance difference and the subtest scatter? Isn't it true that my child is very bright and that his scores are suggestive of a learning disability? His full-scale IQ of 106 is not valid and should not be used to judge his performance." Not only are you helping your child, but you are giving notice to the school professionals that you are an informed consumer and that you will be an assertive advocate for your child.

The specific test used to evaluate a student for a learning disability will vary over time. New ones are developed; new editions of old ones are available; different school systems select their own battery of tests to use. Thus, I will discuss the broad issues involved in testing. I will then review the more traditional current tests. It is possible that I won't mention the test used for your child. If so, ask the evaluator questions about the test. What does it measure? How are the results given? What do the results mean?

The basic assessment includes both psychological and educational tests. Thus, the term for these studies is a psychoeducational evaluation.

The Psychoeducational Evaluation

The primary purpose of the psychoeducational evaluation is to identify your son's or daughter's areas of learning strength and any areas of learning weakness or disability. The major goal of such testing is to bring to light what can and should be done to intervene in the areas of weakness and disability and to establish the necessary school programs to help the student overcome, compensate for, and/or acquire accommodations for these difficulties.

These studies might be done by a special education diagnostician, a psychologist, or by both. In general, three areas of study are done:

1. Assessment of intelligence.
2. Assessment of achievement levels in school skill areas.
3. Assessment of the student's ability to receive, process, and express information, noting strengths and weaknesses.

Assessment of Intelligence

The first task is to assess an individual's potential for learning. The IQ (intelligence quotient) test used to accomplish this is usually given by a psychologist. These studies are designed to be as culturally and linguistically sensitive to different ethnic groups as possible. However, if a school system feels that the tests are biased, other methods of assessing intelligence will be used.

FREQUENTLY USED INTELLIGENCE TESTS. The two most frequently given tests of intellectual ability are the Stanford-Binet and the Wechsler intelligence tests. The Kaufman Assessment Battery for Children (K-ABC) may be used as well. The Wechsler tests come in three different units: the Wechsler Pre-School and Primary Scale of Intelligence (WPPSI), the Wechsler Intelligence Scale for Children (WISC), and the Wechsler Adult Intelligence Scale (WAIS). Each is timed so that a standardized score for the person's age can be determined.

Stanford-Binet Intelligence Scale: This test, in its fourth edition, consists of fifteen subtests grouped into four areas: verbal reasoning, quantitative reasoning, abstract/visual reasoning, and short-term memory. It is standardized for age two to adulthood and emphasizes verbal responses more than nonverbal. Thus, if a child is tested on the Stanford-Binet Scale when she is a preschooler and then on the more nonverbal Wechsler scale several years later, the two IQ scores may not be comparable. The child might appear to have dropped in IQ, especially if she has motor problems.

Wechsler Pre-School and Primary Scale of Intelligence (WPPSI): This test, for ages four to six and a half, measures verbal and nonverbal reasoning and perceptual motor abilities. The results are given as three scores—the verbal IQ, the performance IQ, and the full-scale IQ.

Wechsler Intelligence Scale for Children (WISC): Used for ages six through sixteen, this test measures general intelligence. Three scores are provided—the verbal IQ, the performance IQ, and the full-scale IQ. Five parts (subtests) measure verbal abilities, and five parts measure nonverbal or performance abilities. These two scores are mathematically combined to produce the full-scale score.

Wechsler Adult Intelligence Scale (WAIS): This test is used for age seventeen and above. The scores are given in the same way as with the WISC. High school juniors and seniors are often given this test. It is based on adult standards; thus the IQ scores might appear to be lower than previous scores from the WISC.

Kaufman Assessment Battery for Children (K-ABC): Using a different assessment approach, this test focuses on intellectual abilities such as sequential processing or simultaneous processing. Should this test be used for your child, ask for an explanation of the results and how they are interpreted.

These intellectual assessment tests provide more than an IQ score. Equally important, the results assist in the diagnostic process. Children and adolescents with learning disabilities will do well on the parts of the test that utilize their areas of strengths but do poorly on the parts that tap their areas of disability. When the differences between the verbal IQ and the performance IQ or the differences among the separate subtest scores (called subtest scatter) are compared with the rest of the results of the educational evaluation, the picture of the learning disabilities and the reasons for poor classroom performance become clearer. For people with learning disabilities, the IQ test in isolation cannot be used. The scores simply do not truly measure intelligence. The subtest scores do, however, help to identify areas of weakness and do suggest intellectual potential.

THE WECHSLER INTELLIGENCE SCALE FOR CHILDREN. The Wechsler Intelligence Scale for Children, or WISC, is most frequently used for school-age children and adolescents. The subtest results can provide much meaningful information. Thus, I want to look at this test in more detail.

The WISC, in its third edition, has a verbal and a performance (nonverbal) component. Each component has five basic parts (subtests) plus an optional supplemental part.

WISC Verbal Scale

    Information
    Similarities
    Arithmetic
    Vocabulary
    Comprehension
    (Digit span)

WISC Performance Scale

    Picture completion
    Picture arrangement
    Block design
    Object assembly
    Coding
    (Mazes)

The score for any subtest can go from 1 to 19. A score of 10 is considered average. The scores for each of the subtests under the verbal scale are averaged using what is called a weighted system, producing the verbal IQ. The same process is done to produce the performance IQ. Then, the verbal IQ and the performance IQ scores are averaged using a weighted system to produce the full-scale IQ. (These processes of averaging are not done in the usual mathematical way, and the results are not a true average of the subtest scores.) Average IQ is 100, with scores between 85 and 110 considered to be within the average range.

There is no consistent set of guidelines used. In general, if there is more than a 10- to 15-point difference between the verbal IQ and the performance IQ or if there is greater than a 5- to 8-point difference between subtests (called the subtest scatter), the results will be considered suggestive of a learning disability.

Each subtest measures a different intellectual function or cognitive task. Each score is based on the expected normal performance for a person of similar age. Each area of function, and therefore each score, can be affected by learning disabilities or ADHD. Some of the subtests measure knowledge learned in school. Thus, if your son was held back a year and is a year older than expected for the grade, it is important that the results be based on his age then scored again for his grade. Unless this is done, some of the scores might reflect that he does not know some of the things a student his age should know. Table 13-1 explains each subtest.

Table 13-1 WISC Subtests

INFORMATION

Format: The examiner asks a series of questions about common events, objects, places, and people. The child's answers indicate knowledge about this common information.

Assessment: This subtest measures the amount of general knowledge a person has acquired both in school and as a result of life experiences in the family and elsewhere. Children with learning disabilities who do poorly in school may have picked up a lot of general information in the classroom and outside of school and may do well on this subtest.

SIMILARITIES

Format: In this test the examiner orally presents a series of pairs of words. The child explains the similarity of the common objects or concepts the words represent. (For example, the child explains in what way an apple and an orange are alike.)

Assessment: This subtest measures abstract thinking and the ability to comprehend concepts. It may measure basic native intelligence that is separate from learned knowledge.

ARITHMETIC

Format: This test is a series of orally presented arithmetic problems. The child mentally solves the problems and responds orally.

Assessment: This subtest measures numerical reasoning ability through the use of verbal problems; that is, story problems written out in words. The expected level of performance is based on grade-level knowledge. Thus, if a child is behind in math (or, because of being in special education classes, has not had the same level of math as others), the score on this subtest will be influenced.

VOCABULARY

Format: This test is a series of orally presented words. The child orally defines the words.

Assessment: This subtest requires a child to define or explain the words given. It measures general exposure to vocabulary as well as to words learned in school.

COMPREHENSION

Format: This is a series of orally presented questions. Formulating the answer requires the child to solve everyday problems or to understand social rules and concepts.

Assessment: This subtest measures abstract thinking and the ability to comprehend concepts. It may measure basic native intelligence that is separate from learned knowledge.

DIGIT SPAN

Format: This test is a series of orally presented number sequences. The child must repeat verbatim the number sequences for digits forward and in reverse order for digits backwards.

Assessment: This subtest requires a child to remember a series of numbers. For example, "I am going to give you three numbers. I want you to wait until I tell you to answer and then give them back to me." Later, "I am now going to give you three numbers. When I tell you, give them back to me in reverse order." This subtest is sensitive to problems of staying on task and to problems with auditory short-term memory.

PICTURE COMPLETION

> *Format:* The test consists of a set of colorful pictures of common objects and scenes, each of which is missing an important part. The child identifies the missing part.

> *Assessment:* This subtest requires the ability to analyze a total picture and to identify what is missing. Thus, it is a measure, in part, of the ability to look at a whole concept and to break the concept down into its parts.

PICTURE ARRANGEMENT

> *Format:* This is a set of colorful pictures presented in a mixed-up order. The child rearranges the pictures into a logical story sequence.

> *Assessment:* This subtest requires the ability to pick up the story line or social cues in order to help place a series of pictures in their proper sequence of events. (For example, there might be four pictures like a cartoon strip. If placed in the proper order, they would show one picture of someone walking up to a car, one of this person getting into the car, one of this person starting the motor, and then one of this person driving away. The pictures are mixed up on the table.) This subtest is sensitive to the ability to pick up social context and the ability to go from part concepts to whole concepts.

BLOCK DESIGN

> *Format:* This test consists of a set of modeled or printed two-dimensional geometric patterns. The child replicates the patterns using two-colored cubes.

> *Assessment:* The child must analyze the whole complex picture, and then break down the pattern into its parts so as to know which blocks to use to reconstruct the pattern. This subtest measures in part the ability to break a concept down into its parts and then to rebuild the concept back into a whole.

OBJECT ASSEMBLY

> *Format:* This is a set of puzzles of common objects, each presented in a standardized configuration. The child assembles the puzzle parts to form a meaningful whole.

Assessment: In part, this subtest requires the opposite ability as needed for the subtests of picture completion and block design. Here the parts must be analyzed and then put into a whole concept.

CODING

Format: This test consists of a series of simple shapes or numbers, each paired with a simple symbol. The child is required to draw the symbol in its corresponding shape or under its corresponding number according to a key.

Assessment: This test is timed; the better the child can remember the code, the faster he or she can go. The test measures visual short-term memory.

MAZES

Format: This test, printed in a response booklet, is a set of increasingly difficult mazes. The child solves the maze using a pencil.

Assessment: This test requires visual perception, visual-motor, and fine motor skills. Thus, children with difficulties in these areas might not do well.

With the WISC, remember that if your daughter has any language disabilities, the scores on the verbal subtests might be influenced because she did not understand the instructions or could not express the answers. If she is distractible, the scores on these tests might be influenced because she may have had difficulty attending and staying on task. If your daughter has visual perception, sequencing, organization, visual-motor, or motor disabilities, she may do poorly on the performance part of the test. Many of the subtests in this part are timed. Thus, if your daughter processes information slowly, she might do poorly as well.

Each subtest requires different abilities and accomplishments. Some require auditory and verbal skills, and others require visual and motor skills. Some require basic knowledge, and others require acquired knowledge. This acquired knowledge might be learned in or out of school. Some tests require short-term memory, sequencing, integration, or abstraction abilities.

Children with learning disabilities may do well on those subtests where their problems do not interfere, and their scores in these areas should suggest their intellectual potential. They usually do not do as well on those subtests that demand performance in their areas of disability. These scores, perhaps, best reflect how the child is performing in the classroom but not the child's true intellectual potential.

ADHD can influence the child's score. If the child is inattentive or distractible, the test results might reflect the inability to focus and to stay on task rather than true ability. If he or she is impulsive, the child might say or use the first answer that occurs, correct or not. Planning ahead, such as with the blocks, might be difficult.

I would like to illustrate the impact learning disabilities might have on the WISC by discussing twelve-year-old Tom. He has good auditory perception; auditory sequencing, abstraction, and organization; auditory memory; and expressive language skills. However, Tom also has visual perception; visual sequencing, abstraction, and organization; visual memory; fine motor; and visual-motor disabilities. He has been in a special education program for years. On the WISC he scored:

Verbal IQ	128
Performance IQ	88
Full-scale IQ	108

To say that Tom is of average intelligence (i.e., an IQ of 108) is misleading and incorrect. What can be said, perhaps, is that he shows evidence of superior intelligence based on subtest scores where he had no disabilities. He is bright, but frustrated in school because of his disabilities. In most school efforts requiring visual and motor skills, he probably performs at a below-average level.

Let me go through Tom's test results (in Tables 13-2 and 13-3) to illustrate how to understand the scores. The numbers in the middle column below are his subtest scores. These scores are based on charts standardized by age. A score of 10 is average. Scores can go down to 1 and up to 19.

Table 13-2 Tom's Verbal WISC Subtest Scores

Test	Score	Possible Meaning of Score
Information	14	Suggests a child of superior intelligence who is learning through school and in general life experiences.
Similarities	15	Suggests a child of superior intelligence with good reasoning and abstraction abilities.
Arithmetic	9	Suggests that the level of math learned in special education programs was not at the expected (sixth-grade) level.
Vocabulary	17	Suggests a child of superior intelligence who is learning through school and in general life experiences.
Comprehension	13	Suggests a child of high-average to superior intelligence.

NOTE: Tom's verbal IQ is 128, in the superior rage. Yet he has a lower math score, probably because of his learning disabilities and his being in a special education program. This score of 9 is averaged with the others in establishing his verbal IQ; thus, his true verbal intelligence is probably higher than 128.

Table 13-3 Tom's Performance WISC Subtest Scores

Test	Score	Possible Meaning of Score
Picture completion	8	Suggests that his visual perception and visual-motor disabilities interfered with this task. He scored in the low-average range.
Picture arrangement	10	This is an average score; yet, for a boy of his superior ability, it would be seen as underperformance. Probably his visual perception and sequencing problems interfered.

Block design	7	This low-average to borderline score probably reflects his visual perception, visual memory, and visual-motor disabilities plus his anxiety with a timed test.
Object assembly	10	This is an average score but an underperformance for him. The same learning disabilities noted above probably interfered with his performance.
Coding	3	His anxiety plus his visual perception, visual memory, and visual-motor disabilities combined to result in a performance that would be scored in isolation as in the retarded level of functioning.

NOTE: His performance IQ scores as 88, the low-average range. Perhaps this score reflects his level of performance in the classroom with timed and written tests. *It in no way reflects his level of intelligence.* The full-scale IQ of 108 is a reflection of *averaging* his verbal and performance scores. All of his excellent scores are "washed out" by the low scores.

Tom's scores suggest a boy of superior intellectual ability who has learning disabilities that interfere with certain test performances, resulting in lower scores on some subtests. These lower scores suggest the types of problems he might have in school. The difference between his intellectual ability and his school performance may explain his frustrations and poor self-image.

Never let someone give you only an "IQ score," especially only the full-scale IQ. You must look at the full test and the scores on each subtest. To say that Tom was of average intelligence would be inaccurate. To conclude that his C average in school matches his intellectual ability, and thus that he does not have learning disabilities, is wrong. For the school to design an appropriate program for him based on the average IQ rather than on his superior IQ potential would be equally wrong. Only a full understanding of all the test results and their meaning can lead to a proper interpretation and to appropriate program planning.

Assessment of Achievement Levels

Once intellectual potential is measured, it is necessary to compare this assessment with the true performance to see if the student is achieving or underachieving. Standardized achievement tests are given by the special education diagnostician to measure where the child or adolescent is performing in specific academic skill areas— reading, writing, and math. The results may be presented either in terms of grade-level performance or in terms of percentile levels for one's age. Percentile levels compare your child's performance to all other children in his or her grade or for his or her age. Suppose your daughter performs at the 75th percentile. This means that 25 percent of children her age (or in her grade) would perform better on the test than she does. A score in the 25th percentile means that 75 percent of children would perform better.

It is important to understand the difference between the demands of these tests and the demands of the real classroom. Some children or adolescents will do well on a reading comprehension test that requires them to read a paragraph and then to respond to verbal or written questions. However, in the real world, where they have to read pages and pages of material, their level of comprehension might be much lower. The same might be true with math. Your son might be able to do well on the test because he can figure the answer in his head. Or the results might be better because the problem is printed on the page and he does not have to first copy it from a book onto a page. But in the classroom, the child must write out each step and show how he got the answer. Here, the child's disabilities might interfere.

In general, these tests measure four areas of achievement:

Reading: Reading tasks measure the ability to decode familiar and new words as well as nonsense words. Next, there is an assessment of reading comprehension. Finally, there might be an assessment of the ability to use the information obtained in the written task to answer questions.

Writing: Writing tasks measure the ability to write (i.e., form, space, print versus cursive). Next, there is an assessment of spelling, grammar, punctuation, and capitalization as well as of the organization and quality of the language used.

Math: Math tasks measure basic math knowledge as well as knowledge of math skills for each grade level. There might be an assessment of the child's ability to apply math skills to new tasks.

General Knowledge: These tasks measure the level of general knowledge acquired for each grade level as well as knowledge learned elsewhere.

There are several popular tests in use today to assess achievement levels. I will briefly describe each. Should your son or daughter be given a different test, ask about the test and how the results are interpreted.

Metropolitan Achievement Tests: These tests are used for grades one through eight and are given to a group of children at the same time. They assess levels of achievement in a wide range of language and arithmetic skills. Because they are given in a group setting, ADHD can affect the results.

Peabody Individual Achievement Test: This test is used for age five to adulthood to measure general academic achievement in reading mechanics and comprehension, spelling, math, and general knowledge.

Stanford Diagnostic Achievement Tests: These tests are used for grades one through twelve to assess mathematics and reading skills. They also provide instructional objectives and suggestions for teaching.

Wide-Range Achievement Tests: These tests are used from kindergarten through college. They cover oral reading, spelling, and arithmetic computation. Scores are by grade level for each skill.

Woodcock-Johnson Psychoeducational Battery—Tests of Academic Achievement and Interest: These tests are used from preschool through adult levels to measure achievement in reading, math, written language, and general knowledge. These tests also assess the level of academic versus nonacademic accomplishments.

There are also specific achievement tests that focus on reading, spelling, writing, written language, arithmetic, and oral language. The results of these tests may be expressed as a grade equivalent or as a percentile ranking. These tests are also used to assess strengths and weaknesses in order to plan remedial instruction.

Assessment of Processing of Information

If there is a discrepancy between your child's intellectual ability and his or her performance level, the evaluation team must find out why. Several broad-based tests assess each aspect of learning, looking for input, integration, memory, and output abilities and disabilities. Each school system has its own preferred or required battery of such tests.

I will discuss in more detail the one test that is popular in most school systems. It is the *Woodcock-Johnson Psychoeducational Battery—Tests of Cognitive Ability*. This test can be used with individuals from ages three to eighty. It can be administered by specially trained teachers as well as by professionals. The scores can be used individually or can be clustered. A discrepancy analysis can be developed by comparing aptitude and achievement scores.

These tests "put the brain under a microscope." Specific studies are done on how the individual brings information into the brain (auditory and visual), how he or she processes (integrates) this information, how the information is stored and retrieved (memory), and how the information is gotten out by either verbal or motor tasks (output). If these diagnostic tests show areas of disability, further studies might be done to focus in more detail on a specific area of disability. There are tests to assess each area of potential disability.

The completed evaluation should clarify the areas of learning disability as well as the areas of learning ability. The results should lead to recommendations for appropriate academic programs, including the type of program and the specific services that are needed.

It is important to understand the difference between your child's being diagnosed with a learning disability and a school system's professionals concluding that your child is qualified to be *coded* as having a learning disability and thus that your child qualifies for special education services. In the public school system, a child or adolescent could be found to have a learning disability but still not be eligible for services. Eligibility is based on the concept of a *discrepancy;* that is, the extent that the individual is behind for his or her age and grade. Each school system has its own formula for determining the individual's degree of discrepancy. Each school system can determine the extent of discrepancy needed to be eligible for services. This concept of discrepancy will be discussed further in Chapter 21, on legal issues.

I am concerned that in some school systems there is an inverse relationship between the school budget and discrepancy. The more the budget goes down, the higher (or greater) the discrepancy requirement goes up.

The Mental Health Evaluation

The mental status of the child or adolescent is done by a mental health professional who is trained to work with children and adolescents. The assessment should focus on several levels of psychological functioning and on the interrelationships among them. Any neurologically based disorders must be identified and integrated into the other observations and conclusions.

The intrapsychic assessment notes the issues of emotional conflict that are faced by the child or adolescent and the coping techniques (defense mechanisms) that he or she has called into play in order to deal with them. The clinician will note whether the areas of concern and conflict as well as the coping techniques used are age-appropriate or not.

The interpersonal assessment focuses on the child's or adolescent's styles of interacting with parents and other adults and with siblings and peers. Conclusions will reflect whether these styles of interacting are positive or negative, helpful or not helpful, successful or not successful.

The behavioral assessment tries to clarify which behaviors the child is using that are successful and which are not. If the behaviors are unsuccessful, where were they learned and reinforced? What might be done to build on positive behaviors, to teach other, possibly more successful behaviors, and to minimize or get rid of negative behaviors?

The systems assessment focuses on the child's or adolescent's roles in the family as well as in other important systems—the school or the neighborhood. The clinician determines how the roles that the child plays in one system influence or interact with the roles he or she plays in other systems. For example, a child might learn a way of acting or reacting within the family. He or she might use these behaviors in school, where they are not accepted or may be disruptive. The clinician will also observe if the behaviors in school are a reflection of family stress or a cause that contributes to family stress.

These evaluations should help the mental health professional to conclude whether the child has emotional, social, and/or family difficulties. The next critical question is a familiar one to you. Are the emotional, social, and/or family problems causing the academic difficulties, or are the emotional, social, and/or family problems a consequence of the academic difficulties and the resulting frustrations experienced by the child, adolescent, and parents?

The Medical Evaluation

Your family physician should evaluate your son or daughter to clarify if he or she has any medical or physical difficulties. Other professionals will examine your child if any hearing, vision, or other difficulty is suspected. A neurological evaluation may be requested if there is a specific concern or if your school system requires such an evaluation.

Your physician might do such assessments as part of routine well-child care. Possibly, you have been talking to your doctor for several years about your concerns. If not, bring him or her up to date and clarify whether further medical studies are needed. Keep your family physician informed of the other studies being done and of the results.

After the Evaluation—A Final Note

Once again, let me stress that you must learn everything you can about the evaluation process and procedures. And you must share these facts with your son or daughter as well as with the rest of the family. If necessary, find someone who can help you understand the results of the studies.

Of equal importance, insist on a written report of each evaluation as well as a summary report of the findings and recommendations. Read each report and be sure that you understand what is written. If you find something that is different from what was said verbally, question the professional who did the test. Be assertive. You must understand the information.

Keep a file of every evaluation that is done, year after year. Keep notes of each meeting. This information will be useful in the future, should further evaluations be needed or should you find that you must go through an appeals process.

The Diagnosis of Attention Deficit Hyperactivity Disorder

At this time there are no formal tests to establish the diagnosis of attention deficit hyperactivity disorder (ADHD). Unfortunately, there are no specific physical examination findings or blood, urine, brain imaging, brain wave, or other neurological findings that establish the diagnosis. There are excellent psychological tests, computer-based tests, and rating scales in use today. These evaluation approaches might clarify that a child or adolescent is hyperactive and/or inattentive, and/or impulsive. However, none of these evaluations will clarify the reason that this individual has one or more of these behaviors. The problem we have is that there are many causes of hyperactive, distractible, and impulsive behaviors with children, adolescents, and adults. To make the diagnosis, we must clarify the reason for the behaviors. And the only way we currently have for doing this is by the clinical history. It is the information obtained from parents, teachers, and previous records, along with information learned from the person being evaluated, that leads to the diagnosis. This chapter will help you make more sense out of the diagnostic process and will help you participate in this diagnostic process.

The frequency of articles in newspapers and specials on TV would suggest that ADHD is the "disease of the nineties." Many people seem to have it, think they have it, or wish they had it so there would be an explanation for their problems. It is true that the number of individuals diagnosed with ADHD has increased significantly over

the past ten to fifteen years. However, the reason for this is consciousness raising and education. Through the efforts of parent organizations, the print and electronic media, and a plethora of books,
more parents and classroom teachers have learned about ADHD and
what behaviors suggest that the child or adolescent might have this
disorder. Thus, more students have been recognized and referred for
evaluation. And more physicians, having learned about ADHD,
make this diagnosis rather than a behavioral diagnosis. Further, in
the past ten years, the concept that adults can have ADHD has been
communicated to professionals. Thus, more adults are now diagnosed.

In Chapter 6, I introduced the issues to be considered in making a
diagnosis. As I said, the problem is this: The most common cause of
hyperactivity, distractibility, or impulsivity with children, adolescents,
and adults is anxiety, not ADHD. When you are anxious, you cannot
sit still or pay attention. You may feel irritable and snap at people.
The second most common cause of these behaviors in any age group
is depression. Some people have what we call an agitated depression.
They are restless, try to get their mind off of their worries but can't
focus on anything, and may be irritable. Others may have what is
called a psychomotor retardation form of depression. They are withdrawn and may not want to get out of bed or leave home. If they're
with people, they feel that they are walking around in a cloud and
have difficulty listening or talking to others. These people appear to
be inattentive and not focusing. The third most common cause of
hyperactivity, distractibility, and impulsivity in any age group is one
of the other neurologically based disorders discussed in this book. A
child with learning disabilities might appear to be not paying attention or not staying on task because of the impact these disabilities
have on learning. A child with sensory integration disorder and tactile sensitivity might be fidgety and squirmy. A child or adolescent
who has obsessive-compulsive disorder might be distracted by her or
his intrusive thoughts or behaviors. The least common cause of hyperactivity, distractibility, and/or impulsivity in any age group is
ADHD.

Perhaps the reason some children and adolescents are misdiag-
nosed with ADHD is that the clinician involved does not know of this
differential diagnostic issue and does not use the appropriate approach for making the diagnosis. A teacher tells a parent that her child

cannot sit still and pay attention. This parent goes to the family doctor and repeats these concerns. The family doctor prescribes Ritalin.
I often say this to family doctors: If a child came in with the complaint
of lack of energy and listlessness and you saw that the inner lining of
his eyelids were pale, would you conclude that the child was anemic
and start treatment? No, you would get the necessary blood and
other studies done first so that the correct diagnosis could be made.
The same approach must apply with the child or adolescent who
comes into the family doctor's office with the complaint of overactivity or inattentiveness or impulsivity. This information *starts* a diagnostic process. It is necessary to collect the other essential
information before making the diagnosis. Not all children who are
hyperactive, inattentive/distractible, and/or impulsive have ADHD.
Again, ADHD is the *least* common cause of these behaviors.

I want to explain first what the official criteria are for diagnosing
ADHD. Then I will review the differential thinking to clarify if the
person with these behaviors has an anxiety disorder, depression, another neurologically based disorder, or ADHD, or to clarify if the
person has ADHD plus one or more of these other areas of difficulty.

The Official Criteria for ADHD

The official guidelines used by physicians and other professionals to
diagnose ADHD are found in the official classification system, the
Diagnostic and Statistical Manual of Mental Disorders. Published by
the American Psychiatric Association, this manual is now in a fourth
edition; thus, the brief name for it is DSM-IV.

Don't let the title of the manual upset you. Because ADHD is
identified as a psychiatric disorder, it is listed in this publication. Perhaps you would like to know how this happened. The World Health
Organization has members from each nation. One of the goals of the
organization is to have a common definition for all medical disorders
with specific criteria for diagnosing each. In this way there can be
uniformity around the world in diagnosing diseases; thus, there can
be uniform data collected on diseases. These guidelines are developed and finalized by committees made up of representatives from
around the world. Once definitions are agreed upon, each member
nation must follow these guidelines. About every ten years the World

Health Organization publishes an updated set of guidelines called the *International Classification of Diseases*. The current publication, in its tenth edition, is called ICD-10. When a new edition is published, each nation must modify its own classification system to conform with that of the ICD. In the United States, the American Medical Association is given this task. The modified American form of the ICD is the *International Classification of Diseases—Clinically Modified*, or ICD-CM. The current edition is the ICD-CM-10. The American Medical Association assigns different parts of the diagnostic system to the appropriate specialty organizations to prepare the revised publication. The World Health Organization defines what is a "mental disorder." The American Medical Association assigns these disorders to the American Psychiatric Association to update the existing guidelines to conform with the new guidelines. These changes are published as the *Diagnostic and Statistical Manual of Mental Disorders*.

Much of what we knew and practiced in the past when working with mental disorders was based on our understanding of the mind. Knowledge of the brain was not yet available. With the major explosion over the past twenty to thirty years of knowledge of the brain and of mind-brain relationships, many mental disorders once thought of as psychologically based are now understood to be neurologically based with possible psychological consequences. ADHD is one of these disorders. Thus, it may not be inappropriate to have ADHD listed in this manual.

In the DSM-IV, ADHD is clarified using five major steps, each with specific criteria:

Diagnostic Criteria for
Attention Deficit Hyperactivity Disorder

A. Presence of either (1) or (2) as listed below.
   1. Six (or more) of the following symptoms of *inattention* have persisted for at least six months to a degree that is maladaptive and inconsistent with developmental level:

INATTENTION

    a. Often fails to give close attention to details or makes careless mistakes in schoolwork, work, or other activities.

b. Often has difficulty sustaining attention in tasks or play activities.

c. Often does not seem to listen when spoken to directly.

d. Often does not follow through on instructions and fails to finish schoolwork, chores, or duties in the workplace (not as a result of oppositional behavior or failure to understand instructions).

e. Often has difficulty organizing tasks and activities.

f. Often avoids, dislikes, or is reluctant to engage in tasks that require sustained mental effort (such as schoolwork or homework).

g. Often loses things necessary for tasks or activities (e.g., toys, school assignments, pencils, books, or tools).

h. Is often easily distracted by extraneous stimuli.

i. Is often forgetful in daily activities.

2. Six (or more) of the following symptoms of *hyperactivity-impulsivity* have persisted for at least six months to a degree that is maladaptive and inconsistent with developmental level:

HYPERACTIVITY

a. Often fidgets with hands or feet or squirms in seat.

b. Often leaves seat in classroom or in other situations in which remaining seated is expected.

c. Often runs about or climbs excessively in situations in which it is inappropriate (in adolescents or adults this may be limited to subjective feelings of restlessness).

d. Often has difficulty playing or engaging in leisure activities quietly.

e. Is often "on the go" or often acts as if "driven by a motor."

f. Often talks excessively.

    g. Often blurts out answers before questions have been completed.

    h. Often has difficulty awaiting turn.

    i.. Often interrupts or intrudes on others (e.g., butts into conversations or games).

B. Some hyperactive-impulsive or inattentive symptoms that caused impairment were present before age seven years.

C. Some impairment from the symptoms is present in two or more settings (e.g., at school [or work] and at home).

D. There must be clear evidence of clinically significant impairment in social, academic, or occupational functioning.

E. The symptoms do not occur exclusively during the course of a pervasive developmental disorder, schizophrenia, or other psychotic disorder and are not better accounted for by another mental disorder (e.g., mood disorder, anxiety disorder, dissociative disorder, or a personality disorder).

In the DSM-IV, there are three types of ADHD. The clinician must clarify which type the individual has:

Attention Deficit Hyperactivity Disorder, Combined Type: Both Criteria A1 and A2 are met for the past six months.

Attention Deficit Hyperactivity Disorder, Predominantly Inattentive Type: Criterion A1 is met, but Criterion A2 is not met, for the past six months.

Attention Deficit Hyperactivity Disorder, Predominantly Hyperactive-Impulsive Type: Criterion A2 is met, but Criterion A1 is not met, for the past six months.

One word of caution. There are many books available today for parents to read about ADHD. Most are good. Some are excellent. Popular books do not have to meet the same standards as professional books. Thus, you might read a book that uses the term *attention deficit hyperactivity disorder* or *attention deficit disorder*. However, the author presents his or her own criteria for this diagnosis. Some let you know in the beginning that the author does not follow the DSM-IV guidelines; however, some do not. Thus, you will find books that do an excellent job of describing many aspects of ADHD. However, the author's criteria for saying that someone has ADHD are not the same as the official guidelines. I have seen many adults or parents who read one of these books and conclude that they or their son or daughter has ADHD. The individual meets the characteristics described in the book but does not meet the official criteria; thus, I cannot make the diagnosis.

The Differential Diagnostic Process

The three presenting behaviors are inattention, hyperactivity, and impulsivity. Let's look again at each of these behaviors before focusing on the possible causes.

Hyperactivity

Most hyperactive children and adolescents don't run around the room or jump on the furniture. Some might, but most don't. What we see is fidgety and/or squirmy behavior. Their fingers are tapping; their pencil is moving; their leg is swinging; they are up and down from their desk or the dinner table. Something is always in motion. Parents may report that the child is equally restless at night, moving about the bed. Some may show what appears to be "verbal hyperactivity." They seem to talk constantly.

Inattention

In all previous editions of the *Diagnostic and Statistical Manual of Mental Disorders,* this behavior was listed as *distractibility*. In the DSM-IV, the name was changed to *inattention*. There is no clear explanation of the difference between these two terms. Many professionals use them interchangeably.

Before being specific, I want to review the broader concept of attention and attentional disorders. Researchers on attentional disorders clarify that there are three tasks involved in attending:

TASKS INVOLVED IN ATTENDING

1. The ability to seek out what needs to be attended to and to attend.
2. Once attending, the ability to maintain this attention.
3. Once the task is completed, the ability to stop attending and move on to something else.

The most common cause of problems with the first task, *seeking out and attending*, is avoidance. Your daughter knows there is homework to do but keeps putting off (procrastinating with) the task. "I just want to watch one more TV show" or "I'll do it soon. I promise." Or she might start to do the homework and then get up to get a drink, later to get a snack, later to call a friend, later to take a break. (When you have several tasks to do, somehow the one you least want to do keeps being bumped to the bottom of the list.) We can understand avoidance best by looking at what is being avoided. Perhaps your daughter does not know how to do the homework or has learning disabilities. Avoidance is not ADHD.

The second task is the ability to *sustain one's attention* once the task is initiated. Children and adolescents who are anxious or worried or depressed might have difficulty maintaining attention. If the environment is too noisy or stimulating (doing homework at the kitchen table as dinner is being prepared or trying to work in a too noisy classroom), it will be difficult to concentrate. If the work is too hard or not understood, the child's attention will wander. If the individual has difficulty screening out unimportant stimuli from what is being focused on, sustaining attention will be hard. Only the last of these examples might be ADHD.

The third task, *breaking away from the task* and moving one's attention to another task, might be a result of the current task being too much fun. Your son is watching TV and you say it is time to go to bed, so he must turn off the TV. He will not want to do so. Or your child is playing a computer game and you tell him to turn it off and start homework. There are neurological disorders that result in the difficulty of stopping one task to start another. This difficulty is called perseveration. It is not common.

Looking at the full picture of attentional problems, it is clear that ADHD is only one of the possible causes for problems with the second task, sustaining attention once a task is started. Often, avoidance or not wanting to stop something that is more pleasant is misinterpreted as ADHD.

Now back to inattention or distractibility. There appear to be two general groups of problems. Some may show evidence of external distractibility, and others evidence of internal distractibility.

EXTERNAL DISTRACTIBILITY.   Some children have difficulty screening out unimportant sounds or sights. They have auditory or visual distractibility. Children or adolescents (or adults) with auditory distractibility seem to hear everything. Your daughter is sitting in a room doing homework and hears a car going by outside, or her sister talking in the next room, or the phone ringing, or the dog's tail thumping. In school, she is distracted by the sound of footsteps in the hall. College students often say they have to study in a small room on the top floor of the library with the door shut. If they study in the main area of the library, they hear the person next to them turning the page or the sound of the pencil on the page. Adults report that they can work only when their door is shut or that they wait until everyone goes home until they can work. The sound of talking, the hum of the computer, and the whir of the printer distract them.

Individuals with visual distractibility will notice everything around them. Your son is working and starts to look at the design of a rug or a poster or out of the window. He is talking to friends in the cafeteria and begins to look at what other people are wearing. He is playing soccer and starts looking up at the sky or down at the grass. You may find that he has difficulty getting dressed in the morning. He starts to dress and you leave the room. Then he sees something and starts to play with it. Then, it's on to something else he spots. You go back into the room and find your child playing and begin to yell, "I told you to get dressed." Your son is sent to get something by a parent or teacher and never seems to get there. On the way, he sees something (a book or game) and starts to use it. Then, he moves on to petting the cat or looking out the window, and the task is forgotten. Adults with ADHD know this problem well.

I am reminded of a mother who described what happened several days prior to our meeting. She went into the kitchen to start dinner. As she walked in, she saw some papers on the kitchen table and decided to sit down and go over them. As she was working on these papers, she looked up and noticed a note attached to her phone and remembered that she needed to make a phone call. As she was on the phone, she looked across and saw something on a counter. When she got off the phone, she went to the counter. At this point, her children came in and asked when dinner would be ready. She had forgotten it entirely.

Some children with both auditory and visual distractibility might show what is called sensory overload when in a very stimulating environment—a birthday party, a busy shopping mall, the circus. It is as if so much is coming in and bombarding the brain that they're overloaded. They might be irritable or cry or hold their ears, or want to leave.

Occasionally, parents describe their adolescent's study habits and question my saying the child has auditory distractibility. Their teen can only study with music playing in the background. I have had so many adolescents describe why they do this in the same way, I must believe their reason. If they study in total silence, they hear every little blip or sound in the house. The music acts like white noise. They get used to it and do not pay attention to it. The music helps them *not* be distracted by other sounds.

INTERNAL DISTRACTIBILITY.   This form of distractibility is not fully understood; thus, different professionals may define it differently. It is more commonly found with adolescents and adults, less seen with children. I want to share my understanding of this problem. I see two types of internal distractibility. I've termed these two types *drifting* and *jumping*.

Drifting means daydreaming. We all daydream at times. However, for these individuals, the daydreaming occurs all of the time—in school (or at work), with friends, with family. It is the consistency over time that is different. The adolescents or adults might start to read a page. Their eyes go down the page, but their mind is someplace else. They have no idea what they read. They are in class and the teacher is talking. They mentally wander off and miss what is said. They are with friends and everyone is talking. Their thoughts wander off and they miss the conversation. Parents, teachers, friends, and employers might see that "glassy" or blank look in the eyes. Some are called "airheads" or "space cadets." One girl joked that her friend often said, "Earth to Susan. Earth to Susan. Come in, Susan." Any of these examples might be seen with everyone. Again, it is the consistency over time in all situations that distinguishes drifting from normal daydreaming.

Jumping behavior is something that confuses others and frustrates the person with the problem. Our mind is always busy. We have many thoughts going on at the same time. Most can screen out all but the thoughts that we need to focus on. Individuals with the jumping form of internal distractibility cannot. They have multiple thoughts going on at the same time, and their thoughts jump from one to another. They might make a comment from three thoughts out, and everyone looks puzzled about what the comment has to do with the current conversation. These individuals may start to do something; then their thoughts jump to something else. Thus, their activity shifts to another task or activity. Another jump and they change again. Their life is full of piles of incomplete activities.

Impulsivity

Impulsive behavior is usually described as being unable to or finding it difficult to stop to reflect before speaking or acting. Some with ADHD will have difficulty stopping to think before speaking. Others may have difficulty stopping to think before acting. Most have both problems.

Your son might interrupt in class, calling out before being called on. Or he might blurt out an answer or interrupt a teacher who is working with another student. At home, this is the son who continues to interrupt you while you are on the phone or talking to someone else. He hurts friends' feelings by speaking before thinking. As soon as the words are out, he is sorry; but it is too late. Adolescents and adults often become aware of this problem in themselves and work at controlling it.

Some act before thinking. A young child might grab something, knock someone else's blocks down, push into line, or hit. Older children might continue these behaviors. Or they might write down or say the first answer they think of on the test without reflecting first. Older individuals might engage in dangerous behaviors because they do not think before they act. Adults might buy something before thinking through if they can afford it or quit one job before getting another.

Children and adolescents who are impulsive are at risk for certain other behaviors. We do not understand the connection, but we look for them. They might still be bed-wetters. They might be fascinated with fire or matches. Or they might have a problem with stealing.

Making the Diagnosis

Earlier, I described the main problem in making the diagnosis. The most common causes of inattention/distractibility, hyperactivity, and impulsivity are anxiety, depression, and one of the other neurologically based disorders. The least frequent cause is ADHD. Psychological test results, data from specially designed computer performance tests, and scores on rating scales will clarify if someone has one or more of these three behaviors. But this information will not clarify if the behaviors are due to anxiety, depression, learning disabilities, obsessive-compulsive disorder—or even pinworms.

The Other Causes of These Three Behaviors

The most frequent causes of ADHD-like behaviors are anxiety and depression. These reasons for the behaviors must be considered in the diagnostic process.

ANXIETY.   The most common cause of inattention/distractibility, hyperactivity, or impulsivity is anxiety. Anxiety can be a reflection of psychological stress or conflict, or reflective of a specific anxiety disorder. The psychological stress might be the result of an academic problem. An anxious child or adolescent might be in constant motion. As with adults, anxious feelings result in the need to be active. Also as with adults, when anxious, kids find it hard to pay attention or maintain focus. Daydreaming or escaping into TV are not uncommon. If your son has learning disabilities, he might become anxious when asked to perform in his areas of weakness. Thus, he begins to fidget during reading group. When sitting at the desk doing a worksheet, he looks around the room or out of the window. He might have no problems sitting or attending when the tasks relate to strengths. For example, he might have excellent language skills and have no problem sitting still and attending during class discussion.

DEPRESSION.   Again, the depression might reflect a psychological conflict or stress, or might reflect a specific mood disorder. This psychological stress might be a poor self-image and low self-esteem resulting from learning disabilities. In Chapter 6, I described both the agitated and the psychomotor retardation phases of depression. Depression can be experienced at all ages. Sometimes it is difficult to clarify whether the child or adolescent is primarily depressed; whether the depression is a result of the learning disabilities; or whether both are present, possibly along with ADHD. Here is Chris's story.

Chris was ten years old and in the fifth grade when I was asked to do a consultation. He had been in individual and group therapy for two years because of emotional problems and depression. He was unhappy in school and not doing his class work or his homework. A psychological and educational evaluation done by his school system eighteen months earlier showed evidence of learning disabilities. However, the team of evaluators concluded that "his weaknesses were not great enough nor his skill levels behind enough to qualify for services."

A review of his school records plus the history provided by his parents revealed that he had been labeled as hyperactive and distractible in preschool and kindergarten. The first-grade teacher described him as overactive and unable to stay on task. The second-grade teacher made the same comments. Third grade was described as terrible. He got into fights, disrupted the classroom, and did not complete his work. Fourth grade was similar. He was falling further behind in school skills and strategies. The teachers blamed this on his behavior and his "refusal" to sit still and pay attention.

The clinical history added to the diagnostic process. Chris was adopted by his family at age four and a half. He had been in a foster home for one year prior to this adoption. He had been removed from his mother because her boyfriend had sexually abused him. His mother had been neglectful and had often left him alone. The social service agency's records noted that his mother had used alcohol and drugs during her pregnancy. Chris was in both individual and group therapy to help him cope with his past. All of his academic and behavioral problems were seen as secondary to his emotional problems.

During my assessment sessions with Chris he spoke openly of his past. He knew about it and felt that he no longer worried about it. "I talked it all over in my therapy. It is behind me, and this is my family now and forever. I like them." I could find no evidence of emotional conflicts relating to his past. He did speak of his frustrations in school. He did not like school and he believed he was not as smart as the other kids. Chris was aware that it was difficult to sit still in class. He also was aware of his easy distractibility by any noise or activity. He blamed the fighting on the other kids teasing him.

I found Chris to have a chronic and pervasive history (as far as such a history could be obtained) of hyperactivity, distractibility, and impulsivity. Thus, I had to consider the diagnosis of ADHD. His mother's use of alcohol and drugs during pregnancy certainly placed him at risk for ADHD and/or learning disabilities. However, his history also suggested that he might still be dealing with what is called a post-traumatic stress disorder (discussed in Chapter 7). The hyperactivity, distractibility, and impulsivity might be reflective of anxiety and/or depression.

After discussing the clinical issues with his therapist, I presented these diagnostic questions to Chris and his parents. We agreed to a trial on medication to help clarify the issues. He was started on Ritalin. The dose was adjusted. He became calmer, more on task, and less impulsive at home and in school. All of his teachers as well as his parents noticed the significant improvement. His level of work at school improved as well.

After his parents advocated for more services, school professionals agreed to identify Chris as having learning disabilities. He began to receive services and classroom accommodations. His grades went up. The fighting and other disruptive behaviors stopped.

In conclusion, Chris may be struggling with anxiety and depression relating to his past life experiences. But, he also had ADHD and learning disabilities.

Diagnosing ADHD

The only approach we have to the diagnosis of ADHD is the clinical history. If the behaviors observed started at a certain time or occur in certain situations we must think of anxiety, depression, or another neurologically based disorder. Billy is first described as hyperactive and impulsive in third grade. We learn that his parents separated during the summer before or that a favorite grandmother died. Allison is only inattentive/distractible in reading group or when sitting at her desk working on a report. She is very attentive when there is class discussion. José seems to be distracted when doing homework but at no other home time. These children do not have ADHD.

ADHD is present at birth or during the early years of life. Thus, for a diagnosis of ADHD, the behaviors must be both chronic and pervasive. This makes sense. The child is born with the problem and the brain is with him or her throughout life; thus the behaviors are seen year after year. This brain is with the child or adolescent every minute of every day; thus, the behaviors occur all day.

The history is *chronic*. A mother might typically tell me that her son was very active in utero or has been active all of his life. "He started walking at ten months, and at ten months and one minute my life became hell. He never stopped running." A mother might go to a school conference for her third-grade daughter. The teacher comments that the girl doesn't stay in her seat or pay attention. The mother says, "You think you have problems. Her second-grade teacher complained. Her first-grade and kindergarten teachers complained. She was kicked out of nursery school because she would not sit in circle time and pay attention." Adults with ADHD will describe their problems as having been present since adolescence or childhood. With some effort, the clinician can usually find evidence to support the chronic nature of the problems.

The child's problems are *pervasive*. The morning teachers complain about his or her behaviors. The lunchroom monitor complains as do the afternoon teachers. The tutor complains. The piano teacher complains. The soccer coach complains. Sunday school teachers are not allowed to complain; but they let you know. These behaviors are not just school problems. They interfere with friends, family life, and after-school activities.

To make the diagnosis, then, the clinician must take the following steps:

1. Confirm the presence of the criteria in the DSM-IV to establish the presence of one or more of the three behaviors.
2. Show through the clinical history that these behaviors have been present throughout life—they are chronic.
3. Show through the clinical history that these behaviors are present throughout the person's present life—they are pervasive.

The DSM-IV requires this chronic and pervasive history. The behaviors identified must have been present before age six. And these behaviors must interfere with functioning in two or more areas of the person's life.

Test Instruments Used as Part of the Diagnostic Process

Professionals might use rating scales or computerized tests to assist in establishing the diagnosis of ADHD. These test instruments are helpful but do not make the diagnosis.

Rating Scales

Rating scales are popular when assessing children's behaviors. These behavioral rating scales might be completed by parents, teachers, and/or the child or adolescent being evaluated. The results can be analyzed and compared to established norms. Important information can be obtained in an efficient way. These findings provide a baseline so that any changes can be compared.

The difficulty is in using the results to make the diagnosis. The results will clarify if the individual is hyperactive, inattentive/distractible, or impulsive. However, the results will not clarify the reason for these behaviors.

My bias is not to use rating scales. I have great respect for them. However, I learn more by spending time with the parents and child or adolescent and then talking to the teacher or teachers by phone. This process might take more time, but it is worth it. I can learn more by talking with a teacher for five minutes than I can learn from any rating scale.

Rating scales are two-dimensional. The results are reported as a behavior or behavioral cluster being present at a significant level or not. When I talk to the teacher, I can pick up more. For example, the teacher might report to me that the child is hyperactive and inattentive. She or he would have marked the rating scale accordingly. But, as we discuss the child, I learn that these behaviors are only noticed during certain activities and not during others. Or they occurred after something happened at home, or they are more likely to be seen when the child is at one parent's home than when at the other's home. I also can pick up the teacher's affect, that is, how upset or angry the teacher is about these behaviors. "He is so disruptive that I can't teach my class!" tells me more than a check on a rating scale saying the child is impulsive.

I must admit that I am in the minority. Most professionals like rating scales and use them as part of the diagnostic process. The Conners series of parent and teacher rating scales are probably the most popular. There are other behavioral rating scales in use. New rating sheets are developed all of the time, and some professionals have their own. Some school systems use standard rating scales that have been modified to fit the school's needs. If your professional uses a rating scale, ask her or him to explain what it screens for and how to interpret the results.

Computer-Based Tests

Several tests have been developed using the computer to assess the child's or adolescent's ability to pay sustained attention. The results will suggest that this individual has difficulty sustaining attention or that he or she shows evidence of impulsivity.

There are professionals that insist that they can make the diagnosis of ADHD based on the results of these studies. They cannot. The results are to be used as part of the diagnostic process. The results might provide an excellent baseline to be used later in assessing the impact of medication on these behaviors.

The Continuous Performance Test (CPT) and the *Test of Variables of Attention* (TOVA) are the most frequently used. For each, vigilance is assessed by having the child respond to an auditory or visual stimulus by pressing a button. The stimulus is in the background of similar signals. For example, letters appear on a visual screen and the child is asked to respond when a certain letter appears. The tasks are monotonous and require constant attention. The speed or complexity of each task can be increased. ADHD children or adolescents perform more poorly than normal children. They might make more errors of omission (missed signals) and errors of commission (pressing the button in error). Errors of omission are seen as reflective of inattention. Errors of commission are seen as reflective of impulsivity.

In Summary

Not all children, adolescents, or adults who are inattentive/distractible, hyperactive, and/or impulsive have ADHD. In reality, ADHD is probably the least common cause for these behaviors. A clear differential diagnostic process that takes into account all possible causes for these behaviors is needed before a diagnosis can be made. There must be a chronic and pervasive history of the hyperactivity and/or inattention/distractibility and/or impulsivity.

Because individuals with ADHD have a higher likelihood of having learning disabilities than other children and adolescents, if someone is diagnosed with ADHD, the possibility of a learning disability must be considered. So, too, the possibility of one of the modulating disorders or a tic disorder must be considered.

If there are emotional, social, or family problems, the clinician must help in clarifying whether these problems are causing the behaviors or these problems are secondary to the ADHD and the resulting emotional and behavioral problems.

F I V E

Treatment

15

Your Role in the Treatment of Learning Disabilities

As discussed in Chapter 3, the processing problems involving language, motor, cognitive, or executive functions that result in learning disabilities are the result of specific areas of the brain being wired differently. Once a brain is wired this way, we do not know how to "rewire" the brain. Thus, the treatment for learning disabilities involves "habilitation" of the brain. We cannot say "rehabilitation" because we are not trying to return function that was lost. We are trying to develop function that never developed or that developed incompletely. These efforts are a long-term process. Some individuals may make enough progress to no longer need help by a certain age. Many individuals may need help throughout their education, including college and beyond. Most develop strategies for success that work for a time. Then new learning challenges come up, and additional help may be needed.

Nowhere is understanding your total child or adolescent in his or her total environment more important than when you are dealing with learning disabilities. As you know by now, learning disabilities do not interfere just with reading, writing, and arithmetic. They interfere with all aspects of life—at home, in the neighborhood, at religious education, in sports, at clubs, and with other organized activities. Wherever your son goes, you must be an advocate for making the most of his strengths. You must see to it that he has as many positive experiences as possible. How do you build on his strengths and minimize the impact of his weaknesses? Who might work with you at school, at home, and outside of the home? I need to help you answer these questions.

Much of your son's life is spent in school. What help will he need in school? How do you get this help? How do you make sure that the help is adequate and working? These questions have to be asked often over each school year. I need to help you answer these questions as well.

As a start, do you know where your child's learning disabilities and learning strengths are? If not, ask to meet with the special education team at your school or, if the evaluations were not done by the school professionals, with the special education diagnostician or psychologist who did the testing. You might want to review Chapter 4 on learning disabilities and Chapters 12 and 13 on the diagnostic process and procedures. Go back over previous tests and your notes from meetings. Don't stop until you have the information you need to be able to list your child's strengths and weaknesses.

Because the treatment of learning disabilities centers primarily on the school, I will focus on the school environment first. Later, I will discuss the treatment of learning disabilities within the family.

Treating Learning Disabilities in the School

Ideally, your school system is as concerned as you are about developing the necessary help and the proper programs for your son or daughter. These school professionals might contact you before you feel a need to contact them. If your system is so overloaded that only those students who get into major trouble or who fail get noticed or if you are in a system that makes a minimal effort to identify students who are struggling, you may have to be very assertive to get what you need. In Chapter 21, I will discuss education and civil laws and how you go about getting what you need.

The treatment of choice for a student with learning disabilities within the school system is special education. This statement might seem so obvious that it need not be noted. Yet, I find often that this obvious statement is not followed.

This special education help might be offered at different levels of intensity. Depending on your school's facilities, approach to learning problems, and budget, your son or daughter might be placed in a regular classroom or a special education classroom. (It is clear to me that what dictates education policy is partly philosophy of education but primarily the budget.) Education law requires that the placement be in the "least restrictive environment" for that student. For most students, this environment will be the regular education classroom. For others, the least restrictive environment might be the most restrictive environment. It may only be in a small, structured special education class that some students will feel safe enough to take risks and work on their disabilities. These students might feel overwhelmed in a regular classroom.

Procedures for Obtaining Services

The process for obtaining services varies from state to state and often from school system to school system. Here I will describe the general flow of this process. These steps are discussed in greater detail in Chapter 21. Your school system might use different terms for the various steps I will describe. Remember, if your child or adolescent is in a private school, you are still eligible for services. For you, the process starts with the principal of the neighborhood public school your son or daughter would have attended.

STEP 1.   You make a request *in writing* to the principal of the school that a conference be scheduled to discuss the need for your son or daughter to be evaluated for possible learning disabilities. It might be that the principal identified this need first and requested that you come in for this school conference. If you had testing done privately and sent the results to the principal, the request would be for a conference to discuss these tests. In most school systems, once a request is submitted in writing, the principal must respond with a conference within thirty working days. (Thus, put your request in writing to force the school administration to start the process.)

STEP 2.   This conference is scheduled. It is often called an *education management team,* or EMT, meeting. Prior to this meeting, the special education person and school psychologist should have reviewed your request and any test results. They should also have spoken with the classroom teacher and have observed your son or daughter. In some school systems there is a preliminary EMT meeting to discuss the parents' request and a second EMT meeting after the professionals read the reports, talk to the teacher, and observe in the classroom.

At the meeting, the professionals decide whether an evaluation is needed. If they decide in favor of an evaluation, they should explain what studies will be done and why. They should offer a time frame for completing the test. If you agree, you will be asked to sign a release giving the school professionals permission to do the tests. If these professionals decide that testing is not needed, you should be informed of your right to appeal this decision. Under education law, the school system has up to sixty working days to complete the testing.

STEP 3.   Once the studies are completed (or the school professionals have reviewed the private evaluations and added selective studies of their own), the evaluation team meets with you, the parents, to discuss the findings and recommendations. In many school systems this meeting is called an *admissions, review, and dismissal* (ARD) meeting. (It is here that a student is admitted into special education; or, if already in, his or her progress is reviewed; or if significant progress has been made, he or she is dismissed from special education.) At this meeting, three major decisions are made. Each requires parent approval to be adopted.

Does your son or daughter have a disability. If so, what kind or kinds?

If he or she has a disability, what level of service should he or she have and which professionals will be involved (e.g., special education, speech-language, occupational therapy)?

Where will these services be provided (e.g., in the neighborhood school or in another school)?

STEP 4.   Once answers to these three questions are agreed upon by both the school professionals and the parents, a written contract is prepared and presented to the parents. This contract between the school and the parents, which clarifies exactly what the school will do, is called an *individualized education program* (IEP). The IEP identifies each area of difficulty, describes how each difficulty will be addressed, and reviews how progress will be assessed. If you disagree with any part of the IEP, you will be informed of your right to appeal. Included at the end of this IEP will be a time frame for reviewing progress. For example, "A meeting will be held ninety days into the next school year to review progress."

Levels of Services

The names for these levels of services vary from school system to school system. Thus, I will describe them and you will have to match my list to your school's definitions.

Level One: The child is in a regular classroom, and any professionals that are needed will work with and through the classroom teacher.

Level Two: The child is in a regular classroom but is pulled out for up to one unit of time a day for special education services.

Level Three: The child is in a regular classroom but is pulled out for two or more units of time a day for special education services.

Level Four: The child is assigned to a special education program (often called a resource room) and may be mainstreamed (placed in a regular class program) as appropriate.

Level Five: The child is assigned to a special education program full-time with no mainstreaming. This program might be part of a regular school facility or might be in a special facility.

Level Six: Some school systems use this level for students assigned to a special education program full-time in a self-contained special education program or school. Such a school might be public or private.

Alternative Options for Parents

Should you decide to provide the necessary help on a private basis by paying a special educator or other professional to work with your son or daughter, it is critical that these efforts be coordinated with the classroom teacher and with any school professionals who might be working with your youngster. An alternative plan is to place your child or adolescent in a private school that is willing to work with students who have learning disabilities and then to supplement this program with private special education tutoring.

You might decide to send your child or adolescent to a private school for students with learning disabilities. Sometimes, because of your location, you must consider a boarding school for such students. Ideally, your public school will agree to the need and fund the program. If not, you will find the financial cost high. Should you want to consider a private placement and not know where to find one, ask someone in the special education program of your school. A list might be obtained from your local chapter of the Learning Disabilities Association or from its national office. Another option is to look in specific directories in your library or to order the directories of such schools. (See the appendix for more information.)

Remember that there is nothing magical about a private school. Not just any private school will do, either. A private school that provides general education may turn out to cause more stress for your child than your public school. You may get smaller classes and more structure, but with it may come a higher level of academic demand or an excessive emphasis on grades and college preparation. Also, in a small class your son or daughter will find it harder to hide and not be noticed.

A school that is designed and staffed to work with students with learning disabilities or a regular private school that has the resources and staff to address the needs of those students with learning disabilities is what you need. Know what you are getting. Talk to parents of children at the private school about academic demands, number of hours of homework, and flexibility of teachers. Ask other parents of children with learning disabilities for advice about what to do and what not to do, and weigh their experiences when you make your choice.

If you find that you cannot get the appropriate special education help in your school system or community, you may find yourself considering a boarding school. To me, this is always the last choice and should be considered only if it is absolutely necessary. Boarding schools can be excellent, and some have excellent special programs for students with learning disabilities. However, if your son or daughter is to live away from home, you must weigh the loss of the security and strength that the family provides against whatever your child or adolescent will gain from the programs at that facility.

If you cannot find any local programs that are tailored to help with the learning disabilities or if your child's behavior at school or at home is so problematic that you must consider a boarding school or residential treatment center, get the best help you can in selecting a good one, one that will be most likely to help your son or daughter.

The School-Based Treatment Program

Before discussing the specific interventions in the regular classroom and provided by specific professionals, I want to offer some advice on monitoring these services. You must be alert and aware of everything. The best plans on an IEP written in the spring will go out the window the next fall if the resources are not there.

If your daughter is in a regular class and is pulled out for special services, watch her carefully. How much time does she really have in the special programs? Is she seen alone or in a group? One study looked at a group of five children with learning disabilities who were in a regular classroom but pulled out for work in a resource room. The plan called for the five to be seen together for thirty minutes a day. It sounded great. The study found, however, that on an average five minutes were lost coming in and getting the students and taking them back to the room. Another five minutes were lost ending early enough to get the students back to the classroom at the end of the thirty minutes. The twenty minutes a day spent in the resource room had to be designed to meet the needs of all five students. The study results showed that on an average each student received seven minutes a week of individualized help specifically designed to address his or her learning disabilities. A variation of this problem often is seen in high school. The student with learning disabilities is assigned to a resource room one period a day. There might be fifteen to twenty students in the room. At best, the teacher can address general issues or help with homework. There usually is no individualized help.

Another concern with the pull-out programs is that the special education teacher, speech-language therapist, occupational therapist, remedial reading teacher, and other professionals work closely with the classroom teacher or teachers. Without this interaction, the class-room teacher may not know how to compensate for or accommodate the needs of the student during the time in the regular program. Sometimes the student is expected to make up the work missed while in a special education program. He or she might have to do the work at home or during recess. Explore whether you think this is fair, and dicuss the situation with the team of people who are involved. I have seen children fall between the cracks. They are pulled out each day during the time the classroom teacher does social studies or math. Suddenly, later in the year everyone realizes that the student never learned this subject. I think that public school teachers really want to understand and help our children and adolescents. However, some-times "the system" or other pressures interfere. You have to be on guard to catch the difficulties so that you can speak up.

Monitor the program continually. In September, your son may be getting everything that she was promised in the IEP. As the school year goes on, the case load for each professional might build. Gradu-ally, the amount of time for your son may decrease or the number of other students in the program may increase. Ask your youngster from time to time how often she is seeing the tutor or speech teacher and how many other students are with him. If you learn that the pro-gram is being diluted, speak up. The shortage of personnel may be real; but this shortage is the school's problem. Your problem is as-suring that your child gets what she is supposed to get.

Don't be afraid to monitor. Keep informed. Ask if the special edu-cation person is trained and certified to work with children who have learning disabilities. Expect and ask for conferences between the class-room teacher and special education professionals on a regular basis to learn of your child's progress and problems. If you have not heard from the school professionals by early spring about planning for the next school year, remind them of the need for such a meeting.

Another service should be available if needed. It is called the ex-tended school year (ESY) service. These are services provided be-yond the school year that are designed to meet specific objectives in a student's IEP. They are offered over the summer months. ESY eli-gibility and services should be determined at the annual review meeting held to develop the next year's IEP. The guidelines for eligi-bility may vary from school system to school system. In general, they are as follows:

1. Without ESY services, there is a likelihood of substantial regression of critical life skills caused by the summer break and a probable failure to recover those lost skills in a reasonable time following the school break.
2. Without ESY services the student's limited degree of progress toward reaching the IEP objectives will prevent the student from receiving some benefit from his or her educational program during the next regular school year.
3. The student is seen as near a breakthrough point with specific life skills, and an interruption of instruction on these objectives caused by the school break is likely to prevent the student from receiving full benefits during the next regular school year.

Specific School Interventions

In general, there are three types of interventions provided to students with learning disabilities:

Remediation
Compensatory strategies
Accommodations

The remediation and compensatory strategies interventions are provided by specific professionals trained to do this. They might be the special education (or learning disabilities) specialist, the remedial reading teacher, the speech-language therapist, the occupational therapist, or others. The knowledge and skills needed to teach remedial and compensatory strategies are significant. Please do not allow your school system to assign these tasks to a volunteer grandparent or a peer tutor. You need the most skilled person doing this work, not an untrained volunteer. Accommodations are provided by the classroom teachers who must know how to build on the student's strengths and to accommodate the weaknesses.

REMEDIATION.   A student who is having difficulty learning a specific skill using the standard teaching approach might succeed in learning that skill if a different or remedial approach is tried. These remedial approaches focus on the student's strengths in an effort to break through where the weaknesses prevented progress. For exam-

ple, a student might have auditory processing problems, thus difficulty with awareness of the subtle differences in sounds (phonological awareness). The first step in learning to read requires this phonological awareness. The child may not make progress. A remedial
approach might be to use a multisensory model that uses the visual, tactile, and kinesthetic (muscle movement) senses in an integrated way.

COMPENSATORY STRATEGIES.   This approach helps the student learn how to learn. Given his or her strengths and weaknesses, what is the best way to read a book and retain the information? What is the best way to take notes in class? What is the best way to organize material? What is the best way to study? Specific strategies are tried until the ones that work best for a specific student are determined. The student then learns to apply these strategies.

ACCOMMODATIONS.   All regular education teachers learn where the student's strengths and weaknesses are and how to accommodate the weaknesses while maximizing the strengths. The special education team usually helps to define the accommodations needed for each learning situation. Later, I will discuss the parents' roles with homework. The concept of accommodations is as critical with homework as it is with classwork.

It is important that classroom teachers know that accommodations are needed and how to do them. The IEP might list the accommodations to be provided. The special education professional should work with the regular education teacher to implement them. You must check to see if they are in place with every teacher. The sensitive, well-informed classroom teacher can do much to help your son or daughter. The teacher can teach to your child's strengths and find ways to accommodate or compensate for the weaknesses. An insensitive or poorly informed classroom teacher can frustrate your son or daughter and give lower grades for work that should have been presented differently or accommodated to.

Examples of accommodation would be allowing extended time on written tests, checking to see that a student understood the verbally given lesson plan, providing a copy of what was put on the board so that the student doesn't have to copy it, not marking off for spelling, permitting a laptop computer in class, or permitting the use of a calculator. Don't let a teacher say it isn't fair to treat your child or adolescent differently than the other children. The disabilities may appear invisible, but they are there. If a teacher doesn't cooperate, speak to the special education teacher or to the principal. Don't let a child or adolescent suffer because of an uncooperative teacher.

There is a seventh-grade teacher in a local middle school that I am fond of because of his sensitivity to the needs of students with learning disabilities. I remember a visit to his school. We were chatting in the hall. He excused himself as a boy passed by to enter his class. He said, "Ralph, later this period I am going to call on students to answer the questions at the end of the chapter you read last night. I want to tell you now that I will call on you to answer question four." After Ralph entered the classroom, I asked the teacher why he had said this. He explained that Ralph had an expressive language problem. If he did not know when he was to be called on, he would have been anxious and less available for the whole class. By getting this information in advance, Ralph could prepare to answer question four and do it well. He would be able to relax and learn during the rest of the period. This teacher represents what we want from the classroom teacher.

Art, music, and physical education teachers must be knowledgeable as well. Each class might require a different set of accommodations. Be sure each teacher is informed.

Assistive Technology

Students with learning disabilities face many challenges in school, challenges that largely result from difficulties in acquiring the requisite skills associated with a particular task that the classroom demands; for example, reading, writing, listening, speaking, thinking. Fortunately, recent advances in technology—assistive technology devices and services—have provided new opportunities for students and adults with learning disabilities to compensate for such deficient skills and to access information that was formally inaccessible. Such an opportunity to learn is helpful not only when doing homework. It is helpful in the classroom if incorporated into the curriculum and teaching methods.

Passed in 1988 and amended in 1994, the Technology-Related

Assistance for Individuals with Disabilities Act (known as the Tech Act) helps states to develop and facilitate usage of such technology. The most recent 1997 amendments to the Individuals with Disabilities Education Act (IDEA) require school systems to incorporate these assistive technologies into a student's individual education program (IEP). It is important that parents know of this opportunity and know to ask for the addition of such assistive technology.

Assistive technology is used for two purposes. First, it can augment an individual's strengths so that his or her abilities counterbalance the effects of any disabilities. Second, technology can provide an alternative mode of performing a task so that disabilities are compensated for or bypassed entirely. Some of these technologies have been used for years. Students with difficulties in reading may be able to capitalize on good listening skills and listen to books on tape rather than reading the print versions. Individuals with poor computational skills might use a handheld calculator, and those with poor spelling might write with a word processor that offers spelling assistance. Others might use the computer's grammar aids for editing assistance. For those who cannot master typing, there is the voice-activated word processor.

Newer technologies include gaining new information by listening to audiotapes, audio CDs, and radio as well as by watching films, videos, and television. Today, with the increased use of CD-ROM techniques for interactive teaching, many students with learning disabilities can take advantage of these multisensory models. Some of these programs analyze the student's area of weakness and divert to a program that compensates for this weakness. Then, the program returns to where it was prior to the shift. These approaches have been especially helpful to the individual with a math disability. The newest planning aids are computer programs that assist writers in the planning stages of the writing process. With such a program, the writer can brainstorm ideas and arrange them in some sort of visual display, such as an idea map, cluster, storyboard, or flowchart. The program can then transform the visual display to a standard outline.

The future is exciting. I encourage parents to ask about assistive technologies at the time of the IEP meeting. Under IDEA, such technology devices and services must be included in the IEP. Unfortunately, in a time of declining fiscal resources for education, assistive technology for students with disabilities may not be a high-priority budget item for school systems. There is another problem. Even if the equipment is made available, it is necessary to have trained professionals who know how to use such equipment. And, it is necessary to retrain classroom and special education teachers to incorporate such technologies into the teaching programs.

School Interventions at Home—Homework

What about homework? Who is responsible for what? What do you do when homework time is a battle zone and is causing tremendous stress between you and your child or within the family?

All youngsters need help from time to time with their homework. Those with learning disabilities may need extra assistance. I believe, however, that the main role for parents is to help their children feel good about themselves. This means helping them to build a good self-image, encouraging their feelings of acceptance, seeing that they feel loved. For some children and adolescents, being able to work with their parents on schoolwork is a positive and sought-after experience. Some, however, become so dependent on parents to do the work for them that they may take advantage of the situation, and this ultimately erodes their self-esteem and your patience. Others do not like to explose their weaknesses or reveal their problems, so they resist help or say they don't have any homework.

Suppose you find yourself wondering about such problems. You may want to talk to your son's teachers as well as to your son. Let the teacher help you decide what to do. How much homework should your child be doing? How long should it take? How much should you be helping? Don't let your son browbeat or nag you into doing his homework with or for him.

You might request a meeting with the teacher and your child. Perhaps the teacher is giving a twenty-minute assignment without realizing that it takes this child an hour. Homework, of necessity, involves reading and writing. If these are the child's areas of weakness, what alternatives could be arranged. Maybe you need to ask whether in addition to the assigned homework, the teacher expects students to complete all uncompleted class assignments. Because of the learning disabilities or the time spent in a pull-out program, your son might have twice as much work to do at home as the other children. Explore, then negotiate solutions.

If you must help your child do homework or certain assignments
and your approach only leads to frustration, speak to the special education professionals. You may need to learn the best approaches to
use when teaching. For example, if you are helping your daughter
memorize a spelling list, should you call the words out, use flash
cards, or ask that she copy them over ten times? The answer is not
based on what worked best for you or for another of your children.
The answer might be based on whether your child's strength is in
auditory short-term memory or visual short-term memory.

To help with the process of doing homework and with preparation
for school, you can do some activities that do not require sitting
down and doing the child's work. Your knowledge of his or her
strengths and weaknesses will enable you to individualize the help to
meet your child's specific needs. Here are a few examples:

1. Help your child to organize materials for school. The youngster may be keeping English papers in the math section or
   today's work with old returned papers. Work with your son or
   daughter to set up a system of organization, and ask the
   teacher to help.

2. Some youngsters have trouble organizing their life. They forget to bring home what they need, they forget to take to
   school what they need, and they misplace or forget to turn in
   work that they did. They lose things, including the key to their
   locker. They might need an assignment book completed and
   monitored by the teacher. They might need a large backpack so
   that they can carry everything in it. They might need a second
   set of books assigned so that they can keep one set at home all
   of the time. Their assignment book can have two columns. The
   left one lists the assignments by subject or class. The right one
   lists what needs to be taken home for these assignments. Thus,
   when they go to the locker at the end of the day, they only
   have to run down the right column and fill their backpack.

3. You may need to set up specific schedules and tasks to help
   with organization. Before going to sleep each night, make sure
   the backpack is filled with everything that will be needed the
   next day. It is too hectic in the morning to do this. Attach little

notes to remind your child of morning tasks—take lunch, take permission slip, take gym shoes.

4. You may need to help your child plan his or her time. Many students with learning disabilities have difficulty planning ahead. Sit down and map out a time plan. Start from the end. For example, "Your book report is due on this date." Have him or her think through with you from finish to start how long it will take to type the final draft, to go from the first to second draft, to read the book. Mark off each date a task should be completed. You will end up with an organized plan your child can follow step by step.

5. Make sure the child understands homework instructions. Memory problems, poor handwriting, or ADHD may result in an incomplete or incorrect idea of what to do at home. The youngster may cover up this problem by saying there is no homework or may do only part of the assigned work and believe that all of the work is done. Suppose the teacher told the class to read Chapter 6 and answer the questions at the end of the chapter. Your son, who has an auditory short-term memory problem, does not write down the assignment. That night he reads the chapter and believes he completed all the homework. The next day the teacher asks for the answers to the questions and your child doesn't have them. In this instance, an assignment sheet or book may help. The child must write down each homework assignment, and the teacher must initial it to show that it is correct. You can use the list to check if all work is done.

6. If you feel that too much homework is being assigned, meet with the teacher or teachers. Discuss what you feel your child can handle. Work out a plan before the overload frustrates him or her and results in the child's being turned off.

7. If your child has ADHD as well, distractions may be a problem when he or she is off of medication. Help find a quiet, less cluttered area with few distractions. In general, TV and homework do not go well together for these students.

8. You may find it helpful to set aside a specific time each day or weekend day for doing homework. Allow for time to relax, play, and unwind after getting home from school. It is difficult for a child to spend a full day in school and then be expected to do homework as soon as he or she comes home. If possible, let your child have some control. Sit down when the child gets home and help plan out the evening. Depending on what he or she has to do and how long it will take, would your child like to do all or part of the homework before dinner, or after dinner but before his or her favorite TV show?

If your son seems to have little or no homework, while his teachers complain that he doesn't turn in work or comes to class unprepared, ask for a conference with the teachers and your youngster. Set up a plan with consequences. If playing police officer each night results in battles and anger, suggest to the teacher and to your child that you "resign." Work out a plan with the school that offers consequences if the child comes to school with work not done. Perhaps he will have to use lunch or recess time or stay after school to complete all homework not done on arrival that morning. At home you can say, "If you want any help, please let me know." Then, stay out of it. If the child doesn't do the work, the school will handle it. Maintain your sanity and the family's peace.

Treating Learning Disabilities in the Home Environment

You want to help all of your children grow up with a positive self-image and confidence. This is difficult enough to do, but it requires even greater effort if your son or daughter has learning disabilities. Don't excuse this child from chores, even though that might be the easy way out. A double standard for this child, one that is different from the expectations you have for other children in the family, will make the other children angry. This behavior also sends a clear non-verbal message that you, too, think that the child with learning disabilities is inadequate. Building on your knowledge of what the child can and cannot do, try to select tasks and activities at which she or he is most likely to succeed. This success builds confidence, and with that confidence comes increasing family and social acceptance.

I will discuss home first, then the neighborhood, clubs, activities, and sports. I cannot give you a ready-made program, but I can suggest an approach—a way of thinking and problem solving. Using this approach, you can write your own book on your own son or daughter.

Your daughter's learning disabilities will be quite apparent at school. Tell her clearly that you understand, and make sure she believes you. Reassure your daughter that you are glad that she is getting help at school. You are also glad that you understand her learning disabilities and abilities. Since these disabilities are life disabilities, you understand that they can interfere with homelife as well as with success with friends or with activities and sports. Ask her to work with you to find ways to maximize her strengths and to minimize or compensate for her weaknesses.

Understanding chores around the house is a good place to start. Make a list of your daughter's strengths and another list of her weaknesses. Next to the list of strengths, think of chores that she could do successfully. Next to the list of weaknesses, list those chores that she would find very difficult to do or write the accommodations she would need to complete the chore. Then, think creatively about what you can do to build on the strengths while helping to compensate for the weaknesses. If you get stuck, ask the special education professional working with your daughter.

Suppose your son has a visual-motor and fine motor disability. You might not ask him to load or unload the dishwasher (unless you have plastic dishes). But he could walk the dog, bring in the newspaper, take out the trash. These chores require gross motor skills and minimal eye-hand coordination.

Let's say that your son has a sequencing problem and has difficulty setting the table. Don't excuse him from this task. Be creative in helping. "Look, I know it is hard for you to set the table because you are confused about where to put the fork, knife, spoon, and glass. So, I just drew a picture of a typical place setting. I will keep it in this drawer in the kitchen. Whenever it is your turn to set the table, feel free to take it out and use it." What are you saying? "You have a disability. I wish you did not, but you do. I would do anything to get rid of it. But I cannot. Since I love you, I will help you work around your disability and be successful. I will not excuse you from life, but I will help you learn how to compensate." What a powerful message to give!

Suppose your young son with sequencing problems has difficulty getting dressed in the morning. You walk in and don't know if you should laugh, cry, or bite your tongue. He has his shirt on and is holding his undershirt. Or he has his pants on and is holding his underpants. Getting the right things on in the right order is not easy. Lay the clothes out on the floor in correct dressing order, and place a favorite stuffed animal at the starting end. Then say, "When you get dressed, start at your teddy bear and work your way down." Help your child learn to compensate. Don't do the tasks for him, and don't excuse him from this life task. If this same child had difficulty with fine motor planning—thus with buttoning, zipping, or tying— be creative as well. Use slipovers or Velcro closures when possible. When not, agree to help. "Richard, put your shirt on and come down to the kitchen. I will help you button it" or "Put on your shoes. I'll help you tie them."

If your son has difficulty with receptive language (auditory perception), be sure to make eye contact with him before speaking. You might want to speak in smaller units and pause at times to ask if he understands. You might not want to give more than one instruction at a time.

If you are in doubt about your youngter's ability to do a particular task—whether he or she might just be lazy or not in the mood—start by assuming that the task can be done and insist on it. Then watch. If you find real problems, you can apologize and discuss ways to help your child do this task.

Chores become a useful activity to help your son or daughter work on learning disabilities. Again, I cannot write out a recipe for doing this. However, I can suggest a way of thinking that you can individualize. Many kitchen activities, for instance, require reading, measuring, counting, and following instructions in a particular sequence. These activities provide good practice in these skills. Chopping and stirring make good gross motor exercises. If you want to improve his or her auditory memory, take the child shopping with you. At first, while near the correct shelf, ask the child to pick up an item, maybe a can of peas. Later, make it two or three items. Still later, make it an item an aisle over, then two aisles. Think of other activities that are fun, can be done together, and can help work on areas of weakness.

What about activities outside of the house? What about sports, clubs, and other programs? Use your knowledge of your child's strengths and weaknesses to select the best activity or to plan the needed adjustments for these activities. Each sport requires different strengths. If your son has visual perception and visual-motor difficulties, he might have difficulty with sports that require quick eye-hand coordination—catching, hitting, or throwing a ball. Avoid baseball and basketball. Look for sports that require more gross motor abilities and minimal eye-hand skills—swimming, soccer, bowling, golf, horseback riding, sailing, canoeing, certain cross-county and field and track events. The child who resists playing baseball might excel at swimming. So let swimming be his or her area of success.

Some children and adolescents find all sports difficult. But it might be possible to improve some of the required skills through practice. Most of the kids his or her own age won't take the time or have the patience to help. However, a parent or an older sibling can go into the yard, or anyplace else where the other kids won't see, and practice catching, throwing, or hitting.

Because they have difficulty following directions or because they simply play more slowly or poorly, some children never learn the basic rules of an organized game. Once again, you or someone in the family may need to sit down and teach the child how to play baseball or hopscotch from the ground up, going back over the rules and actions until the child catches on.

And remember that those children and adolescents with auditory perception or auditory short-term memory difficulties might need help as well. Think of soccer for elementary school children. The coach often runs along the sidelines, calling in instructions. This child might be lost. Thus, the coach might need to learn some hand signals. The coach calls the child's name and then does the signal. Complicated practice drills given verbally might be a problem. Alert the coach, and find a way to work around this problem.

Use this same approach with all outside activities. Build on strengths. Don't magnify weaknesses. For example, picture a ten-year-old girl with fine motor, sequencing, and visual-motor disabilities at a Girl Scout or Indian Princess meeting. Everyone is working on a project—cutting out pumpkins or drawing turkeys—and your child's cutouts or drawings are not very good. She cannot color and stay within the line, or cut and stay on the line. Everybody might laugh or tease. Another failure and the child doesn't want to go to any more meetings. But if the activity leader had known what the child could and could not do, your daughter's gross motor abilities might have been used. She could have handed out the paper, squirted the glue, smeared the paste. Maybe she could have been asked to read about the theme of the meeting or to give an oral report to the group while the others worked on the motor task. On parent night, if you say you will ask the child to demonstrate knot tying, she will resist going. But, let her march in carrying the flag, and all is a success. Turn potential failures into successes.

When such children or adolescents go to the local youth center, don't let them wander around and select what they want to do at random. Whether they should be in arts and crafts or photography or a computer club depends on what they are able to do reasonably well. Many crafts require good visual perception and eye-hand coordination; many aspects of photography involve gross motor skills. Plan ahead for all occasions. Work to make the club, group, or activities leaders into extensions of yourself. Help them to understand what you want to accomplish beforehand. They can help you only if you have advocated for your own cause.

Make sure such people understand if your child does not always hear every instruction given. They must know in advance to check with the child and to repeat instructions if necessary. Your child might appear quiet or indifferent because language does not come easily. Tell this to the people in charge. You may have to explain the whole thing—your child is not retarded, bad, or lazy. The disability is simply invisible. You can and must make the instructor or activity leader sensitive to your child's or adolescent's special needs.

Don't forget Sunday school and religious education programs. Be sure that the staff members know all about your child so that they can work with you in designing appropriate classroom and activity programs.

Choosing a camp, whether day or sleep-away, requires the same attention. You may need to consider a camp that is designed for children with special needs, or you might be able to use a carefully selected regular camp. What strengths and abilities does your son have to have to succeed in that camp, and how do you match them with the offerings of the camp? Some camps focus on drama, arts, or horseback riding. Are these activities that will build on strengths, or will your child sustain more damage because he cannot do these activities well?

Some camps are sports oriented and competitive. Woe to the girl or boy who has visual perception and eye-hand coordination problems and who drops the ball or misses the hit or kick, causing the team to lose the game! But there are camps that focus on noncompetitive activities. There are camps that feature sports or sports-like activities, but are more focused on gross motor skills with minimal eye-hand coordination needed. Your clumsy, nonathletic son might do very well at a camp that focuses on waterfront activities. Swimming, rowing, sailing canoeing—all of these are gross motor activities with no or minimal need for eye-hand coordination.

Before selecting a camp, talk with the director at length. Is this person flexible? Can she or he describe programs that might work for your particular child? Don't hesitate to educate the counselors, either. They will appreciate the information, and your child will undoubtedly benefit from the understanding of such important people.

If your son is going to a sleep-away camp, plan ahead with him for every possible problem. Maybe you need to arrange for your child to call home to problem-solve. Maybe you need to ask the counselor to call if there are difficulties. If your son has major difficulties with reading and writing, corresponding will be a problem. How will he read or write letters? Maybe you can give him a tape recorder, and you can mail him your "letter" on a tape. He can listen to your letter, erase the tape, and dictate a letter back. Creative problem solving before the crises can minimize or avoid them.

In Summary

Learning disabilities are life disabilities. They interfere with school and the family. They can interfere with activities, sports, clubs—with everything. If you can think in a problem-solving way, you increase the likelihood that you will be successful. How do you build on your child's strengths, compensate for weaknesses, and avoid potential failures? No book can give you a list of dos and don'ts. You must write your own book about your own son or daughter.

Whether the location is in school or at home, on the playground or in camp, at a friend's house or at Sunday school, you must plan ahead and anticipate all situations. You must be creative. It will take extra time; but *if you don't do it, who will?*

16

Your Role in the Treatment of Attention Deficit Hyperactivity Disorder

The comprehensive treatment of attention deficit hyperactivity disorder (ADHD) initially involves several models of help, including individual and family education, appropriate school programs, and specific medications. Once the effects of these approaches are clear, other services might be added depending on the need—individual therapy, family counseling, couples counseling, behavioral management programs. Such a multimodal approach is needed because children and adolescents with ADHD have multiple areas of difficulty. As with learning disabilities, the total person must be understood in his or her total world.

As discussed in Chapters 1 and 6, individuals with ADHD might have other neurologically based disorders as well as secondary emotional, social, and family problems. Each problem must be identified during the evaluation process, and each must be addressed in the treatment plan. To treat ADHD with medication only and not address the impact the disorder has had on the parents and family and on school performance will not be successful.

I will discuss the educational process first. Next, I will review the nonmedication treatments at home and in school. Finally, I will explain the medication treatments. The current controversial treatments for ADHD will be reviewed in Chapter 18.

Individual and Family Education

The diagnostic process was reviewed in Chapter 14. Once the diagnosis is made, it is important to educate yourselves on ADHD. The child or adolescent also must understand his or her disability. Siblings, grandparents, and other meaningful adults may need to know and understand.

Different professionals use different approaches to explain ADHD. You may find that if you have done a lot of reading, you know more than the professional you are seeing. I would like to describe how I explain ADHD and its cause and treatment to parents, the child in question, and the child's siblings. The concepts and words used are based on research and are accurate. I do simplify some of the concepts by using symbolic thinking to illustrate the points I want to make. I do believe that I am providing the best information on ADHD. To make the educational process as real as possible, I write the following explanation as if you were sitting in my office and I were speaking directly to you.

Let me review what research strongly supports about our understanding of ADHD. All of the facts are not yet in, but we do know a lot. Your son or daughter has hyperactivity, inattention/distractibility, and/or impulsivity (depending on the specific person being discussed).

First, let's discuss hyperactivity. As you know, we are referring to your child's fidgety, restless behavior. What causes this hyperactivity? There is an area in the brain that stimulates muscle activity. It is in the thinking part of the brain, or the cortex. I call this area the accelerator. There are other areas in the lower parts of the brain that decide how many of these messages will get through to the muscles. I call these areas the brakes. Normally, there is a balance between the accelerator and the brakes, with the brakes appearing to be the controlling factor. Children and adolescents with hyperactivity due to ADHD have brakes that are not working effectively. Thus, the accelerator is not as controlled and the individual has an increased amount of muscle (motor) behavior. I will come back to the brakes and why they are not working effectively.

Then there is distractibility. This distractibility makes it difficult for the individual to filter out unimportant stimuli in the environment and/or to filter out his or her own thoughts so that only one thing can be focused on. The result is difficulty sustaining attention and a resulting short attention span. Our brain has a series of filter systems that screen out unimportant stimuli or thoughts, allowing the person to focus on what is important. In this way, the cortex is not cluttered with too many stimuli and can maintain focus on what is important. In ADHD, the filter systems are not working effectively. Depending on which systems are ineffective, the individual will experience auditory distractibility, visual distractibility, and/or internal distractibility. I will explain why the filter systems are not working effectively in a moment.

Finally, there is impulsivity, the inability to stop to think before talking or acting. We know less about this behavior. It appears that our brain operates somewhat like a computer. Information is entered like data inputted from a keyboard and then relayed to many areas of the brain for a rapid assessment of options. Then, the appropriate decision is relayed through the keyboard leading to actions. For some, this keyboard is not working effectively. Thus, thoughts and ideas come in, and decisions go back out without the brief fraction of a second of reflection needed. The result is impulsive behavior.

If I may continue to use these symbols, the braking system, filter system, and keyboard appear to be in a similar area of the brain. What they have in common is that each uses the same chemical to transmit messages from one nerve ending to another—the same neurotransmitter. We believe this neurotransmitter to be norepinephrine although it might be one of this chemical's precursors—dopa, or dopamine. Individuals with ADHD appear not to produce enough of this neurotransmitter in these areas of the brain. Thus, the systems that use this neurotransmitter cannot work effectively. If the brake is not working effectively, the person is hyperactive. If the filter systems are not able to screen appropriately, the person is distractible. If the keyboard is not operating as it should, the person is impulsive. Thus, depending on which areas of the brain are involved, the individual will be hyperactive and/or distractible and/or impulsive.

What was first learned in 1937 is better understood now. Certain medications can affect these areas of the brain and increase the amount of this neurotransmitter. Once the level is raised to the normal level, the brakes begin to operate effectively and the individual becomes less hyperactive and calmer, the filter systems begin to operate effectively and the individual becomes less distractible with an increased attention span, and the keyboard begins to operate effectively and the individual becomes less impulsive and more reflective. What we understand, therefore, is that these medications do not drug, sedate, or tranquilize individuals. These medications correct an underlying neurochemical deficiency, allowing the individual to function "normally." The effect is analogous to the effect of insulin on diabetes. When a diabetic is given insulin, a chemical deficiency is corrected and the diabetic can function normally. This medication does not cure the diabetes. Thus, when it is metabolized, the person returns to difficulty regulating sugar. When the medications used to treat ADHD are metabolized, the person returns to being hyperactive, distractible, and/or impulsive.

The way I describe the research findings that help us understand ADHD may appear too symbolic to be correct. I am using poetic license with anatomy and physiology. But, like most parents, you probably have not gone through medical school, and these symbols and descriptions may help you understand your son or daughter. Once I introduce these symbols, I can use them during the treatment phase. For example, "He is still more fidgety than he should be. We may need more medication to get the brake working better."

This explanation should help you understand that the purpose of using medication is not to drug your son or daughter so that others can live with him or her. The medications help your child or adolescent function normally so that she or he can be successful within the family, at school, and with friends. You have no reason to feel guilty about placing your child on medication.

Now that you understand that ADHD is a neurochemical disorder, you can see why it exists all of the time. As I will discuss in detail in Chapter 16, to have your child or adolescent on medication only during school hours and school days may make no sense. Yes, the school is delighted with the change, but then your child must continue at home to struggle with the ADHD behaviors and the undone homework.

Nonmedication Treatments—The Family

Frequently, once the medications are working well and the parents and the individual understand the impact of ADHD, the emotional problems and/or family stress decrease or go away. No special help may be needed. Parents may seek out a support group in their community. These organizations provide information, resources, and a chance to meet other parents who share similar problems.

If, after medication and education, everything doesn't improve, it is important to pinpoint the source of what remains. It may be that your son is less hyperactive, distractible, and/or impulsive, but he continues to have a behavioral problem or continues to show emotional stress or peer problems. The emotional damage done before the diagnosis was made might be too great, or it might be difficult for the child to give up learned patterns of behavior without help. Stress on one of the parents might have been so great before the diagnosis and treatment that this parent can't get over it. Or the stress between the couple might remain, resulting in conflicts around parenting and discipline issues or conflict within the marriage. Siblings might still feel anger and react negatively.

Depending on the observed need, you might need individual, group, couples, or family therapy. This help might be in the form of behavioral management, counseling, or therapy. These mental health approaches to treatment will be discussed in Chapter 17.

Whichever form of clinical help you or your child get, it is critical that the clinician managing the medications and the clinician addressing the emotional, social, and family problems communicate with each other.

It is important for parents to learn about the medications used for ADHD. How do they work? How are they regulated? What are the side effects? When should they be used? This information will be discussed in Chapter 16.

Nonmedication Treatments—The Role of the School

Ideally, medication will help your child. If it isn't helping, you might want to discuss this with your physician or get a consultation. If you don't have your son or daughter on medication, it will be necessary for the school to design a program to handle his or her hyperactivity, distractibility, and/or impulsivity.

The roles for the school are as follows:

1. If the student is on medication, the classroom teacher will need to understand the medication, its effects, any side effects, and what observations need to be communicated to the parents and to the physician.

2. If the student is not on medication or the medication is not effective in reducing the behaviors, the classroom teacher and other professionals will need to develop strategies for handling these behaviors.

3. If the student also has learning disabilities, the school professionals will need to provide appropriate special education services and accommodations.

4. If the student doesn't have learning disabilities but has gaps in specific skill or knowledge areas because she or he was less available for learning prior to the diagnosis and treatment, remedial interventions might be needed to fill in the gaps.

School Guidelines and Procedures

The federal guidelines issued by the U.S. Department of Education for school systems to use when working with students who have ADHD reflect the tasks listed above. These guidelines state that there are two primary "decision factors" to use in planning the school program: (1) Is the child or adolescent successfully on medication or not? (2) Does the child or adolescent also have a learning disability?

Schools use two different sets of legal guidelines when addressing these federal guidelines. There are education laws and civil laws. The education law is the Individuals with Disabilities Education Act, or IDEA. The civil law refers to the Rehabilitation Act of 1973, especially to Section 504 of this act, and to the more current Americans with Disabilities Act. Each of these important pieces of legislation will be discussed in detail in Chapter 21.

The regulations for IDEA clarify the criteria to be used to classify (or code) a student as having a disability. If a student is coded, appropriate services and accommodations must be provided in the least restrictive environment. The so-called Section 504 guidelines also clarify what criteria are used to identify an individual as having a disability. If your daughter is coded under IDEA, she will get special education services and accommodations. If she is identified under Section 504 guidelines, your child will receive only accommodations. Thus, it is critical when possible to use the education law and have your child identified under IDEA rather than Section 504. Let me elaborate.

Under the guidelines of IDEA, there is no category for ADHD. Under federal regulations, there are three options for students who have ADHD:

1. If the student also has a learning disability, he or she can be coded as having a learning disability (and thus be eligible for both services and accommodations).

2. If the student has significant emotional problems that make him or her unavailable for learning or that so disrupt the classroom that others cannot learn, he or she can be coded as being "seriously emotionally disturbed" (and thus be eligible for both services and accommodations).

3. If the student does not qualify as having a learning disability or is not seriously emotionally disturbed, he or she may be coded as "other health impaired" (and thus be eligible for both services and accommodations).

If the school professionals do not feel that the student with ADHD meets one of these categories under IDEA, they can use Section 504 guidelines. But here the student will only get accommodations, such as extended time on tests or other helpful adaptations. But there will be no specific interventions. The difficulty is often with the student who has ADHD and learning disabilities, but where the degree of discrepancy is not great enough to code the student as having a learning disability. She or he still needs services, but will not get services under Section 504.

The Role of the School

As noted earlier, the classroom teacher and all other staff working with a specific student need to know about any medication the student is on. The teacher and school nurse must be sensitive to the child's or adolescent's feelings. They should not call out in class "Billy, it's time to take your pill." Or, when Billy misbehaves, call out "Billy, did you take your pill this morning?" Worse is the school nurse who uses the school's loudspeaker system to page: "Will Billy please come to the Health Room to get his medication." These examples might sound so insensitive that no educator or nurse would commit them. However, I mention them because I have heard such examples many, many times.

I'll review general suggestions for the regular classroom teacher first. Then I'll review specific suggestions for specific problems.

GENERAL GUIDELINES: There are four aspects of the regular classroom that should be addressed.

Establishing the Best Learning Environment. The classroom should be modified to address the child's or adolescent's ADHD behaviors. Specific approaches will be discussed later in this chapter. In addition, the student should be surrounded with good role models, preferably students who will not get pulled into inappropriate behavior. The classroom should be as calm, quiet, and organized as is possible for the grade. Additional structure and supervision should be provided during out-of-the-classroom time—in the hall, at lockers, at lunch, on field trips. All teachers, including the art, music, and physical education teachers, should be informed of any special needs or understanding.

Giving Instructions and Assignments. When giving instructions and assignments, the teacher should be sure to have the student's attention and to make the information clear and concise. There should be consistency with daily instructions and expectations. The teacher should be sure that the student understood the directions before beginning the task. If necessary, he or she should repeat the instructions. The student should be made to feel comfortable when seeking help. A daily assignment notebook might be helpful.

Modifying Unacceptable Behaviors. Rules of the classroom should be clear and understood. If the student breaks a rule, the teacher should remain calm, state the infraction of the rule, and avoid debating or arguing with the student. It is helpful to have preestablished responses or consequences for inappropriate behaviors. The consequences should be presented quickly and consistently. It is important that the teacher avoid ridicule and criticism.

Enhancing Self-Esteem.   Building or rebuilding self-esteem is important. The teacher should reward more than punish, and praise any and all good behavior and performances immediately. Ways should be found to encourage the student. If the child or adolescent has difficulty, it is important that the teacher find a way of reestablishing contact and trust so that new solutions can be found and tried.

SPECIFIC GUIDELINES: If the student remains hyperactive, distractible, and/or impulsive, each of these behaviors must be addressed. It is important to plan for each student individually and for his or her specific problem areas. The classroom teacher should try these accommodations. If these approaches do not work, it may be necessary to reconsider if the student can be best handled in a regular classroom setting.

Hyperactivity.   The goal is to channel excessive activity into acceptable activities. If it is possible, this student might be permitted to stand up or walk around the room as she works, and to take more breaks. These breaks might be blended into specific tasks such as taking messages to the office, delivering something to another classroom, or getting something for the teacher. If the child fidgets by tapping a pencil or fingers or by playing with paper clips or other objects, the teacher might try to work out a hand signal. For example, the teacher might place a hand on the student's desk to get the student's attention and then use one hand to tap the other. The student knows this signal means that she is fidgeting and should stop. No one else in the class need know of the interaction.

Distractibility.   The teacher might shorten tasks by breaking one task into smaller parts the student can complete at different times. He or she might give fewer and/or briefer homework assignments. The student might benefit from working with other students to try to increase the interest and novelty of the tasks.

A student who is distracted by sounds might sit in the quietest area of the class, away from windows, doors, or air conditioners. It might be best to have him sit next to the teacher's desk. The teacher might work out a hand signal to point out that the student has been distracted. Perhaps the teacher could place a hand on the child's desk to get his attention, then touch her ear. The student knows what this means and refocuses.

If the student is distracted by visual stimuli, it would be best to decrease such stimuli. He might sit in the front row. (If he is distracted by sounds, sitting in the front row might be a problem in that most sounds are now behind him.) Working in a corner or within a cubicle might help. The other students would have to understand that working in a corner, facing the wall, is not for punishment. The idea of hand signals might work. Here, the signal might be a hand on the desk and then touching an eye.

For the student who is distracted by his own thoughts, the best approach may be to have the desk next to the teacher. The teacher might assist in bringing the student back to task by getting his attention and then either whispering or using a hand signal (maybe touching the top of the head) to alert the student to get back on task.

Impulsivity. Impulsivity is a difficult behavior to manage in the classroom. Efforts might focus on helping the student learn to wait. She might be encouraged to use a piece of paper on the desk to write down what she needs to say or to doodle on until the teacher is free. The student can practice forming a line or handing the teacher a note. A reminder, such as a picture on the desk of a child with a finger over its lips, might help the child resist impulsivity.

Sometimes the teacher can signal the student right after she calls out or interrupts. If the student is receptive, a hand signal might be enough to remind the student that she just acted impulsively. The student might see the teacher turn toward her and place a finger over his lips. The student might be able to say or mouth "I'm sorry" and wait.

In Summary

Ideally, the student should be on the appropriate medication at the right dose so that she or he is not hyperactive, distractible, or impulsive. If this approach is not possible, the above classroom adaptations often will help. If, even with these efforts, the student is unavailable for learning or disruptive in the classroom, it is best if the classroom teacher and parents request a meeting with the other school professionals either to rethink the classroom placement or to consider what additional services might be provided the classroom teacher to help. Examples of such services would be a psychologist who could work out a behavioral management program or a counselor who might try group therapy.

Treatment with Medications

The use of medication to treat what is now called ADHD was first described in 1937. During that year there was an epidemic of viral encephalitis. Some of the children, as they recovered from this disease, were observed to be hyperactive and distractible. A pediatrician, Dr. Charles Bradley, tried a stimulant medication (Benzedrine) and found that the children became less active and less distractible. Stimulants have been used to treat these behaviors since that time. It is important for you to understand that the stimulant medications have been used for more than sixty years. ADHD may be more popular and publicly recognized in the 1990s, but it is not a new disorder.

About 80 percent of children and adolescents with ADHD show improvement on the appropriate medication, used properly. These medications decrease or stop the hyperactivity, distractibility, and/or impulsivity. They do not treat any learning disabilities that may also be present. For some of the individuals with ADHD, medication may result in improved motor control and possibly in improved handwriting. Although scientists don't know why, some children and adolescents with a language disability show improved speech and language when on stimulant medications. However, the underlying processing problems seen with learning disabilities do not improve.

There is no established protocol for treating ADHD with medication. I present an approach I find helpful. The protocol discussed should be seen as one possible model for thinking through each step of the clinical treatment process. Each clinician might use a variation of this model.

One other thought before becoming specific about medication management of ADHD: Some or much of what I present might differ from the views or practices of the physician working with your son or daughter. I believe that I am presenting the most current information. It is possible that your family physician is not as up-to-date. How could this happen? Most physicians work very hard to keep up with their field. They read their journals and newsletters, discuss new medications with pharmaceutical representatives, and attend conferences. They know of the newest concepts and treatments for infectious diseases, metabolic diseases, and other commonly seen problems. However, most of the research and clinical literature on ADHD appears in the child and adolescent psychiatry and general psychiatry literature as well as in some of the psychology journals. Most family practitioners and pediatricians do not receive these publications. Thus, they find it difficult to keep up with the ever-expanding literature on ADHD.

Introduction to the Use of Medication

The material covered in this chapter is not meant to substitute for the decisions made by the family physician or other specialist working with the child or adolescent. This information is meant only to inform parents about the medication used for ADHD. For detailed information on each medication discussed, parents need to read the literature provided by the pharmaceutical manufacturer.

It is important that the necessary differential diagnostic process be considered before establishing the diagnosis of ADHD. If the clinician establishes this diagnosis, it is presumed that the behaviors are not due to anxiety or depression but are neurologically based. Therefore, ADHD is both chronic and pervasive. The behaviors are present not only during school hours but all of the time, every day. There are physicians who insist that children and adolescents take medication only during school hours. They are "off" evenings, weekends, holidays, and summers. However, these children often have behavioral, social, and family problems during these times off medication and have difficulty doing homework. During the summer, they might do poorly at camp or in other activities. Let me use this problem of when to use medication to illustrate the difficulty of keeping all physicians current.

One study done in the 1970s on a small number of children suggested that Ritalin might inhibit the production of human growth hormone and thus "stunt" growth. Vacations from Ritalin were suggested so that the body could catch up with this deficiency. Many physicians heard of this concern and began the practice of insisting on medication vacations. Since this initial study, there have been several major studies that show that Ritalin does *not* decrease the production of human growth hormone. Any decrease in height as a side effect of medication is considered negligible (less than one inch), and even this finding is questioned. The general understanding is that Ritalin does not affect growth and that this medication can be used whenever it is needed. But not all physicians are current on these other studies.

Another example of information not getting out to every practitioner relates to the use of medication following puberty. We used to teach that everyone "outgrew" what is now called ADHD by puberty. Thus, teens no longer needed medications. It became clear in the 1980s that about 50 percent of children continue to have ADHD into adulthood. This is why a parent so often reports that he or she, too, has ADHD. It does not always go away. Some practitioners, not knowing this, take all children off medication when they reach puberty. Not too surprisingly, about 50 percent begin to do very poorly. Adults respond to the medications for ADHD in the same way as do children. Everything I discuss for treating children and adolescents applies equally to adults.

There is one more problem that occurs from time to time in the professional literature. A specific finding is observed and reported. Until this problem is understood, cautious guidelines are appropriately suggested. Gradually, the initial findings are better understood and these guidelines are softened or dropped. Several examples will be given in this chapter where an initial alarm was followed over time with a decrease in concern. It can be difficult to keep up with these changes.

A Clinical Protocol

I find it helpful to have a format to follow in treating individuals with ADHD. In the absence of an established protocol, I will discuss the one I use as a possible way to approach treatment. I try the stimulant medications first. Thus, I call them the Group One medications. If these medications do not help or if the side effects create problems that cannot be clinically resolved, I try a second group of medications, mostly those called tricyclic antidepressants. I call these the Group Two medications. If these medications do not help or help to control only some of the behaviors, I might try a combination of Group One and Group Two medications. Usually, up to 85 percent of correctly diagnosed children, adolescents, and adults with ADHD will respond to one or the other group or to a combination of the groups.

Recall that ADHD is caused by a deficiency of a specific neurotransmitter, norepinephrine. The goal of medication use is to increase the level of this neurotransmitter at the nerve interfaces in the areas of the brain involved. At this time there are two different mechanisms for accomplishing this increase. I like to think of the analogy of a lake without enough water in it. There are two ways you can increase the level of water in the lake. First, you could pour more water into the lake. The second way would be to build a dam. No more water is flowing into the lake than before; but the water flows out more slowly. Thus, the level of water goes up.

One mechanism for increasing the level of this neurotransmitter is to produce more of it. The stimulants (Group One medications) appear to work by stimulating the nerve endings to produce more norepinephrine. The other mechanism, like the dam, seems to decrease the breakdown or metabolism of the neurotransmitter, thus causing whatever is produced to stay around longer. The relative amount of the neurotransmitter then goes up. The tricyclic antidepressants and other medications to be discussed within the Group Two medications appear to inhibit the uptake of norepinephrine, resulting in an increase in the amount at the nerve interface.

Each medication has a generic or chemical name and a trade name. The medications used to treat ADHD are listed in Table 16-1, with the generic name first and the trade name in parentheses.

Table 16-1 Medications Used to Treat ADHD

GROUP ONE MEDICATIONS

Methylphenidate (Ritalin)
Dextroamphetamine (Dexedrine, Dextro-Stat)
Pemoline (Cylert)
Dextroamphetamine and levoamphetamine mixture (Adderall)

GROUP TWO MEDICATIONS

Imipramine (Tofranil)
Desipramine (Norpramine)
Nortriptyline (Pamelar)
Bupropion (Wellbutrin)
Clonidine (Catapres)
Guanfacine (Tenex)

Each of the medications in these two groups will be discussed in detail later in this chapter. But first let me discuss the nonresponder group. The most frequent reason for a child or adolescent not to respond to one of the medications in these groups is that the medication is not being used correctly. Either the dosage or the coverage is not correct. The second reason for not responding is that the role the medication plays is misunderstood. A parent might call me and say her daughter has been on every medication and has not improved. When I ask for more information, I learn that the child is calmer and more focused but still cannot read well or spell. I need to explain that these medications treat ADHD but not learning disabilities. Or a parent might say that his son is better focused but still oppositional and defiant. I need to explain that these medications treat ADHD but not oppositional defiant disorder. A different clinical intervention is needed for this disorder. A third reason noted is that the diagnosis is not correct. The hyperactivity, distractibility, and/or impulsivity is a reflection of anxiety, depression, or learning disabilities but not of ADHD.

There is a small group of true nonresponders. These children and adolescents often have several or all of the previously discussed neurological disorders. They might have ADHD, but they might also have a learning, language, or motor disability, one or more of the modulating disorders, and/or a tic disorder. These medications might be helping the ADHD, but other medications are needed to address the other disorders.

I will discuss treatment with the Group One medications and with the Group Two medications. Then I will discuss indications for combining medications from each group. Later I will discuss the medication treatment for the child or adolescent who has ADHD and other disorders. The proper protocol is to use generic names only. However, parents are more likely to be familiar with trade names. Thus, I will use the trade names in my discussions. Refer to Table 16-1 to find the generic name.

I firmly believe that parents must know as much about the medications their son or daughter is taking as the physician does. Thus, I will discuss each medication in detail, including how the dose is selected and adjusted, what the side effects might be, and how to address these side effects.

Group One Medications: The Stimulants—How They Are Used

It is difficult to predict whether a child or adolescent with ADHD will respond better to one stimulant medication versus another. Some will respond poorly to one and have a positive response to another. Some will have side effects with one and not with another. Clinicians must use their own judgment as to which one to try first.

Each of these medications has shared characteristics, effects, and side effects. Ritalin and Dexedrine come in a short-acting and a long-acting form. Cylert is only long-acting. Adderall lasts for five to six hours.

Caffeine, while also a stimulant, has not proven to be a useful medication for ADHD.

Prior to starting one of the stimulant medications, the child needs a general medical evaluation. This medical workup should include measurements of height, weight, pulse rate, and blood pressure. The physician should note whether the child has a family history of a tic disorder or a personal history of a tic disorder. Medical follow-up visits should include observing for tics and involuntary movements and recording of pulse rate, blood pressure, weight, and height. If Cylert is used, blood studies of liver function should be done every six months. (I'll explain why later in this chapter.)

Stimulant medications may aggravate symptoms of anxiety, tension, and agitation; thus, they should be used with caution in these situations. These medications might also exacerbate a tic disorder, and this possibility must be considered. Cylert should not be given to individuals with known impairment of liver function.

Ritalin is available in 5-, 10-, and 20-mg tablets and in the long-acting Ritalin-SR 20 tablet. Ritalin-SR 20 is designed to release 10 mg initially and 10 mg four hours later (for a total of 20 mg). The short-acting Ritalin tablet lasts an average of four hours; however, for some it may last less time or more time. Although there are references to the amount of Ritalin needed based on body weight, the amount needed by each individual does not seem to relate to body weight. This concept will be elaborated on later in this chapter. The recommended upper limit is 20 mg four times a day.

Dexedrine is available in 5-mg tablets and in long-acting Dexedrine Spansules of 5-, 10-, and 15-mg strength. Each tablet lasts an average of four hours. The Spansule lasts eight hours. Dexedrine is approved for use starting at age three. The upper limit of dosage is the same as with Ritalin, 20 mg four times a day. Dextroamphetamine is also available as Dextro-Stat. It is the same chemical compound manufactured by a different company. Dextro-Stat comes in 5- and 10-mg tablets, each lasting an average of four hours. A new medication in this same group is Adderall. This medication is a mixture of several different salts of amphetamine. Research is not yet available to clarify if this mixture of amphetamine salts offers benefits over the single-salt dextroamphetamine. Adderall comes in 5-, 10-, and 20-mg tablets and is designed to last five to six hours.

Cylert is available in 18.75-, 37.5-, and 75-mg tablets and in a 37.5-mg chewable tablet. It is administered as a single oral dose each morning and lasts for twenty-four hours. The recommended starting dose is 37.5 mg per day. The dose is gradually increased by 18.75 mg each week, with the maximum recommended daily dose being 112.5 mg. Cylert is approved for use starting at age six. During early 1997, several cases were reported of children on Cylert developing acute liver function problems. An alert went out from the manufacturer of this concern. For this reason, many professionals are hesitant to use Cylert at this time. It may be that like other sudden alerts, the problem will be of less concern over time.

Since Ritalin is the most frequently prescribed of the Group One medications, I will discuss it as a prototype of this group of medications. Most of what is presented is true for all of the medications in this group. Exceptions will be noted.

The short-acting Ritalin tablet begins to work in thirty to forty-five minutes and lasts about four hours. It does not accumulate; thus, at the end of four hours it is no longer found in the blood. If a child takes 10 mg three times a day, we do not say that he or she is taking 30 mg a day. We say that at any moment during the day the child has 10 mg in the blood. Studies show that there is little difference between taking Ritalin on an empty versus a full stomach. Food does not impair absorption; thus, it can be given before a meal, with a meal, or after a meal. As noted earlier, the dose is not based on body weight but on how rapidly the medication is metabolized by the individual. It appears that once the therapeutic benefits are noted, the blood level of the medication is the same for the individual who needs 5, 10, 15, or 20 mg per dose.

When Ritalin is used, there are three clinical questions that must be addressed. These same questions are relevant for the other stimulants.

1. How much medication is needed per dose?
2. At what time interval is the medication taken?
3. During what time periods should the medication be taken?

Each of these issues is important to understand.

How Much Medication Is Needed per Dose? It appears that the dose needed to reach clinical benefit is related not to body weight but to how rapidly each individual metabolizes the medication. I have two-hundred-pound adults taking 5 mg and thirty-pound children taking 20 mg. Each person seems to need a specific amount to achieve the benefit. There are no readily available tests to measure the blood level of Ritalin. Thus, clinical observations are used to establish the dose. I start the individual on 5 mg per dose. With very young children, I might start at 2.5 mg per dose. At five-day intervals I get feedback from parents and teachers. If no benefits are noted, I increase the dose by 5 mg each five days until a decrease in hyperactivity, distractibility, and/or impulsivity is reported. There are two side effects that would suggest that the dose of Ritalin or any of the other stimulants is too high for that individual. These are emotional lability (mood swings) and hyperfocused behavior. Unless one of these side effects is noted, I will raise the dose every five days. If I reach 20 mg per dose with no noted benefits, I rethink the diagnosis or the use of the medication. Usually when I increase the dose, I increase it for every dose the child takes over the course of the day. At times I might want to assess the impact of an increase in dose at a specific time. Thus, I might increase the morning dose but leave the noon and afternoon doses the same. Then, I will ask parents and teachers if they notice a difference between the morning and afternoon parts of the school day. If I find that the child or adolescent is doing much better in the morning than the afternoon, I increase the noon and afternoon doses.

Feedback from parents and teachers is critical in adjusting the dose. One efficient way for the physician to do this is to ask a parent to discuss the child's or adolescent's improvement with the teacher at the end of the school day and then to call the physician. In this way, the physician can obtain feedback from school and home with one phone call. Rating scales can be used if a more formal feedback model is desired.

I find it best to start with a short-acting form of Ritalin until the appropriate dose and time of dose is established. Then, if needed, a longer-acting form might be considered. With Ritalin, the long-acting Ritalin-SR can only be used if two consecutive doses are 10 mg. For other doses, the Dexedrine Spansule or Adderall might be needed.

AT WHAT TIME INTERVAL IS THE MEDICATION TAKEN?   The average length of action for a short-acting tablet is four hours. However, for some individuals, the medication may last two or three hours and for others it might last up to five hours. Thus, the dose interval must be established for each individual. There is nothing absolute about using Ritalin every four hours.

The dose interval is determined clinically, using feedback from parents, the individual, and teachers. As an example, John is placed on Ritalin, 5 mg at 8:00 A.M., noon, and 4:00 P.M. daily. If the feedback throughout the day is good, the dose interval in place may be best. But suppose the teacher says, "You know, John is great in the morning. But about 11:00 or 11:30 he begins to wiggle in his seat and cannot stay on task. He is much better after the noon medication is given." This indicates that perhaps the ideal dose interval for John is three hours. He may need his medication at 8:00 A.M., 11:00 A.M., and 2:00 P.M. with a 5:00 P.M. dose added, if needed.

Suppose a teacher reports, "Alicia is great in the morning. But between 12:30 and 1:00 she gets so upset. If I look at her the wrong way, she cries" or "Between 12:30 and 1:00 she appears so spacey that she seems out of it. By 1:00 or 1:30 she's fine again." How do we explain this? There are two behaviors that suggest that the dose of Ritalin (or Dexedrine) is too high for an individual. A child might show one or both. One is being emotionally fragile. The child or adolescent is more irritable or tearful than usual. The other is that the child or adolescent is now so overfocused that she or he appears to be spacey. It is possible that for Alicia each dose lasts five hours. She gets the next dose in four hours, and for about an hour she is on the remains of the first dose plus the second dose. For her, the combined dose is too high and thus she experiences side effects. For her, the doses should be five hours apart.

DURING WHICH TIME PERIODS SHOULD THE MEDICATION BE TAKEN?   ADHD is a neurologically based disorder having to do with how the brain functions. Thus, the behaviors—the hyperactivity, distractibility, and/or impulsivity—will be present throughout the person's day, every day. Thus, the guideline for deciding when medication should be used is: Use medication whenever the hyperactivity, distractibility, and/or impulsivity interferes with that individual's success in life. The purpose of medication is *not* to make parents or teachers happy. Medication is used to help the child or adolescent be successful in the family, in school, with friends, in activities, in sports—everyplace. Some will need medication only during school and homework hours. Most will need medication all day, each day.

As noted earlier, it was the misinformation that Ritalin inhibited the human growth hormone and, thus, stunted growth that led to the concept of vacations from medication on afternoons, weekends, holidays, and summers. For too many children and adolescents, the family physician does not know that the concern about growth is no longer an issue and these youngsters get medication only at 8:00 A.M. and noon Monday through Friday, September through June. They struggle with homework and have difficulty getting along at home, with friends, and everyplace they go.

My preference is to place the child or adolescent on medication all day, every day, and ask parents to observe. If they find that the medication is only helpful related to school, I will set up a plan to cover school and homework time only. Parents are taught how to use a single dose for special occasions like going on a long car ride. More frequently, parents report that the medication helps their son or daughter function better at home and with all out-of-the-home activities. Some note, "He actually sat through a whole meal and talked with us." "She can now entertain herself." "He plays better with his friends." "I asked her to do something and she actually did it." Unless parents can observe their child or adolescent in all situations, it is difficult to assess when medication is needed.

The key is to think of the behaviors—hyperactivity, distractibility, and/or impulsivity. When do these behaviors interfere with success with life? Let me give a few examples. Parents report that the medication works well. Their son Louis gets his doses at 8:00 A.M. as he leaves for school, at noon, and at 4:00 P.M. But between the time he gets up and the time he leaves for school, he is impossible. He plays with his toys rather than getting dressed, runs around the house, jumps on his sister's bed, talks loudly, and gets everyone angry with him. Finally, at 8:00 A.M. mother gives Louis his medication, hands him a piece of bread and butter, and shoves him out of the door. Not good for mother, sister, or Louis. The problem is clear. The first dose is given at 8:00 A.M. From the time he gets up until about 8:45 A.M. when the medication takes effect, he is "very ADHD." The solution is also clear. I asked the mother what time her son gets up on school mornings. She said 7:00 A.M. I asked her to wake Louis up at 6:15 A.M., give him his medication, and let him go back to sleep. He wakes up at 7:00 A.M. pleasant and cooperative. He gets dressed, comes to the kitchen, has a good breakfast, and leaves for school with hugs and kisses. Then, he will get his other doses at 10:45 A.M., 2:45 P.M., and if necessary at 6:45 P.M.

Suppose a child gets her medication at 8:00 A.M. as she leaves for school and the second dose at noon. She is about to be suspended from the school bus because on the morning trip she runs up and down the aisles and won't stay in her seat. The problem is that the medication doesn't start to work until she is already in school. The noon dose lasts till 4:00 P.M. and covers the trip home. She needs the first dose at 7:15 A.M. so that it is working before she gets on the bus.

For some children and adolescents who take their medication at 8:00 A.M., noon, and 4:00 P.M., the difficult time is from 8:00 P.M. until bedtime. They may need an additional dose at 8:00 P.M. The key is that medication should be used whenever it is needed to help the individual be successful in life.

The need for medication might vary depending on the age, grade, school demand, and family style. For example, a first or second grader might have little or no homework. A primarily distractible child will need medication during school hours but not for after-school hours. However, this same child, when older and in a higher grade, might have homework and need medication during after-school hours. A hyperactive child might need medication during school hours. However, if the child is young and spends most of the after-school hours playing outside and if the family does not mind the fidgetiness, medication may not be needed at home. This same child might need medication for these hours when he or she is older and homework or family demands increase.

Think through each situation based on the guideline noted. Suppose your family plans to drive to the grandparents' house, a four-hour car trip. Once there, your son will run around and play with cousins all weekend. Then there is the four-hour ride home. Your child might need medication for the car ride there and back. While there, he might not need medication at all or might need it for the quieter family dinner times.

Group One Medications: The Stimulants—Side Effects and Their Management

Ritalin will again be used to demonstrate the Group One stimulant medications. I will review the possible side effects seen with Ritalin and how they are managed. If there are any unique side effects found with the other medications in this group, I will note them.

The two most frequent side effects found with Ritalin are loss of appetite and difficulty falling asleep at night. Less frequently, some individuals will complain of a stomachache or headache after most doses. Even less frequently, some individuals develop tics (these will be described later in this chapter). I'll note even rarer side effects later in this chapter. As discussed earlier, there are two side effects that suggest that the dose of the medication is too high—being emotional labile and being in an overfocused or cloudy state.

LOSS OF APPETITE.   This side effect may lessen over the first several weeks and cease to be a problem. If it persists, something should be done. First, observe your child's eating patterns. The medication may take the edge off your daughter's appetite; thus, she might not finish her meals but may eat candy, cake, and other more desirable sweets. If you see this, you need to limit such sweets until after meals. Some children on three doses a day eat breakfast (because the first dose has not started to work), show no appetite for lunch or dinner, and then come into the kitchen at 8:00 P.M. starved and eat everything they can find. Try to observe your son's or daughter's eating patterns.

One effort to overcome this problem with appetite is to try to create "windows of opportunity." Try to get a good breakfast into your child before the first dose starts to work. Accept that lunch will be a loser. Maybe he or she will eat part of a jelly sandwich, but more often nothing. Try to hold off the 4:00 P.M. dose until 5:30 or 6:00 P.M. During this time provide more structure and supervision and don't expect homework to be done. Your child's appetite may return in time for dinner. Then give the third dose.

If nothing works and the child is losing weight or not gaining weight, Ritalin will have to be stopped and a Group Two medication tried. For reasons we do not understand, some children will have less of a suppression of appetite on one of the stimulant medications than another. Thus, some physicians might try one of these other medications before moving on to the Group Two medications.

SLEEP DIFFICULTIES. Some children and adolescents on Ritalin have difficulty going to sleep at night. They can stay up for hours before finally falling to sleep. This problem often lessens or goes away over several weeks. If it does not, an intervention is needed. The issue is that for some, it is the medication that keeps them awake, and for others, it is the lack of medication that keeps them awake. Both possibilities must be explored. Each reason leads to a different management approach.

It is not possible to predict which of these situations is the reason for an individual's sleep problem. The only way to clarify is to find out by trial and error. I pick an evening when a sleep problem might not be a disaster since the child can sleep later the next day, maybe a Friday or Saturday night. I ask the parents to give the child another dose at 8:00 P.M. If he or she goes right to sleep, I know it was the lack of medication that caused the difficulty. If he or she is even more wired and unable to sleep, I know it is the medication that is causing the difficulty. (On such a night I do not want the child to be up all night. Thus, I will have the parents use Benadryl to get through that night.)

If the medication only occasionally results in difficulty falling asleep at night, your physician might recommend the use of Benadryl, an over-the-counter antihistamine, to help the child or adolescent get to sleep. A dose of 25 to 50 mg, depending on weight, might be recommended. Your child should know that Benadryl is not a sleeping pill. He or she cannot read or play until he or she gets sleepy. However, if the child waits about forty-five minutes, then lies quietly in the dark and tries to sleep, the medication may help. It is all right to use this medication on occasion with your physician's blessing. If it is used every night, the effect might be lost.

If the sleep problem persists, you might decrease or stop the 4:00 P.M. dose. If this change creates behavioral problems in the afternoon and evening or with doing homework, a change to a Group Two medication may be needed.

For others, it is the lack of medication that causes the sleep problem. A child who takes three doses a day is functioning "normally" from about 8:00 A.M. until about 8:00 P.M. Then, the medication wears off, and she is not used to being hyperactive, distractible, and/or impulsive. In bed, she cannot lie still, hears every sound in the house, and cannot turn her mind off. For this person, a fourth dose at 8:00 P.M. may allow for ease of going to sleep.

If every medication in Group One and Group Two has been tried and it is concluded that Ritalin or one of the other stimulant medications works the very best but causes significant sleep problems, there is a possible approach to use. Catapres, a medication in Group Two, can be added one hour before bedtime. I will explain how Catapres works in this situation when I discuss it later in this chapter.

STOMACHACHE.   The reason for the side effect of stomachache is not understood. No one has suggested a solution that seems to work. If the child takes a dose on an empty stomach, he or she might try eating something first. Usually, if stomachaches persist, it is necessary to change to a Group Two medication.

HEADACHE.   The reason for this side effect is not known either. If headaches persist, it is necessary to move to a Group Two medication.

TICS.   Tics and tic disorders were described in Chapter 7. Motor tics are sudden, involuntary movements of specific muscle groups. The most frequently seen involve blinking or moving of the eyes or twitching of the face, mouth, neck, or shoulder muscles. If the muscles in the back of the throat are involved, the child or adolescent might make sniffing, snorting, or coughing sounds. Sometimes the tics begin immediately or soon after the medication is started. Occasionally, they start later. At times the tics are noted only after the dose has been increased.

If tics occur, it is best to stop the medication and to try one of the Group Two medications. For most, the tics will stop immediately. For others, the tics might last for several months before going away.

If there is a family history of a tic disorder, there is concern that the child or adolescent is genetically loaded to develop a tic disorder. In this case, the medication will trigger this tic disorder earlier than it might have started. Stopping the medication will not stop the tics. Here, the medication did not cause the tics, but the medication caused a disorder that would have happened later to start earlier. For most individuals who are going to develop a tic disorder, the tics starts between the ages of eight and twelve. Thus, the closer the child is to adolescence without evidence of tics, the less likely that Ritalin or one of the other stimulants will set off a tic disorder that was probably genetically determined. Thus, if a child has a family history of a tic disorder, the physician might start with one of the Group Two medications as a precaution. When a child is adopted and no family history is available, this possibility of tics is discussed and the decision to use a Group One medication is decided by the parents and the physician.

If all of the possible medications have been tried and only one of the stimulant medications works but causes tics, a decision has to be made by the parents with the help of the physician. Should the stimulant be used and another medication added to treat the tic disorder? In some cases, the result of not treating the ADHD is so harmful to the child that the decision to continue the medication and to treat the tic disorder is necessary.

EMOTIONAL LABILITY OR SPACEY BEHAVIOR.   As mentioned earlier, these side effects suggest that the dose is too high and the dose should be reduced. Being emotional labile means that, based on that individual's normal behavior, he or she is more tearful or irritable. Spacey behavior means that the child or adolescent is so overfocused that he or she seems to be in a cloud or zombie-like. Sometimes this problem is noted as a blunting of the personality. A parent notes that the spark is missing from the childs personality and that he or she "is so flat."

Neither of these behaviors should be accepted. The dose needs to be lowered. If lowering the dose results in a loss of effectiveness, another medication should be tried. As with the other side effects, it is possible that one of the other stimulant medications might not cause the same side effects and should be tried. Usually, however, if one does, the others will.

OTHER SIDE EFFECTS.   Some children and adolescents show a rebound effect about twenty to thirty minutes after the last dose wears off. For those on three doses a day, this occurs about 8:30 to 9:00 P.M. For half an hour or more they may become very hyperactive and talk constantly or may be excitable or impulsive. If this side effect becomes a concern, the last dose may be reduced. This may make a difference. Another approach, if the medication does not cause sleep problems, is to give a fourth dose at 8:00 P.M. so that the medication does not wear off until the person is asleep.

There are other very uncommon side effects. Some children on Ritalin or one of the other stimulant medications become explosive, with limited ability to control their anger. Some may become depressed or very anxious. Others might become very obsessive (with intrusive thoughts) or compulsive (needing to do certain behaviors or patterns of behavior). With each of these side effects, if the medication is stopped, the behaviors return to normal either immediately or within a few days.

THE USE OF LONG-ACTING STIMULANTS.   Ritalin comes in one long-acting form. It is called Ritalin-SR 20, meaning "Ritalin, sustained release, for a total of 20 mg." It releases 10 mg immediately and 10 mg in four hours. Experience shows that this SR form does not always work as it should. For some individuals, the total effect is only about five hours. For others, each release lasts three hours. Thus, they do well from say 8:00 to 11:00 A.M., then have difficulty until about 12:30 or 1:00 P.M. They then do well for about three hours. We now understand that if the surface of the Ritalin-SR 20 tablet is broken (chewed or cut in half), the whole dose is released at once. The child or adolescent gets 20 mg immediately and nothing four hours later. For some, the effect is emotional lability or spacey behavior during the first four hours and hyperactivity, distractibility, and/or impulsivity during the second four hours.

Dexedrine comes in capsule form called Dexedrine Spansule. There are 5-mg, 10-mg, and 15-mg Spansules. Each does last eight hours and releases the medication reasonably evenly. The capsule can be opened and sprinkled over food if necessary without affecting the absorption pattern and length of action. Another form of dextroamphetamine, called Dextro-Stat, comes in both 5-mg and 10-mg tablets. This is not a long-acting form of the medication. Each dose still lasts four hours. The advantage is that the individual can take fewer pills per dose. Adderall, a mixture of several salts of amphetamine, lasts five to six hours and can be used as a longer-acting medication than the basic Dexedrine.

SPECIAL ISSUES.   At what age can a child be started on the Group One medications? Dexedrine is approved at age three. The other stimulants are approved at age six. However, it is not unusual for all of the stimulant medications except Cylert to be used starting at age three.

Clinical observations to date do not show that children and adolescents on Ritalin or one of the other stimulant medications develop tolerance, requiring a gradual increase in dose. Many individuals need the same dose for years. Since the amount needed is not based on body weight, it is not necessary to raise the dose with growth. For some, the dose may have to be increased slightly over time.

Cylert is long-acting; thus, it is always in the bloodstream. For this reason, it is necessary to monitor liver function. This blood test is usually done every six months. More information on the need to monitor liver function with long-acting medication will be discussed later in this chapter.

Earlier literature has raised the question of what is called "state-dependent" learning. That is, if a child learns something while on a medication, will he or she retain this information when off the medication? All studies show no such problems with any of the Group One medications.

The question of addiction is noted in the pharmaceutical literature. Reference is made to the possibility of abuse. At the doses used, addiction has not been reported to be an issue. Recent articles in newspapers refer to the increased use of Ritalin by students to get high. Most reports note that the user ground up the Ritalin tablet and sniffed it. Thus, the entire dose was absorbed into the bloodstream at once rather than slowly over time as when taken properly. These students report feeling high and stimulated. Such feelings are not reported if the medication is taken properly by mouth. If I might try to summarize my understanding of the literature relating to the stimulants and addiction, it is: If the individual has ADHD and is properly managed on medication as well as with appropriate non-medication help, the likelihood of substance abuse is no greater than expected for that individual's peer group. If the individual has ADHD and is not on medication or not managed properly on medication or the necessary nonmedication interventions are not in place, the likelihood of substance abuse may be higher than what would be expected for that individual's peer group. The conclusion I reach is that using medication to treat ADHD does not increase the possibility of substance abuse. The lack of proper or comprehensive treatment with the resulting frustrations and failures might lead to an increase in substance abuse. It is not the disorder or the medication that is the issue. It is the lack of recognition of the disorder or the absence of or incomplete treatment that might result in substance abuse.

Earlier literature also noted concern with the use of a stimulant medication if the individual had a seizure disorder. The current guidelines suggest that this issue need not be a concern. The use of a stimulant medication with a child or adolescent who has ADHD and a seizure disorder should be decided by the physician on an individual basis.

Parents might be concerned with the long-term use of Ritalin or the other stimulants. How safe is it? We have long-term follow-up studies of children who took Ritalin in the 1960s but stopped by adolescence. No side effects have been noted. However, at this time we might start a person on a stimulant medication as a child and he or she might use the medication into adulthood. We do not yet have this type of long-term follow-up report. The best evidence to date suggests that there will be no long-term side effects. Parents must understand that hard data are not in at this time on using these medications continuously over many years.

Group Two Medications

The Group Two medications are used if the Group One medications do not work or if they produce side effects that cannot be clinically managed. Another indication might be an attempt to obtain a smoother, more even effect from the medication. If the Group One medication lasts only two to three hours, a long-acting Group Two medication might be added to get a more even coverage by filling in the valleys when the stimulant is not working.

Most of the Group Two medications are in a family of medications called tricyclic antidepressants; thus some people refer to the whole group by this name. However, there are several medications in this group that are not tricyclic antidepressants. The common theme for this group is that the mechanism of action results in a decrease in the breakdown or absorption of the identified neurotransmitter at the nerve ending, resulting in an increase in this neurotransmitter.

There are several reasons why the medications in this group are our second choice when treating individuals with ADHD. The first is that they do not always address each of the three behaviors seen with ADHD. With the Group One medications, there is a decrease in hyperactivity, distractibility, and/or impulsivity. For reasons we do not yet understand, the medications in Group Two do not cover all of these behaviors. The tricyclic antidepressants (Tofranil, Norpramine, and Pamelar) and Wellbutrin seem to help with the hyperactivity and distractibility; however, often they do not address the impulsivity. Thus, a second medication might need to be added to address the impulsivity. Catapres and Tenex seem to help with impulsivity but often will not address the hyperactivity or distractibility. Thus, again, a second medication might have to be added.

The second reason that these medications are our second choice is that we have to manage long-acting medications differently than short-acting medications. When a medication is in the bloodstream all of the time (unlike, say, Ritalin, which even if used three times a day is out of the bloodstream half of each day), it is necessary to monitor liver function. This step is a precaution since the liver metabolizes most medications. This precaution is not unique to these medications for ADHD. The same need would exist if the child or adolescent were on medications for asthma or arthritis or other medical disorders. The child, therefore, needs to get a blood test about every six months to monitor his or her liver function. The possibility of damage to liver function is rare, and this time interval is believed to allow for early enough recognition of such a problem to know to stop the medication. On rare occasions, the tricyclic antidepressants might result in a decrease in a particular white blood cell (neutrophil); thus, along with the liver function test, a complete blood count (CBC) is done.

Tofranil (imipramine) is the most frequent medication used in Group Two. Thus, I will use it as the prototype for this group. Later, I will discuss the unique features of other medications in this group.

DOSAGE AND USE.   Tofranil is available in 10-, 25-, and 50-mg tablets. Since it is long-acting, the medication is often taken in the morning and in the evening; the individual thus avoids the need to take medication at school. It can be used in individuals age six and older. As with the stimulant medication, there appears to be no relationship between the dose needed to treat ADHD and body weight. Thus, the dose should be determined by clinical observation. Often with children, 10 to 20 mg twice a day is enough. Sometimes the dose may go up to 100 to 150 mg, given in divided doses.

Tofranil and the other tricyclic antidepressants are also used with adolescents and adults to treat depression. However, the dose needed for depression is often 200 to 300 mg a day. Thus, one cannot use the blood level of Tofranil given in the package literature to determine the dose needed. The range used is based on these higher doses to treat adult depression. Also, the side effects noted in the material provided by the pharmacist is not accurate for our population. Again, these side effects are seen at the higher doses used to treat depression and not at the lower doses used to treat ADHD.

It may take a week or two for Tofranil to begin to work or for it to be possible to observe the effects of an increase in dose. Thus, the dose is usually increased every week to two weeks until the desired effects are noted. If the two doses a day cause fatigue or the child seems to do less well in the late afternoon, the total dose can be divided into three doses a day. For convenience, this can be in the morning, after school, and in the evening.

SIDE EFFECTS. The most frequent side effect is being tired or sleepy. Often this side effect decreases over time as the individual gets used to the medication. If this does not happen, the dose can be decreased or divided into three smaller doses each day. If these shifts do not help, Tofranil may not be the medication to use. As with the stimulant medications, sometimes a different tricyclic antidepressant might work without this side effect and should be considered.

Less common side effects are constipation, dry mouth, or blurred vision. If these occur, another medication should be considered. A very uncommon side effect is morning insomnia. The child wakes up at 4:00 or 4:30 in the morning wide awake and wants to play. Often this problem can be minimized by giving more of the imipramine in the evening. If not, a different medication may be needed.

Tofranil and other tricyclic antidepressants might affect brain-wave activity. Thus, if the child or adolescent has a seizure disorder, there is the possibility that the medication may potentiate a seizure. Your physician should be able to make the proper decision on using Tofranil in this situation.

If a tricyclic antidepressant is stopped, it must be tapered off slowly. If it is stopped abruptly, the child or adolescent might develop flu-like behaviors.

THE TRICYCLIC ANTIDEPRESSANTS AND HEART FUNCTION. These medications might cause a slight shift in the electrical conduction pattern of the heart. Most studies show that this shift is minimal and does not cause symptoms. A very small percentage of children and adolescents have what is called a subclinically abnormal electrical conduction pattern of the heart. That is, there are no observable symptoms of the abnormal pattern. If a tricyclic antidepressant is given to this child, it is possible that the effect of the medication added to the underlying shift might combine to cause a rapid heart beat (tachycardia). The individual complains of his or her heart pounding or racing in the chest and the neck "feeling full." This possibility is uncommon. Some of the literature on this medication recommend that an electrocardiogram (EKG) be done prior to starting the medication and again after the dose is stabilized. Other reports suggest that the possibility of tachycardia is minimal and the impact is not life-threatening; thus, getting an EKG is not considered essential. Clearly, if a child or adolescent has a known history of a conduction problem, these medications should not be used. You will have to discuss this concern with your family doctor.

THE OTHER GROUP TWO MEDICATIONS.   Wellbutrin is related to the tricyclic antidepressants and it works in a similar way as Tofranil and the other tricyclics. Wellbutrin is recommended starting at age eighteen. The side effects are the same. It comes in a 75-mg and 100-mg tablet.

There are two medications, Catapres and Tenex, that are used with adults who have high blood pressure and result in a decrease in blood pressure. At lower doses, these two medications increase the amount of norepinephrine at the nerve endings. The exact mechanism is different than the mechanism in use with the other Group Two medications, but the result is the same. Whereas the other Group Two medications decrease hyperactivity and distractibility but not impulsivity, these two medications seem to have minimal benefit with the hyperactivity and distractibility but do decrease impulsivity. Thus, they are used along with the other Group Two medications when impulsivity is an issue. Catapres comes in a 0.1-, 0.2-, and 0.3-mg tablet. Tenex comes in a 1- and 2-mg tablet.

The main side effect is sedation. With Tofranil, the child will be tired in class. With Catapres, he or she may fall asleep in class. Thus, minimal doses are given. With Catapres, each dose will last about six hours. Often, a 0.1-mg tablet will be used, with one-half or one-fourth of a tablet given in the morning and a similar amount about 3:00 P.M. Even this low dose can be sedating for some children, in which can even lower doses will be tried. With Tenex, often one-half of a 1-mg tablet will be used in the morning and in the afternoon.

If either Catapres or Tenex is stopped, it should be tapered off slowly. If it is stopped abruptly, some children or adolescents complain of headaches or dizziness.

As mentioned earlier, if a child or adolescent has tried many medications and one of the short-acting stimulants seems to be the only one to be of help yet this medication causes problems going to sleep, Catapres can be used at bedtime. We take advantage of the sedating effect and use a slightly higher dose than would be used during the day. This dose, given one hour before the planned bedtime, frequently helps the child or adolescent go to sleep. (There was a brief concern about using Ritalin and Catapres in this way because of one reported case of death. A more detailed study of this case and of the use of these medications resulted in a report that the mixture was safe.)

Catapres also comes in a slow-absorption patch, called a TTS (transdermal therapeutic system) patch. The medication is in a small gauze similar to the center part of a Band-Aid. There is a waterproof cover that can be used. Each patch releases the medication slowly over seven days. These patches come in various doses and can be selected to provide steady coverage over a week with a decreased likelihood of sedation. There are two problems with the patch. Some children do not like them and keep pulling them off. Also, with some, the patch will cause a skin rash that itches. If Catapres is helpful and sedation is a problem, the possibility of using small amounts over a long period of time should be considered.

Other Medications for ADHD

Only the medications discussed above have been found to be effective with ADHD. If a child or adolescent has other problems in addition to ADHD, other medications might be tried. In Chapter 1, I reviewed other neurologically based disorders that might be seen with (comorbid with) ADHD. These include disorders reflecting problems with modulation of anxiety, anger, or mood, and obsessive-compulsive disorder and tic disorders. Each of these problems may need to be treated.

If a child or adolescent has several related disorders, it is important to work with a physician who is familiar with the appropriate medications to use and the interactions of these medications. Often, the child and adolescent psychiatrist is most knowledgeable on these issues.

In Summary

Medication to treat ADHD must be seen as part of a multimodal approach that includes education, counseling, behavioral management, and family work along with the medication. If any of the associated disorders are present, they must be addressed as well.

If your son or daughter has ADHD and needs medication, work with your physician. The information provided in this chapter is meant to help you be informed so that you know what is being done and why. If you find that you now know more than your family doctor, consider lending your doctor a copy of this chapter. If your physician does not believe in medication or seems not to be current on the use of the medications, try to find another physician.

17

Treatment for Emotional, Social, and Family Problems

The critical question is whether the emotional, social, or family problems are causing your child's academic difficulties or whether these problems are a consequence of the frustrations and failures brought on by the academic difficulties. If the problems are a consequence of learning disabilities, the initial focus should be on developing appropriate educational programs and educating the family. If your child has attention deficit hyperactivity disorder (ADHD), he or she may need appropriate medication. After these initiatives are in place, the emotional, social, and family problems often lessen or disappear. If they do not, you and your family may need to seek clinical help.

In this chapter I will discuss approaches for helping parents address the emotional or social problems of their son or daughter as well as possible family problems. First, I will review the types of mental health professionals available to help. Then, I will discuss the types of interventions used. Finally, I will present a model for parents to use to decrease their child's or adolescent's unacceptable behaviors.

The Mental Health Professionals

There are several professional groups providing mental health services—psychiatrists, psychologists, social workers, psychiatric nurses, and mental health counselors. These professionals might be in a private practice, be part of a mental health organization, or be part of the public school system. Each has a core of common knowledge and skills in diagnosis and treatment as well as unique areas of expertise. Each requires different levels of training and certification. Thus, being an intelligent consumer requires that you learn all you can about the qualifications of any clinician who is going to work with your child and your family. Don't be any less concerned about seeking the best-qualified person in the mental health field than you would be in selecting the best person in the health field.

All mental health professionals are not equally competent to help children and adolescents, even within the same profession. In case you are not familiar with the different mental health professions, let me review each.

Psychiatrist

The psychiatrist is a medical doctor, a physician. A general psychiatrist has completed the medical education and training required to become a physician. He or she then does four or five more years of specialized training in psychiatry. Part of this training includes experiences working with children and adolescents. A child and adolescent psychiatrist has completed medical education and training required to become a general psychiatrist and then taken two additional years of training in child and adolescent psychiatry. Because of her or his medical training, the general psychiatrist and the child and adolescent psychiatrist both are familiar with the biological and the psychological aspects of diagnosis and treatment. Of all the mental health professionals, only psychiatrists can prescribe medication or admit patients to the hospital. All psychiatrists are trained to do psychopharmacological treatments as well as individual, group, or family work. The child and adolescent psychiatrist, because of the additional training, may be most qualified to assess and treat the individual with a mixture of neurological, psychological, and social problems.

Psychologist

A psychologist might have a doctorate or a master's degree. Most states require a doctorate degree to be licensed to practice. This doctorate may be in clinical, counseling, school, or developmental psychology, although there are other possible areas. The doctorate-level psychologist has completed four to six or more years of graduate training beyond college, including a year of special clinical training called an internship. The degree might be a Ph.D. or a Psy.D. Because one can be trained in so many areas and because there are so many different types of internships available, any specific psychologist might have differing skills with different age groups or types of therapy. The depth and variety of training with children or adolescents also may greatly vary. The master's-level psychologist has completed a two-year graduate program beyond college. Because training and experience vary so widely, you may want to discuss the background and training of your psychologist before starting any evaluation or therapy. Psychologists have the unique skill of being able to administer psychological and educational tests.

Social Worker

The social worker has completed college plus a two-year master's degree program in a graduate school of social work. Following graduation, he or she must work under supervision for several years before being eligible to take the clinical certifying examination. If the candidate passes this examination, he or she becomes a licensed clinical social worker (LCSW). The level of diagnostic and treatment skills in working with children and adolescents depends on the social worker's additional experience following graduation or as part of other postgraduate training. The kinds of therapies offered will also be based on this required experience or other experience. Thus, not every social worker is necessarily experienced in working with children and adolescents. Parents need to learn what training and experience the social worker has had since graduation from the graduate school of social work.

Psychiatric Nurse

The psychiatric nurse may have completed a training program leading to a certificate as a registered nurse or may have a bachelor's degree in nursing. Some also have a two-year master's degree in psychiatric or mental health nursing. To be certified as a clinical specialist in psychiatric nursing, he or she must have a master's or doctor's degree in psychiatric or mental health nursing or an acceptable equivalent and must pass a national certifying examination. The psychiatric nurse with graduate school training has core knowledge and skills comparable to those of the other mental health professionals with a similar master's level of training but with the special focus based on their training in nursing in a medical setting. Many focus on family therapy, but many are also skilled in other forms of therapy. As with the social worker, parents need to know if the psychiatric nurse has had special training experience with children and adolescents.

Mental Health Counselor

The mental health counselor is more difficult to clearly define. Many have completed a two-year graduate degree in counseling followed by several years of supervised experience. These individuals take a clinical certifying examination following this training. If they pass, they are certified as mental health counselors. The licensing laws in some states permit individuals with less to much less training and experience to identify themselves as "counselors." Thus, it is critical that parents clarify the level of training, the type of certification, and the amount of formal training and experience with children and adolescents.

General Comments

You can see that there are several professional groups within the mental health field. Within each professional group, practitioners have widely different levels of training and experience. Not all are equally well trained to work with children and adolescents. Not all can do psychological testing or prescribe medications. Not all will be familiar with school systems and such problems as learning disabilities or ADHD.

I continue to be upset and surprised when I see people search the country to find the "best" surgeon for a specific procedure or the "best" physician to treat their specific disorder. They might spend hours on the phone or computer tracking down "the best." Yet, these same people will take a family member to the most convenient

local mental health practitioner without asking about training, qualifications, and experience. Are the mind and brain any less important?

Be an intelligent, informed consumer. It is not inappropriate to
discuss a professional's training, experiences, and specialty. Parents
ask me often. I am not offended. If anything, I respect the parents
for caring that much about their child or adolescent. You are entrust-
ing your son or daughter and possibly your family to this clinician.
Be sure you have someone qualified to address the diagnostic or
treatment concerns you have.

The Types of Therapy

The social, behavioral, or emotional problems shown by a child or
adolescent must be seen as clinical clues. These clues along with
other observations and evidence lead to a diagnosis. The diagnosis
leads to a treatment plan and to treatment interventions. Thus, it is
important that the diagnostic process be done by a competent clinician or a team of competent clinicians. The types of interventions
will be based on the diagnosis or diagnoses. These interventions
might be with the individual, with the family, or with the individual
in a group setting. Such interventions might include medications, individual therapy, group therapy, or family therapy. Within each of
these types of therapy there are several approaches to be considered.
If the child or adolescent has a learning disability and/or ADHD
and/or any of the other related disorders discussed in this book,
these problems must be addressed. To treat a secondary emotional
problem without treating the underlying cause will not succeed.
Blowing away the smoke does not put out the fire. If the child has a
poor self-image because of academic frustration and failure, psychotherapy will not improve the self-image unless or until the proper
special education services are provided.

It is critical that the appropriate treatment approach be used.
Sometimes several approaches will be used at the same time or one
following the other. For example, the family might be in such a crisis
that family behavioral therapy is started. Once the family is more sta-
ble, the underlying reasons for the dysfunction might become clear
and other treatment approaches will be used.

Psychoanalytic Psychotherapy

The goal of psychoanalytically oriented psychotherapy is to help the child or adolescent better understand his or her concerns and conflicts and to help him or her develop better methods of coping. This evaluation of the child or adolescent is done by talking about possible worries and problems. For younger children, play materials may be used as a vehicle for communicating. The professional looks at the interactions between the child's internal thinking processes (basic wishes and needs, conscience or value system, and the ability to assess the realities of the outside world). The clinician explores the relative strengths of each process, the coping skills available to handle any conflicts between these processes (called defense mechanisms) and if the conflicts and strategies are age-appropriate and successful.

Behavioral Therapy

Behavioral observations and observational data might clarify that a child has learned inappropriate or unacceptable behaviors, which were then reinforced. If the presenting problems are seen as a reflection of learned patterns of behavior by the individual or by parents, behavioral therapy might be initiated. Different approaches will be used to help the child increase more healthy or acceptable behaviors and to decrease unacceptable behaviors. This therapy might be with the individual, with the parents, or as part of work with the family.

Another form of behavioral therapy might be directed toward helping the individual control anxiety. The child might be taught specific behavioral techniques, including relaxation therapy, to stay calm or better control anger.

Our behaviors can be seen as consisting of feelings, thoughts, and behaviors. If the individual is not able to see the influence one of these three experiences has on the others, cognitive behavioral therapy might be used. The goal is to help the child or adolescent to become more aware of the relationships between feelings, thoughts, and behaviors. The child learns techniques to become more aware of inappropriate feelings, thoughts, or behaviors and how to gain better control over the inappropriate interactions.

Group Therapy

If the child or adolescent is having difficulty interacting successfully with peers, group therapy might be considered. In the therapeutic group setting, patterns of behaviors and interactions can be observed and pointed out. New approaches and strategies can be taught and tried out. For younger children, role playing and practice might be used to learn more acceptable styles of interaction.

A special form of group therapy is a social skill group. Suppose your child, Anita, has social skill problems and difficulty reading social cues. A group setting might be the best place to help her improve her social skills and peer interactions. There are many types of social skill groups. In general, these groups focus on a series of steps. The first step would involve helping Anita to develop an awareness of and sensitivity to her social problems. This step is critical. Some children have only limited awareness of their socialization difficulties and may deny their problems or blame others for their difficulties. The second step would involve having Anita generate alternative solutions for the identified problems. Here, the group leader and other group members can be of help. The third step would involve helping Anita step-by-step through the process of learning the newly identified solution to the problems. Role playing and practice are important ways of learning these new solutions. The final step would be to help Anita link her new knowledge to past events and difficulties as well as to future happenings. She would be encouraged to try out the new social skills in new settings and to report back to the group on her successes and failures.

Family Therapy

If the difficulties are seen as reflective of how the family functions, family therapy might be used. The focus might be behavioral, helping the parents to regain control and teaching the children that they can be safe even if they are not in control. The focus might be on family communication or family interactions. With family therapy the goal is to help all family members find a way to make the family a happier, safer, more positive place to be.

Psychopharmacology

The use of medications to treat behavioral or emotional disorders may be essential. The medication may be to address anxiety or depression, or to treat ADHD or one of the modulating disorders. If a child has several disorders, for example, ADHD, obsessive-compulsive disorder, and a tic disorder, several medications may be needed.

You may find that your son's or daughter's doctor can treat the ADHD. For the psychiatric disorders, it is best, if possible, to work with the most skilled person in psychopharmacology. This professional is usually a child and adolescent psychiatrist.

Medication should not be used in isolation. Education, counseling, or other interventions might be needed as well.

General Comments

There are many approaches to therapy and several types of therapy within each approach. It is important that the mental health professional or professionals doing the evaluation select the most appropriate intervention for your son or daughter. At times, several approaches will be needed. As progress is made, changes in the approach might be appropriate.

Some mental health professionals believe in a type of therapy that requires minimal or no contact with the parents. "Therapy is between your child and me, and it will interfere with our therapeutic relationship if your child knows I am talking with you." I must respectfully state that I have difficulty with this approach. Parents are lost and hurting. They need help in helping their daughter or son. They must be given guidance along with any individual therapy for their child or adolescent. I find that once a trust is established, the child or adolescent is not threatened if I talk with parents. Confidentiality is defined and respected. But I can still help the parents help me in the therapeutic process. If you are working with a clinician who sees your son each week, week after week, and you are lost as to how you are to manage his unacceptable behaviors or how to help when he is angry, crying, or upset, speak up. If the clinician insists she cannot work with you, ask that someone else be identified to help you understand how to help your son.

Family Behavioral Programs
to Address Unacceptable Behaviors

I will teach you a model for assessing behaviors within your family and for setting up your own behavioral program to change unacceptable behaviors. It should work. If it does not, you may need to seek help from a professional. Let me describe the types of problems, the models for clarifying what needs to be changed, the basic model for demanding change, and additional models that might be used as necessary.

These ideas are to be actively applied. If you read this section and say "This is what I need," try it. Go step-by-step. If it doesn't work, rethink your strategy and try again. This approach will work with most children and adolescents. But it takes time, effort, and commitment. And this commitment must be by both parents.

Sometimes a parent calls me and describes his son. The child sounds like a tyrant who must have his way or all hell breaks loose with screaming, throwing things, hitting sister, messing up his room, or "something." Later, I meet this "tyrant"—a four-foot, seventy-pound little boy with a sweet smile who could be picked up and carried under one arm. Where is the monster?

Then I begin to work with the family, and I soon find out. This child's behavior does dominate the family. The parents avoid too many confrontations because they do not want to face the consequences. They look the other way until pushed so far that they have to react. By that time, they feel helpless; their only possible reaction often is anger. They yell, hit the child, or give out a punishment like "no television for one week." They then have to back down because they have no way to enforce the punishment or because enforcing it leads to more confrontations and fights.

As my evaluation progresses, I gain clues or clarify the dynamics within the child or within the family that explain the behaviors. More often, I cannot clarify the underlying issues but can see that something has to be done—and quickly. One has to "put out the fire" before an in-depth assessment can be considered. What is clear is that the child is in control and the parents are not in control or are equally out of control. What may also be clear is that the parents disagree and, rather than supporting each other, they are split and fighting with each other. This situation in the family is anxiety producing for the child and not compatible with healthy psychosocial development. This situation is dysfunctional for the parents and for the other members of the family as well.

Perhaps I will find patterns. Without meaning to do so, the parents are reinforcing the very behaviors they do not want. Their daughter acts badly and gets a lot of attention—negative attention. The parents get upset, and this proves to the child that she can control one part of the world—her family. This, along with getting what she wants, is the reward for bad behavior. The other children see the parents forced to give in. They become angry. Soon, they may learn that the only way to get attention or to get what they want in this family is to behave badly.

Whatever the dynamics or initial cause, the family dysfunction must be addressed first. Parents must regain control. The child must feel that he or she can be controlled. These changes are essential for the parents, for the child, and for the family. Such negative control of parents is unhealthy and unproductive for children. They must learn different behavioral patterns before they generalize out to the school, to peers, or to the community.

Once the behaviors are under better control, the child can begin to learn new and better techniques to function within the family and to cope with stress. Parents and children can rework styles of interacting and roles within the family. First come the behavioral changes; then come awareness and insight.

Related to this goal is an important concern when the child or adolescent also has ADHD and is impulsive. Behavioral programs do not work well with individuals who are impulsive. The goal of the program is to help this individual think before he or she acts. "If you do this behavior, you will have to spend time in your room." Someone who is impulsive acts and then thinks. The consequences are remembered after the act. Children and adolescents with ADHD who are impulsive must be properly medicated before a behavioral program will be successful.

It is not uncommon to find that the same child who is out of control at home is functioning very well in school, at friends' houses, or when playing with friends away from the house. Sunday school teachers, activity leaders, sports coaches, other parents think your son is great and a gentleman around them. In this case, you might assume that the behavioral difficulties are not neurologically driven or they would occur in every setting. If the behaviors are expressed only at home, it is possible that they reflect family dynamics or conflict. It is also possible that your son holds in all of his frustration and anger all day so as not to get into trouble. He comes home where it is safe to let out these feelings, and any little frustration leads to an explosion. As one child told me, "I can't act this way at school. The principal will suspend me. But my parents love me and will never get rid of me. So, I can get away with acting this way at home." Another possibility is that your child has ADHD and is on the appropriate medication and dose during the time he is out of the house. Thus, there are no behavioral problems. However, if the medication only covers school hours, this child is off medication when at home and the hyperactivity, distractibility, and/or impulsivity cause behavioral difficulties. The addition of the medication for evenings and weekends might lead to a significant improvement in home behaviors.

If the unacceptable behaviors are found at home only, a behavioral management program will be needed for the home and family. If these behaviors expand into the school, a similar program might be needed at school. If these behaviors expand also into after-school activities or settings, a behavioral program may be needed throughout each day.

Basic Concepts of Behavioral Management

Any behavioral plan, to be successful, must be based on two basic behavioral concepts:

1. One is more likely to succeed in changing behavior by rewarding what is seen as desired behavior than by punishing what is seen as undesirable behavior.

2. For a plan to work, the responses to acceptable and to unacceptable behaviors must be consistent and must occur each time. Inconsistent response patterns may reinforce the negative behaviors.

As parents, you must learn that there is no right or wrong way to raise children. You must collaborate in developing a plan with which you both can be comfortable and can agree. Once decided upon, the plan must be practiced in a consistent and persistent way. No more splitting. No more parents disagreeing in front of the family about how best to handle behaviors. The child experiences the same responses from both parents. This concept is harder to accomplish, but must also be the goal, in divorced families when the children share two households.

Initially, it is important that you be omnipotent. No more reasoning, bargaining, bribing, threatening, or trying to provoke guilt or shame. Parents make the rules; parents enforce the rules; parents' decisions are final. "Life may not seem to be fair as you see it; but this is what I expect." As parents you must learn that if you "step into the arena" and agree to debate or argue with your child, you will lose. If you say it's time to go to sleep and the child says "But can I stay up fifteen minutes more," your answer must be "I did not ask you what time you wanted to go to sleep. I said it is bedtime." Argue about the fifteen minutes and it will become twenty minutes, then thirty minutes. Soon, your frustration and anger will result in fighting. Later in the plan you can be flexible, but not at the beginning.

Developing the Initial Intervention Strategy

Initially, parents are usually overwhelmed. They have exhausted their choices of action, and none have worked. They may feel helpless and like failures as parents. If there are two parents in the family, there may be stress between them as they disagree on how to handle the behaviors or blame the other for the problems. One, often the father, may feel so frustrated and unsuccessful that he finds ways of working later and later, coming home after the kids are in bed. Try to develop and follow the plan I suggest. If you are too worn out or overwhelmed or if the stress between parents is too great, seek professional help.

The first step is to collect data on your observations of the behaviors. Each parent should collect data separately. The differences between the two will be very useful. Don't be embarrassed by what you do. Record what really happens without worrying what someone will think. We already know that things are not working well. Just record what happens so that you can begin to change things.

You will need a structure to collect these data. The easiest model to use is called an ABC chart. You record three things: A, the *antecedent* to the behavior; B, the *behavior* observed; and C, the *consequences* of the behavior. The chart headings will look like this:

Date/Time	Antecedent	Behavior	Consequence

An example of an ABC chart might read like the one in Table 17-1.

Each parent may have different lists. In part this reflects when each is home and with the child. One may be the firm disciplinarian, and the other the easy-going, "give them another chance" type. Each parent will see and list different things. Each has different experiences and expectations. Possibly father comes home at 6:30 P.M. looking forward to being with the children and playing with them. Frustrated and short of temper, mother may have had it by then and want the kids to be quiet and to get their homework and other chores done so that they can go to bed.

Neither parent is right or wrong. The important goal is that both parents agree on their expectations and be consistent in asking that the expectations be met. Consistency is the key. Inconsistency reinforces the behavior; consistency lessens or stops the behavior.

Certain patterns should become clear for each column and for

Table 17-1 Billy's Chart

Date/Time	Antecedent	Behavior	Consequence
Monday 4:30 P.M.	Don't know; not there.	He hit sister; she hit back.	Told both to go to room.
6:00 P.M.	Talking to sister.	He teased her; she cried.	Yelled at Billy.
9:00 P.M.	Told him to get ready for bed.	Refused to take bath, get in PJs; yelled at me when told.	Took 30 min. of reminding; finally hit him and he went to take his bath.

overall behaviors. Certain antecedents lead to certain behaviors. The consequences that follow the same behaviors are inconsistent. Or one parent gets mad and yells at everything, or other family members seem to get punished as much as the child who caused the problems. A common theme may be that when your child does not get what he wants or is asked to do something he does not want to do, he misbehaves.

Once the data is collected, analyze it. Seek out patterns. The first task is to clearly define the unacceptable behaviors that need to be changed. Often, parents start with a long list of behaviors. Once the data is studied, the behaviors can be clustered into two or three major areas. By doing this, you will not be as overwhelmed. You are not dealing with an impossible list of problems but can focus on a few major areas.

Frequently, the unacceptable behaviors fall into one of three basic groups. Try to see if your list can be divided into one of these groups.

Physical abuse: This group includes hitting, threatening to hit, breaking something or threatening to break something. Thus, hurting a pet or damaging property would be included.

Verbal abuse: This group includes any words, tone of voice, or sounds you wish to identify as verbal abuse. Yelling, cursing, teasing, and taunting could be included. At any time a parent can include something as verbal abuse by saying "The next time you do that I will call it verbal abuse."

Noncompliance: This group includes not completing a required or requested chore, not listening to what is said, or refusing to do what a parent requests. Often, three warnings are given. Following the third, action is taken. "If I have to ask you to hang up your coat again, it will be for the third time and the consequence for noncompliance will be given."

Once the behaviors are identified, it is useful to study the relationship between the antecedents and the behaviors. Look for themes. Perhaps the behaviors are more likely to occur if your daughter is tired, hungry, or about to be sick. Perhaps the behaviors are more likely to occur during the first hour after coming home from school, or during times of transition, whether leaving the house or returning to the house. Or if routines are disrupted or planned activities have to be changed. Or when she is off medication or the medication is wearing off. Or if she does not get what she demands. Or if she is asked to do something she does not want to do. You might find that the behaviors relate to your child's learning disabilities or sensory integration disorder. Maybe you gave her too many instructions at once. Maybe the chore is too difficult. Maybe she is frustrated with homework or wants to avoid doing homework because she doesn't understand it or finds it too hard.

These themes might lead to possible interventions. They also will make you more sensitive to the times or situations when problems are most likely to occur. Try to identify these themes and think of how this information can be helpful in both understanding and addressing the problem behaviors.

Finally, study the pattern of consequences. Are you consistent? Do you use consequences and later give in and not carry them out? Do you use consequences you cannot enforce and thus have to back down on?

Setting Up the Initial Program

Once you have a clearer idea of the behaviors that need to be changed, a plan can be developed. Define the behaviors as clearly as possible, and work out a consequence that can be consistently imposed and that is compatible with your family's philosophy and values. Work out the plan in great detail; then introduce it to the family. The plan should be for all siblings. Even if the other children do not cause problems, it will not negatively affect them to be part of the program. The plan might benefit them by rewarding them for their good behavior. It might have been that the "bad" child took so much attention that the "good" child was ignored or not thanked for being good. This plan will help you remember to reward good behavior. If a sibling is provoking or encouraging the negative behavior, that will become clear if he or she also is on the plan.

As parents, you need to understand that there are several basic principles to reverse the pattern of punishing bad behavior and usually ignoring, or inconsistently rewarding, good or positive behavior. This plan will reward positive behaviors and withhold rewards for negative behaviors. Furthermore, you will have preplanned responses that can be used every time. Your child cannot catch you off guard, making you feel helpless and therefore angry. Each time a behavior occurs, there will be the same response from either parent.

Let me illustrate this point about consistency. Suppose a boy hits his sister five times in a week. On one occasion the mother was in such a rush that she yelled at him but did nothing about the hitting. On another occasion she was tired and did not want to deal with him so she pretended she did not see what happened. On the other three occasions she did punish him by making him go to his room. If this child gives up hitting his sister because mother tells him to, he has to give up hitting her 100 percent of the time. If he continues to hit her, he has a 40 percent chance of getting away with it. He is only punished three out of five times. He would be a fool to give up the behavior. If a parent is consistent, the behaviors will decrease and then stop. If the parent is anything less than consistent, the behavior might persist or get worse.

STEP ONE.   Divide the day into parts. For example, on a typical school day there will be three parts: (1) from the time the child gets up until he or she leaves for school; (2) from the time the child returns from school until the end of the evening meal; and (3) from the end of this meal until bedtime. Weekend, holiday, or summer days can be divided into four parts by using meals as the dividers: (1) from the time the child wakes up until the end of breakfast; (2) from the end of breakfast to the end of lunch; (3) from the end of lunch to the end of dinner; and (4) from the end of dinner until bedtime.

STEP TWO.   Make a list of the child's unacceptable behaviors. This list should be brief and limited to the major problems. If the basic three noted earlier are used, a list might read as follows:

1. No *physical abuse* (define this in detail for the child; for example, no hitting your brother, pulling the cat's tail, kicking your mother, breaking toys).

2. No *verbal abuse* (define this in detail for the child; for example, no cursing, calling someone "stupid," teasing).

3. No *noncompliance* (define this in detail for the child; for example, refusing to do what you are told to do). For younger children, the term *not listening* might be used. Make it clear that you will make a request several times. Then you will say, "If I have to ask you again, I will call this noncompliance." Any behavior that continues after this warning is considered noncompliance. In this way the child can never say "But you never told me I had to do this."

STEP THREE.   The purpose of the plan is to reward positive behaviors. Negative behaviors are not mentioned as such. Your child or adolescent can earn one point for each behavior he or she *does not do* during a unit of time. Later we will discuss "time out." With time out, too, the focus is on the positive and not the negative. The wording is important. The parent says, "What you did is so unacceptable in this family that you must go to your room and think about the need to change what you do." The parent does not say "Go to your room!" with the connotation that doing so is punishment.

The child can earn points by not doing the unacceptable behaviors. He or she can earn one point for each negative behavior not done during a unit of time. For example, suppose a boy gets up in the morning, does all of his chores, and gets to breakfast on time. He does not hit anyone, but he does call his sister "stupid." As he leaves for school, the parent would say "I am pleased that you earned two points this morning. You followed all rules, and you did not hit anyone. I wish I could have given you the third point, but you did call your sister a name and that is verbal abuse." This parent might say to the sister, "I am happy that you earned all three of your points. Thank you for not calling your brother a name when he called you one." Remember, behavior is changed by rewarding what you want and not by punishing what you do not want.

Use a book or chart to record the points. If the child is too young to understand points, use a calendar or chart to paste stars on. For some, a more concrete approach would be to have a jar and fill it with marbles to represent each point earned.

Each part of the day is handled in the same way. In the model designed above with three units of time on school days and four units of time on the weekend, the maximum number of points that can be earned on a school day is 9 and the maximum each weekend day is

12. The total for a week will be 69 points. These points can be used in three ways:

A daily reward
A weekly reward
A special reward

Count the points daily and then continue to count them weekly or accumulatively. The child or adolescent should participate in developing the rewards. Parents make the final decisions, but suggestions are welcome. If the child or adolescent says "This is stupid. I won't participate," the parent replies "The plan starts tomorrow. Either you suggest what you might like to work toward, or I will make the decisions for you."

Each reward must be individualized for each member of the family and must be compatible with the family's philosophy and style of child rearing. Rewards that involve interpersonal experiences are preferred to material rewards. The daily reward could be an additional half hour of television time that is watched with a parent or permission to stay up thirty minutes later to read a book or play a game with a parent, or thirty minutes of special time with one parent. For example, let's say that your daughter is expected to be in her room by 8:30 P.M. with lights out by 9:00. Normally, you and your child spend the half hour in the room with quiet activities like talking or reading together. If your daughter earns the daily reward, she could stay up until 9:30 and have an extra half hour with a parent. However, if she did not earn the daily reward, she must be in the room by 8:00, and lights out is 8:30. She loses a half hour of time with the family.

Again, we are trying to reverse the pattern of rewarding unacceptable behavior that results in having to spend time with the child when this occurs at the price of other members of the family. Often less time or no time is spent when the child acts appropriately. Now, if he or she acts appropriately, there is special time together. If the child acts inappropriately, there is less time with the family.

The weekly reward might be going to a movie, or out to eat with the family, or having a friend sleep over, or any other special activity. If possible, the activity is decided on earlier in the week. "On Sunday, the family is going to the park to play and then have a picnic." Points are counted from Saturday morning to Friday night; thus, you know if your son has enough points to "earn" the picnic before the weekend starts. In this way, a sitter can be lined up to stay home with the child or other arrangements can be made before any family activity begins. In the past, your son might have been impossible all week, yet he would still get to go out with the family on the weekend—reward for negative behavior. Moreover, his behavior might spoil the fun of this weekend activity. Now this child stays home and misses time with the family while those members of the family who earned their points get to spend positive time with the family. An adolescent might miss doing something with the family or with friends or might not have the privilege of using the car.

A special reward might be something important that must be worked toward. A new bicycle, a special toy, or a special trip might be selected. It should be planned so that at least a month or more will be needed to accumulate enough points for this reward.

For the daily and weekly rewards, set a goal initially of earning 80 percent of the maximum number of points possible. After several months of success this goal might be increased to 90 percent. It is best not to set the goal at 100 percent. No one can be perfect all of the time. Any negative behavior early in the day or week could destroy all hope of a reward, and the child might give up.

For the plan described earlier, the child or adolescent would need seven points each weekday evening to get the reward (80 percent of 9 points). He or she would need 55 points by Friday night for the weekend reward (80 percent of 69 points).

TIME OUT.   Before starting the plan, define which behaviors will be considered so unacceptable to the family that they will result in the child's not only not earning a point but also being removed from the family for a period of time so that he or she can think about the need to change this behavior. I always include physical abuse as "so unacceptable that you must spend time in your room thinking about the need to change." You could consider using time out only for these behaviors.

You might start by telling your daughter that time out can be spent in a different part of the house than the rest of the family is in as long as she is quiet and stays isolated. If you feel a need to do so, you can pick a guest room or the laundry room. If she cannot handle this location, she might have to be in her room. If she cannot stay in the room with the door open, the door will be shut. You might be concerned that your child's room is full of fun distractions and that she will not sit quietly and think. That is okay. The main theme is that the child loses time with the family. While she is in her room, the rest of the family is interacting.

Your child is to spend this time out quietly thinking about what happened and why she needs to change behavioral patterns. Quiet time means quiet time. If she calls out or yells, the timer is reset. If she comes out, she is sent back and the timer is reset. (Later we will discuss what to do if you cannot get your child or adolescent to go into the room or to stay in the room.)

It is important that this time to think not be too short. Except for young children, a few minutes have little meaning. For children over eight, I often suggest thirty minutes. For adolescents, I suggest one hour. If they will not be quiet or stay in the room, the initial thirty minutes might turn into hours.

Time out can be used out of the home as well. Try to plan ahead. "We are going to Aunt Sara's house. I spoke to her, and she told me that if you need a time-out room to think about your behavior while we are at her house, you can use the guest room." If you are at a restaurant and it is safe, ask your child or adolescent to sit in the waiting area at the front of the restaurant. If you're in a shopping mall and it is considered safe, place the older child or adolescent on a bench and move to another area of the mall but within eyesight. There will be times when you cannot use time out immediately, for example, in the car. As soon as you return home, the child is expected to go to the time-out site for the time assigned.

For the plan to work, it must be exact as to expectations, behaviors that are rewarded, and consequences. Once your plan is initiated, I can promise you that your son or daughter will find loopholes in the plan. That's okay. Put your head together with your spouse's and find a way to close the loophole. You are in control not the child.

DEALING WITH RESISTANCE.   It is important to solve issues that prevent this plan from being implemented prior to starting it. The most common problem is having a child who will not go to his or her room for time out or will not stay in the room. You do not want to have to chase your son around the house and table. You do not want to have to drag him to the room, often fighting all of the way. You do not want to have to hold the door shut as he bangs and tries to open the door. You must find a solution to this problem and be prepared to implement it. If you find that there really is no way that you can control your child, you will need professional help.

For the child who will not go to his or her room, I usually recommend a plan that requires the cooperation of only one person, the parent. I assume that mother or father only has control over mother or father. This plan has two parts to it. The plan is discussed before the full program is implemented and is used whenever the child or adolescent refuses to go to his or her room or stay in the room.

First, announce how much you think is an acceptable amount of time for your child to get to his room. "I will give your three minutes to get to your room so that you can begin to think about the need to change." Tell your son that every minute it takes him to get to his room beyond this announced time will be doubled and added to the original time. If the original time is thirty minutes and it takes the child thirty minutes to give in and go to his room, he now must spend ninety minutes in the room.

The second part of the plan may sound difficult; but it is not. Tell your son that you will always love him. Love is unconditional. However, during the time that he chooses to abuse you as a parent by not listening to you, you choose not to parent him. You do not take away your love, but you take away being a parent. The message is clear. If you abuse me as a parent, I choose not to parent you. What does this mean? You do not talk to your son or interact in any way. When mealtime comes, you set a place for everyone in the family but your son. If he wants to eat, he can make his own meal and sit somewhere else. If you were to carpool the child to a meeting or sports practice or game, you do not do so. Your child will have to face the consequences of not attending. You do not write an excuse. If his unacceptable behavior persists until bedtime, you do not respond to him or put him to bed. When it is time for you to go to sleep, you turn out the lights and go to your bedroom. The child is left in the dark and alone. Once your son goes to his room to spend the quiet time, your parenting starts again.

Suppose your son would run outside if told to go to his room. Then the plan must include informing him that if he runs outside, you will not chase him. The time it takes for him to come in and go to his room will be counted, doubled, and added to the original amount. If it gets dark, you will call the police and report a missing child. It is no fun hiding behind a bush as it gets dark and cold if no one is going to chase you.

Some parents find that the "I love you but if you abuse me as a parent I do not choose to parent you" approach too painful to consider. I remind this parent that allowing the unacceptable behaviors and teaching the child that he or she can be in control is more painful and potentially more harmful to the child than the model suggested.

If your son will not stay in his room, you have a problem. It may be possible to put a lock on the door. (Buy a bathroom door set, and install it in reverse so that the lock is outside.) Should you need to lock the door, be sure to remain in the hall to listen in case it becomes necessary to go in. Your son may put up a real battle not to let you win. If locked in the bedroom, he might trash the room. The next day, while he is in school, take everything out but the mattress on the floor, and place the removed items in another room. Let your son earn back the furniture one piece at a time.

DEALING WITH LOOPHOLES.   I have been teaching this model in various forms for thirty years. Thus, I can tell you that there are other frequent loopholes. For example, with physical abuse, your son does not earn a point and must go to his room for a given unit of time. For any further such behaviors during the same time unit, he will have to return to the bedroom. But what about verbal abuse? For the first event, he will not earn a point. What do you do for the remainder of the time in this time period if your child is verbally abusive again? I suggest that for the second occurrence and for every other occurrence during the time period, your son must have a time out. I usually use half of the time assigned for physical abuse. If the child is verbally abusive all the way to the room, by the time he reaches the room, the time to be spent might be four or five times more than when you started with the first event.

What about noncompliance? You ask your child to do a chore and he refuses. He does not earn the point for that time period. What then? He already did not get the reward so why should he listen to you? Do you now have to do the chore? Later in this chapter I will suggest strategies to use for noncompliance.

This reward-point system along with the time out plan will work.

The key is to be consistent. You must develop a plan that is feasible and then implement the plan. Your child or adolescent will test and test. But stick to the plan. No child or adolescent wants to give up being the boss of the family. It will take time, but the plan will work. Once the external controls work and your son or daughter begins to have internal controls, everyone will be happier and less frustrated. If you notice this improvement, continue the plan. If you stop it too soon, the behaviors will return. If the plan does not work or your child sabotages every effort, seek professional help.

Setting Up the Second Phase of the Plan

The goal of the second phase of intervention is to help the child or adolescent internalize his or her controls. The first phase provided external controls. Now the effort shifts to helping build these controls into the behavioral patterns of the child. The first phase continues; however, now parents use a more interactive rather than omnipotent approach.

Once the unacceptable behaviors are under better control, you can introduce reflective talking. Initially, these discussions are held after the fact. The best time might be at night when you and your child are sitting on the bed and talking. Your daughter was in a fight or a yelling match, and spent time in her room. Later in the evening you sit with this child in private and discuss what happened. For example, "You know, all day long at work I just could not wait to come home so that I could spend time with you. I feel so disappointed that your behavior resulted in your being in your room so that I could not spend that time with you. What else could you have done?" Or "I am sorry you had so much trouble this afternoon. I love you, and I do not like being angry with your behavior or having to ask you to remove yourself from the family. What do you think we can do to stop such things from happening?"

Let your daughter talk. At first she may only make angry accusations of unfairness or of others causing the trouble and getting away with it. The parent might respond, "I don't know whether your brother was teasing you before you hit him or not. I was not there. But let's suppose that he did. What else could you have done? By hitting him, you got into trouble and he did not. There must be a better way. Maybe you could have told me what you thought he was

doing." Such conversations may have to occur many times as you try
to get your daughter to accept responsibility for her behaviors and to
think about the need to change. It is always important not only to
point out the behavior but to offer alternative solutions.

Gradually, you will be able to point out themes, then suggestions.
"You know, Mary, I notice that you are most likely to get into difficulty right after you come home from school. Do you suppose that
you hold in all of your problems with the schoolwork or the kids
until you get home so that you will not get into trouble at school?
Then, you let it out the first time you are upset at home. If so, maybe
you and I can do something to help. Maybe, as soon as you come in
the house, we can sit in the kitchen and have a snack. We can talk
about your day, and you can tell me about the problems you have
had. You may feel better and then won't have to let your unhappy
feelings out at the family."

Soon you will be able to do the reflective thinking before the fact.
"John, you and I both have learned that if you keep playing with your
brother once the teasing starts, there will be a fight. Do you remember what we talked about? What else could you do? Isn't this a good
time to try out that new idea?" Or "Juanita, you are forcing me to be
a police officer and to yell at you or punish you. I do not like doing
that. I'd rather enjoy being with you than yell at you or punish you.
Why do you think you force me to be a police officer? Remember
what we talked about the other night? Do you want to try some of
the ideas we talked about? For example, why don't we both take a
five-minute break to calm down and then try to talk about the problem." Gradually, your child will begin to try the new behaviors.

Children can also learn from hearing parents openly discuss feelings and thoughts. Let them understand how you feel—angry, sad,
afraid, worried. You can model with your spouse how to handle
these feelings. "I am so angry about this situation that I cannot talk
to you now. I am going into the other room to calm down. Can we
agree to talk later?" Not only will you feel more in control later, but
you have demonstrated a way to handle angry feelings.

It is important for parents to begin to explain or model acceptable
ways for their child to handle feelings. Many parents are quick to tell
their children how they may not show anger, sadness, or disappoint-
ment, but they do not teach their children acceptable ways of showing these feelings. Anger is a normal feeling, and children and

adolescents must learn how to handle this feeling in an acceptable way in the family. Can they yell as long as they do not curse? Can they stamp their feet or slam the door shut as long as they don't break anything? Watch out for confusing messages. One parent in the family yells or throws things when angry. The other parent pouts or goes to a room alone when angry. But when children get angry and start to yell, they are told, "You may not yell at me." If they walk off pouting, parents say, "You come back here. I am talking to you." It is acceptable for families to have different rules for the adults than for the children. However, parents must then teach their children or adolescents what would be acceptable ways to express feelings within the family.

Handling Noncompliance

The reward system may not work if the child or adolescent has caught on that once the point is not earned, there is no reason to comply. "You put away the toys! I lost my point, so why should I do it now?" Let me suggest a few strategies to try. You might come up with approaches of your own.

HANDLING CHORES.   To avoid any confusion about chores or other duties expected by the family, you must make a detailed list of expectations. For example, individual chores might include putting dirty clothes in the hamper, making one's bed, and picking things up off the floor. Family chores might include setting the table, loading or emptying the dishwasher, and vacuuming. Place the list in an obvious place. Clarify if these chores are to be rewarded by money or if they are expected as part of family responsibility. If the family chores are to be shared on different days, make a list that is clear as to what each child is to do each day. For example, Francine clears the table on even-numbered days and Charlie clears the table on odd-numbered days.

If the expected chores are not done, what will be the consistent consequence? What can you do if the child "forgets" or does not do an expected chore? Should you continue to nag, then shout? Several models are suggested below. Each gives the parents the controls. If a task is not done, there is a clear consequence. The choice is for the child. If the child does the chore, there is the expected reward. If the child does not do the chore, there is the expected consequence.

Maid Service.   Establish that not all parent services are supplied free of charge. If a child's chores are not done by a preset time, a parent will do the chores, but not for free. Make a list of the chores expected and the exact time expected; for example, the bed must be made before leaving for school, the dinner table must be set by 6:00 P.M., the bike must be in the garage by the time it gets dark. Set a reasonable fee next to each chore if a parent must do it. Be realistic for the age and financial resources of the child or adolescent. For example, 50 cents to make the bed, 25 cents for picking up things from the floor of the child's room, 50 cents for putting a bike in the garage. Stop arguing, reminding, or nagging your son or daughter. If the chore is done by the preset time, fine. Your child earns a point and a thank-you. If it is not done, do the chore without comment. At the end of each day or week, submit a bill for the service. If your child gets an allowance, you might present a bill at the end of the week; for example:

Allowance	$ 5.00
Maid service	−3.75
Balance due	$ 1.25

Your daughter might get upset and ask how she will be able to buy lunch snacks or drinks. You reply calmly, "Think about that next week when you decide not to do a chore." If your child does not get an allowance, you might be able to use her birthday or savings money. If there is no such money or if your daughter owes much more than the allowance, give her specific work details to earn the money she owes. "I will pay you three dollars an hour to clean the garage. You owe me three dollars; so, I expect you to work one hour this weekend."

If using money is not possible, explore bartering. For example, consider using television time or time playing computer games in exchange. "You are entitled to play five hours of computer games a week." Then, instead of money, list units of time next to each chore. At the end of the week, the bill for maid service might read:

Computer time allowed	5 hours
Maid service	−3 hours 15 minutes
Computer time remaining	1 hour 45 minutes

She will get upset. All the same, the computer game is locked up and given out for only the amount of time earned that week.

No more getting angry. No more reminding. No more fights. Children have two choices—to do their chores and get the rewards, or to not do the chores and pay someone (you) to do them.

The Sunday Box. Set up a box in a secure place. A closet or room that can be locked, or the trunk of a car, will do. Make it clear that any items (e.g., toys, bike, books, coat, shoes) left where they should not be after a predetermined time of the day will be placed in this box. (For bicycles, put the front wheel in the box.) The box is emptied every Sunday morning. This means that if a favorite game or bike or piece of sports equipment is left out or not put away on time, it is lost until Sunday. If the objects are clothes or shoes and cannot be done without, the child or adolescent must pay a fee to retrieve them early.

This plan worked so well in one family that the mother placed the father on the plan as well. His clothes, work papers, and other objects that had been left lying around disappeared into the Sunday box.

HANDLING PROPERTY DAMAGE. The initial response from parents regarding property damage will be based on the plan in place. If this behavior is called physical abuse, your son will not earn a point and must spend time in a quiet room thinking about his behavior and the need to change. More might be needed. Your son could be made to pay to repair or replace the item. Money could come out of an allowance. If the amount is large, the money might come out in installments until it is paid off. If this model for payment is not possible because your son doesn't have an allowance or birthday money, given him a way to earn the money. Assign him other than expected tasks and pay by the hour—cutting the grass, washing clothes, washing the kitchen floor, cleaning the garage, helping a neighbor, or doing community service. The first time your child gets angry and kicks over a lamp, breaking it—then learns that it will cost $50 to replace the lamp and that he will have to work for twenty hours to pay for the damage—may be the first time that he starts to think before acting. This is the goal, getting the child or adolescent to stop before acting and to think about the consequences of his or her behavior.

HANDLING DAWDLING.   Many parents reinforce dawdling by reminding, nagging, yelling, screaming, and then, in anger, doing the task with or for the child. All this behavior does is teach the child that he or she can get away with poor behavior, force the parents to help, or succeed in getting a parent upset. Instead, define the limits for a behavior and then establish clear consequences.

Let's say your child doesn't get dressed on time. She is not openly oppositional, but is so busy playing or looking out the window that the tasks just never get done. As the time for the school bus gets closer, she hasn't yet dressed or eaten because she is dawdling and playing. You probably go into the bedroom, yell at the child, and quickly dress her so that there will be time to eat and then catch the bus. Your child has succeeded in getting you upset and angry, and in getting you to help. It is important in this situation to think through if the difficulty getting dressed might relate to a learning disability (e.g., sequencing, organization, or fine motor problems) or be due to ADHD behaviors present because the child is not on medication prior to leaving for school.

For this type of behavior, you might first establish the rules. For example, the kitchen is open until 7:30 A.M. You must be dressed to enter. If you come in before 7:15, you may have a hot breakfast. If you come in after 7:15, there is time for only cold cereal. No food is served after 7:30. You will have to go to school hungry and wait for lunch. You are expected to be ready to leave for the bus by 7:40.

What do you do if it is 7:40 and she is still not dressed? Tell an older child or adolescent that if she misses the bus or car pool, you will not be able to take her to school, or you can take her but not until later, when you were planning to go out. She can use public transportation. Moreover, you will not write a note if she is late or absent; thus, there might be detention. Comment, "The problem is yours, not mine. Maybe tomorrow you will get dressed on time." Another plan to consider if family location and circumstance allow involves using a taxi. If parents must leave early as well, arrange for a contract with a reliable taxi service. This means that your daughter can call a cab when she is ready to go to school and has only to sign a voucher to pay the driver. This child is expected to pay you back or work off the cost of the cab. Again, no written excuses for being late. Accept the consequences.

If the older child or adolescent decides to stay home, she must be in her room with no television or interaction with parents during school hours. No written excuse will be provided to explain the absence.

If the child is young and the school personnel are willing to cooperate, another plan can be developed with the help of the bus driver, the classroom teacher, and the principal. The child is told the plan in advance. When it is time for your child to leave for the bus, quietly take all of the clothes that she has not yet put on and place them in a bag. Wrap the child in a robe or coat, and walk her to the bus, pajamas and all. The bus driver, having been briefed, smiles and says hello. The child gets on the bus with the bag of clothes. The parent then calls to alert the principal. If the child finishes dressing on the bus, fine. If she arrives at school in pajamas, the teacher quietly says, "Would you like to go to the bathroom and get dressed?" The child will not starve without breakfast on this day. She will not have succeeded in defeating you. This child will learn that dawdling no longer works. Only she is affected by the behavior.

This approach might work in other situations. At bedtime, whether in pajamas or still in street cloths, put the child in bed and turn out the lights. When the family is ready to leave for a movie, a visit, or a shopping trip and the child is not ready by the requested time, you should leave with the rest of the family. If the child cannot be left alone, have a sitter on call for the early phase of this approach so that you can follow through with the plan. Once the sitter is called, it is too late to change plans. Even if he or she quickly dresses, the child still stays home. After a time or two, when the child or adolescent loses rather than the parents or the rest of the family, this individual will get the message. "Finish your tasks on time or accept the consequences. You lose, not the rest of us."

When a consistent behavioral plan is used in a family, unacceptable behaviors begin to change to more acceptable behaviors. Both parents regain control and confidence in their ability to parent. Children and adolescents learn that they can be controlled and that they will not be overwhelmed by not being in control. They are usually happier. Now all of the positive experiences within the family reinforce the behaviors as well.

If this plan does not work or does not work as well as desired because the child's learning disabilities and/or ADHD are not fully managed, those issues must be addressed. If the plan does not work because one or both parents don't follow the plan or defeat the plan or because the child has such emotional problems that he or she cannot give up being in control or the need to be bad or be punished, more intensive help will be needed.

In Summary

The child or adolescent with learning disabilities and/or ADHD often develops secondary emotional, social, and family problems. Sometimes a parent or both parents will become as stressed or dysfunctional as the child or adolescent.

Try the plan described for addressing unacceptable behaviors. If the child or adolescent can change and parents can feel more competent, this might be enough. If not, seek professional help.

I reviewed which professionals are available to help and what types of help are available. Don't be hesitant to admit that your son or daughter, your family, yourself, or your marriage is in need of help. Seek competent professionals to help you assess the problems and to provide the needed interventions.

18

The Controversial Therapies

Our knowledge of learning disabilities and attention deficit hyperactivity disorder (ADHD) is not complete. We do have approaches to treatment that are based on research and are considered to be accepted practices. These interventions have been discussed in this book. I would like to discuss the less acceptable, or more controversial, approaches to treatment. The controversy might be based on the theory behind the treatment, on the way the treatment is done, or on the lack of research data to support the findings reported by the people using the treatment approach.

Controversial therapies have been with us throughout history. Perhaps you have heard claims for curing cancer or other diseases that are challenged by the medical profession. Remember ground-up apricot pits to cure cancer? Professionals who study controversial therapies comment on specific themes that exist for most, whether for cancer or learning disabilities:

1. The individual who publicizes and pushes for the treatment claims to have research to prove what is being stated; yet, no research is provided from respected journals.

2. The individual stresses that "traditional medicine" is too conservative and refuses to accept anything that does not fit what they already know.

3. Claims for cure or improvement are made with literature provided by that individual to prove these claims. One is left to wonder why, if what is claimed is accurate, the treatment is not used by most professionals in the field.

4. The person seems to be saying "I'm a genius or I'm a quack" and it is up to the public and the establishment to prove which is true.

Often parents turn to their family physician for guidance only to learn that their doctor does not know any more than they do. The difficulty is that there are many professionals and nonprofessionals proposing approaches for helping. Medical research done to support a particular approach is published in professional journals that are carefully reviewed to assure that the results reported are accurate. Usually, other researchers try to replicate the findings found by the first researcher. If others support the treatment findings, the approach is accepted by the professional groups. When the information appears *not* in professional journals but *only* in books written and published by the person making the statements or in other popular books, newspapers, or popular magazines, or is discussed on a television show, it is difficult for professionals to evaluate the claims. Thus, professionals know only what they read or hear through these popular sources or from parents who tell them about the treatment.

I will discuss controversial approaches to treatment that have been proposed and are still being used. I will not review controversial research that focuses on causes but that has not resulted in proposed treatment approaches. Where there is research to show that the proposed treatment does not work, I will present this. When all of the facts are not yet in or agreed upon, I will review the information known from both perspectives and let you decide for yourself.

Learning disabilities are lifetime disabilities. The habilitative approaches we now use take time and money and must be done over years. The treatment for ADHD works only during the hours the child or adolescent is on medication. Let the medication wear off and the child is ADHD again. Thus, I can understand why parents would want to try almost any approach that might work better and faster for their son or daughter. I can especially understand parents wanting a cure rather than an intervention. But parents must be informed and intelligent consumers. Before committing yourself and especially your daughter or son to any new or different approach, ask questions. Remember this general rule of thumb: If the treatment approach you are about to try is so successful, why isn't everyone in the country using it? No professional, regardless of discipline, would avoid using a treatment that has been shown to work.

I find it helpful to group these controversial therapies by the disorder treated—learning disabilities or ADHD. Within each group, it is helpful to further group them by the proposed mechanism of action—physiological changes or chemical changes. A few proposed treatments do not fit this model and will be listed separately. *Physiological changes* refers to the concept that by stimulating specific sensory inputs or exercising specific motor patterns one can retrain, recircuit, or in some way improve the functioning of a part of the nervous system. *Chemical changes* refers to the concept of orthomolecular medicine. This concept, introduced by Dr. Linus Pauling, involves the treatment of mental disorders and other disorders by the provision of the optimum concentrations of substances normally present in the human body. (See Table 18-1.)

Table 18-1 The Controversial Therapies

LEARNING DISABILITIES	ADHD
Physiological:	Physiological:
Patterning	Biofeedback
Optometric visual training	
Vestibular dysfunction	
Applied kinesiology	Chemical:
Auditory processing training	Megavitamins
	Trace elements
Chemical:	Food additives
Megavitamins	Refined sugars
Trace elements	Herbs
Other approaches:	Other Approaches:
Allergies	Allergies
Tinted lenses	

Patterning

The theory and the technique were initially developed by Dr. Glenn Doman and Dr. Carl Delacato. The underlying concept is that a child's failure to pass properly through a certain sequence of developmental stages in mobility, language, and competence in the manual, visual, auditory, and tactile areas reflects poor "neurological organization" and may indicate "brain damage." The proposed treatments involve repetitive activities using specific muscle patterns in the order the child should have learned if development had been normal; for example, rolling over, then crawling, then standing, then walking, and so forth. The method is described in their literature as reaching "all of the stimuli normally provided by this environment but with such intensity and frequency as to draw, ultimately, a response from the corresponding motor systems."

Reports from the American Academy of Pediatrics and other professional organizations, based on a review of all the literature, express concern about the effectiveness of patterning. These reports from the American Academy of Pediatrics conclude "that the patterning treatment offers no special merit, that the claims of its advocates are unproven, and that the demands on families are so great that in some cases there may be harm in its use."

This approach remains popular in the United States and around the world. I do not believe that patterning will improve children's learning disabilities or ADHD.

Optometric Visual Training

Although this treatment approach for learning disabilities is popular, there are professionals who believe that it is controversial and that it does not work. Parents are often caught in the middle. Ophthalmologists (physicians who specialize in eye diseases and their treatment) believe that this treatment approach does not improve reading and should not be used. Many optometrists (professionals with a doctorate in eye diseases and their treatment) believe that it is effective and should be used.

Both professional groups believe that if a child has a learning disability, it is important to rule out or treat any refractory problem (e.g., nearsightedness, farsightedness, astigmatism), any imbalance in the use of the eye muscles that might interfere with vision, pursuit of visual stimuli, or convergence, or any other medical problems. After this process, ophthalmologists believe that the treatment of choice for learning disabilities is special education and that the child should be referred for this help. Many optometrists believe that visual training will be of help in treating learning disabilities.

Optometric visual training focuses on visual perception and on the ability of eye muscles to pursue visual stimuli and to converge. Other educational and sensory-motor training techniques might also be done.

The ophthalmological literature questions the benefits of visual training, stressing that reading is a central brain process and not an eye process. There are papers showing that optometric visual training does not work. The optometric literature presents research to support the theory and benefits of this therapy.

You, the parent, will have to make your own decision. Perhaps you can discuss the proposed visual training treatment with your special education professionals or your family physician. Read what you can find. Try to be as informed as you can before investing your time and money in any treatment approach.

Vestibular Dysfunction

Several investigators have suggested that the vestibular system is important in learning. The vestibular system consists of a sensory organ in each inner ear that monitors head position and the impact of gravity and relays this information to the brain, primarily to the cerebellum. These investigators claim that there is a clear relationship between vestibular disorders and poor academic performance involving children with learning disabilities.

The first to stress this view was Dr. Jean Ayres. She proposed a theory of sensory integration needed to allow for the development of higher learning and intellectual functioning. Her theories propose the interrelationship between the visual, vestibular, tactile, and proprioceptive senses. Much of her research and that of others explore these interrelationships. There is controversy about aspects of her theory of sensory integration. These aspects will not be discussed since the focus of this chapter is not on theory but on treatments. The treatment model that evolved from her theories is sensory integration therapy. There are individuals who question the usefulness of this therapy approach for children and adults with learning disabilities who have visual perception, motor planning, vestibular, and tactile difficulties. However, the majority view of the field is positive about sensory integration therapy. (See Chapter 4 for a fuller discussion of sensory integration disorder.)

Dr. Harold Levinson has written several books describing his views on the causative role of the vestibular system and the vestibular-cerebellar systems with dyslexia. He proposes the treatment of dyslexia with anti-motion-sickness medication to correct the vestibular dysfunction. Most of the research presented is his own, published in his books rather than in scientific journals. There is little evidence to support his theory or the effectiveness of his treatment. In one of his recent books he proposes multiple other interventions along with the anti-motion-sickness medication, including many other medications and special education.

Much research has been done on the vestibular system. The consistent finding is that there are no significant differences either in the intensity of vestibular responsivity or in the prevalence of vestibular dysfunction between children who are normal learners and those with learning disabilities. Furthermore, these researchers point out that the technique used by Dr. Levinson to diagnose vestibular dysfunction (i.e., a rotating cylinder with a picture on it with the child reporting when the picture is no longer clear) is a measure of "blurring speed" and, thus, a measure of visual stimulation and not of vestibular stimulation.

Dr. Levinson continues to write and publish his books. Much of the publicity for his approach is through these books and appearances on television talk shows.

Applied Kinesiology

Years ago several chiropractors and chiropractic clinics in the United States actively advertised that they could cure dyslexia and learning disabilities. The literature that was distributed referred to the use of "applied kinesiology" and to the work of Dr. Carl A. Ferreri. The claim was that this treatment could result in an astounding reversal of all dyslexic and learning disability conditions. Often it was stated that "This technique produces measurable results immediately, that is, after just one treatment."

The basis for the theory and treatment was a book by Dr. Ferreri and Dr. Richard Wainwright, *Breakthrough for Dyslexia and Learning Disabilities*. This book was published by a local publisher and distributed by Dr. Ferreri in his own center. It presented no research data. There was one reference cited over and over as proof, a paper written by Dr. Ferreri. I tracked down this article. It was in a free, unedited publication distributed to chiropractors. The paper was one page long, and it simply described Dr. Ferreri's theory.

In their book, the authors theorize that learning disabilities are caused by two specific bones of the skull shifting out of position and applying pressure on the brain. They also discuss an imbalance within the "reflex centers" of the pelvis, inner ear, head, and neck. The treatment consists of manipulating the bones of the skull, especially those around the eyes, as well as other bones and muscles of the body. I saw videotapes of Dr. Ferrari doing this treatment. It appeared painful to the child.

The proponents of this approach report that once specific bones of the skull are back in place, the child's learning disabilities disappear. They report that the child will need special education tutoring to correct the problems that existed before the cure and that the bones might slip out of place again, requiring further treatment in the future.

This proposed treatment is not based on any known research. Some of it is based on anatomical concepts that are not held by the majority of anatomists. I could find no research published by others that supports the proposed cures, nor have I found any follow-up studies to document the claimed results. The professional organization of chiropractors became critical of Dr. Ferreri and his proposed treatment. Thus, less is heard of this treatment at this time.

Auditory Processing Training

Several treatment approaches for improving auditory processing have become known in the United States within recent years. Some organizations have offered auditory processing training as a treatment for learning disabilities and ADHD. Their flyers and other advertisements offered no research and none is known to have been published. Yet, as with other promised treatments, many parents have read the flyers and started their child or adolescent in treatment at a not inexpensive fee.

One treatment is called auditory integration training and is based on the theory of Guy Bernard, a physician in France. The second is the listening training program and is based on the theory of Alfred A. Tomatis, also a physician in France. The first approach uses amplified sound, and the second method focuses on proposed overly sensitive hearing.

The only literature available for study was the advertising flyers and instruction booklets supplied by the providers of the service. Two reviews of these approaches were published by the Edmonton Canada Public School System and the Manitoba Canada Speech and Hearing Association. Each of these reviews expressed caution about the treatment approaches and concern about the lack of research data. I will describe the methods and the concern with the lack of research.

Dr. Bernard's auditory integration training is based on the theory that some individuals have auditory perception defects such that they hear distortions of sound, have unusually sensitive hearing, or have uneven patterns of auditory sensitivity that are within the range of normal hearing yet are uncomfortable. Auditory testing is done with a device called an audiokinetron to determine at what frequencies a person has hyperacute or hypoacute hearing. On the basis of this audiogram, various compact disks are selected containing music determined to be the best for the person receiving the training. This music is played through the audiokinetron, which has been set based on the individual's audiogram to amplify some frequencies and to filter out other frequencies of the sound spectrum. During twenty half-hour sessions (two per day), the frequencies that are hyperacute and painful are filtered out. This approach is described as similar to the procedure of immobilizing painful joints or muscles until they heal. The researchers report that after the treatment, the audiometric curve tends to flatten, and hearing is normalized. It is proposed that this treatment allows the auditory cortex to reorganize. In addition, the exercise is said to strengthen the muscles that control the three bones of the middle ear, preventing sensory overload.

The Tomatis method is based on the theory that some children lose or turn off their ability to listen to certain parts of the normal sound spectrum. They do not, therefore, effectively absorb, comprehend, and interpret what they hear. Thus, these children's normal language development and, therefore, their relationship to the world beyond themselves can be affected. The intervention is done through a controlled process of auditory stimulation using sophisticated electronic equipment and special control interviews with the child and the parents. Treatment typically involves a three-week treatment session followed by a six-week rest period and then another three-week session. During the sessions, the child listens to filtered music and other sounds to "help the ear focus on the sounds he hears." In the later phases of treatment, the child is to repeat what is heard through earphones in order "to strengthen the now sensitized ear."

The ads and flyers are full of claims of success. No research supports the theory or claims. It may be too early to report whether these approaches help students with learning disabilities. These treatments are controversial because they are being used before any research has shown validity for the theory or benefit from the treatment.

These two methods of treatment should not be confused with the newer auditory processing training programs for reading based on improving phonological awareness. These approaches are founded on solid research and follow-up studies and do appear to be helpful.

Megavitamins

Using massive doses of vitamins to treat emotional or cognitive disorders was first proposed in the 1940s for the treatment of schizophrenia. It was argued that this disorder was the result of a biochemical problem and could be avoided by the use of massive amounts of vitamins, especially the B vitamins. No research supported the theory or the treatment, and few professionals consider using this approach today.

In the early 1970s, Dr. Allen Cott proposed that learning disabilities could be successfully treated with megavitamins. He presented this concept in his own book, citing no research to support his ideas. In 1976, the American Academy of Pediatrics issued a report specifically focusing on megavitamin therapy to treat learning disabilities. The conclusion: "There is no validity to the concept or treatment."

Within the past several years the concept of megavitamins to treat learning disabilities (and ADHD) has surfaced again. These approaches will be discussed later in this chapter, in the section on herbs.

Trace Elements

Trace elements are chemicals found in the body in minute amounts that are essential to normal functioning. They include copper, zinc, magnesium, manganese, and chromium along with the more common chemicals, calcium, sodium, and iron. In recent years iodine, aluminum, and cadmium have been discussed in connection to learning disabilities.

Individuals are evaluated for the level of these trace elements in their body. Hair or nail clippings are used for this analysis. If deficiencies are found, replacement therapy is given. No data has been published to support the theory that deficiencies in one or more of these elements is a cause of learning disabilities. No formal studies by professionals other than those offering the diagnosis and treatment have validated the proposed successes.

This concept remains popular in this country. Centers are available to diagnose deficiencies and to treat learning disabilities with trace elements.

Allergies

Professionals who work with children have reported for many years that they see in their practice a higher percentage of children with allergies who also have learning disabilities and/or ADHD than children with allergies who do not. Most studies have been done on the possible relationships between allergies and learning disabilities. Dr. Benjamin Feingold, a pediatric allergist, focused on ADHD and will be discussed later in this chapter.

There does appear to be a relationship between allergies and brain functioning. However, no clear cause-and-effect relationship has yet been clarified. Two clinicians have written about specific issues relating allergies to learning disabilities and ADHD. Each has proposed a treatment plan. As with other approaches, the theory and treatment concepts are presented in books written by these clinicians, sometimes published by the clinician. Little, if any, research is presented. The established profession of pediatric allergy does not accept these treatments. Since you might learn of these clinicians or of their approaches, I would like to review their theories.

Dr. Doris Rapp believes that there is a relationship between food or other sensitivities and learning as well as with hyperactivity. She proposes a diet that eliminates the identified foods or the avoidance of other suspected allergens as a treatment. She believes that the traditional allergy skin testing for foods does not always detect the foods that cause problems. Her critics say that her challenge test, with a solution placed under the tongue, is not a valid measure of allergies.

Dr. Rapp identifies certain foods or food groups that children might be allergic to: milk, chocolate, eggs, wheat, corn, peanuts, pork, and sugar. She suggests that parents try a specific elimination diet described in her books. This diet consists of eliminating all of the possible allergy-producing foods, and then adding one back each week to see if there is a change in behaviors.

She studies other possible allergens by using a food extract solution placed under the tongue in her tests. If the child is found to be sensitive to certain foods or chemicals in the environment (e.g., paste, glue, paint, mold, chemicals found in new carpets), these items are eliminated or avoided. She reports an improvement in the behaviors of the child. Most specifically, she reports less aggressive or oppositional behavior and less hyperactivity. Other professionals have not been able to duplicate her findings or claimed successes. Some parents have found her approach very helpful.

Dr. William Crook has written extensively on the relationship between allergies and general health, learning disabilities, and ADHD.

He writes of the "allergic-tension-fatigue syndrome." He also reports that specific allergies can result in hyperactivity and distractibility.

Many of his more recent publications and presentations focus on a possible allergic reaction to a specific yeast and the development of specific behaviors following a yeast infection. He reports that treatment of the yeast infection improves or corrects the problem. I know of no clinical or research studies that have confirmed his theories or proposed treatment program.

Tinted Lenses

Helen Irlen proposes the treatment of certain types of dyslexia with colored or tinted lenses or templates. She specifically focuses on a group of problems she refers to as "scotopic sensitivity syndrome." Individuals with this syndrome show difficulty in six areas: (1) photophobia, or sensitivity to light; (2) eyestrain; (3) poor visual resolution; (4) a reduced span of focus; (5) impaired depth perception; and (6) poor sustained focus. She points out that her proposed treatment is not a substitute for corrective refractive lenses if needed.

Her papers and other publications cite her research. This reference is to a paper presented at a national meeting, not to a paper published in a professional journal. In this presentation she proposes that a small percentage of individuals with dyslexia have scotopic sensitivity syndrome. For this group, the use of tinted lenses will improve the dyslexia. Her treatment with tinted lenses was demonstrated on the television show *60 Minutes*. A child who could not read used the proper tinted lenses and then began to read. Ms. Irlen became very popular.

Since her paper, there have been studies testing this treatment approach. Some published papers support her concept, and some do not. The final facts on the concept or the treatment are not in.

The controversy is that before the facts are in and the effectiveness of this treatment has been studied, Irlen Centers have opened around the country. A screening test for scotopic sensitivity syndrome is done. Tinted lenses are sold. Of further concern is that Ms. Irlen initially reported that a small percentage of individuals with dyslexia, those with scotopic sensitivity syndrome, would benefit from tinted lenses. How objectively is dyslexia being diagnosed and this syndrome identified before lenses are sold? Should any treatment be advertised and sold before the facts are in?

Biofeedback

It has been proposed that ADHD is a result of an altered pattern of brain waves and that this pattern can be identified on an electroencephalogram (EEG). This approach is presented as a diagnostic instrument. It is further proposed that by using a biofeedback technique, an individual can learn to change his or her brain wave pattern. Once the pattern is corrected, the ADHD is improved or treated.

There is controversy about the theory relating both to diagnosis and to treatment. However, there is greater controversy relating to EEG biofeedback as a treatment for ADHD. Yet, the equipment is sold and many professionals throughout the United States do this form of treatment.

Recently the Professional Advisory Board of the organization Children and Adults with Attention Deficit Disorder (CHADD) published a position statement on biofeedback. These professionals reviewed all of the literature on these concepts. In their statement, they challenged the use of EEG biofeedback for ADHD and advised parents not to use this treatment approach.

Food Additives

In 1975, Dr. Benjamin Feingold published the book *Why Your Child Is Hyperactive*. He proposed that synthetic flavors and colors in the diet were related to hyperactivity. He reported that the elimination of all foods containing artificial colors and flavors as well as salicylates and certain other additives stopped the hyperactivity. Neither in this book nor in any of his other publications did Dr. Feingold present research data to support this theory. All findings in the book were based on his clinical experience. He and his book received wide publicity. Parent groups advocating for the Feingold diet formed all over the country. It was left to others to document whether he was correct or incorrect.

Because of a hope that he might be correct and a need to either counter his claims or to prove he was correct, the federal government sponsored several major research projects to study this theory and the treatment. In 1982, the National Institutes of Health held a consensus conference on this issue. A panel of experts were brought together. They reviewed the results of these major research studies, read all available literature, held hearings to allow anyone who wished to present to do so, and questioned experts. The panel members then spent time synthesizing what was known and finally wrote a consensus on the topic.

They concluded that there does appear to be a subset of children with behavioral disturbances who respond to some aspects of Dr. Feingold's diet. However, this group is very small, possibly one percent of the children studied. They also commented that with notable exceptions, the specific elimination of synthetic food colors from the diet does not appear to be a major factor in the reported responses of a majority of these children. They concluded that the defined diets should not be used universally in the treatment of childhood hyperactivity.

Two studies done after this consensus conference reached the same conclusions. The Feingold diet is not effective in treating hyperactivity in most children. There may be a small group, perhaps 1 percent, who appear to respond positively to the diet for reasons that are not clear.

There is no way for physicians to identify in advance which patients might be part of this 1 percent group. Sometimes parents report that if their child eats foods with specific food colors (e.g., Kool-Aid, Hawaiian Punch, certain cereals) or takes a medication with specific food colors (e.g., penicillin with red or yellow food dye), the child becomes more hyperactive. Perhaps this is the child with ADHD who might respond to a diet that eliminates that specific food color. The basic ADHD would still be present and need treatment.

Refined Sugars

Clinical observations and parent reports suggest that refined sugar promotes adverse behavioral reactions in children. Hyperactive behavior is most commonly reported.

Several formal studies have been done to clarify and/or verify these parent claims. Each used what is called a challenge study. Children who were reported by parents to become more hyperactive when they ate refined sugar were given either refined sugar (glucose), natural sugar (fructose), or a placebo. The results failed to support the parents' observations.

Another study explored whether the reported increase in activity level with children who ate a high-sugar snack or meal might be related to the amount of refined sugar eaten and not to the exposure to the sugar. In this study, each child was given breakfast. This breakfast was high in either fat, carbohydrates, or protein. The children were then given the challenge test with either refined sugar, natural sugar, or a placebo. The researchers found that some children appeared to be more active after a high-carbohydrate breakfast and exposure to refined sugars. Possibly, then, some children with ADHD will become more hyperactive if they eat high levels of refined sugar in foods and snacks throughout a period of time (sugared cereal for breakfast, cookies for snack, jelly sandwich and candy for lunch, cake for after-school snack, etc.).

Herbs

The use of alternative medicines is popular around the world. Herbs, spices, and other ingredients have been know to be therapeutic in certain situations. The concept of using herbs as a treatment for ADHD and possibly for learning disabilities have become very widespread within the past several years. As with most of the controversial treatments discussed in this chapter, most of what is known is found in flyers and advertisements distributed by the individuals selling the product. No research is presented, yet claims are made about the effectiveness of the treatment.

In preparation for the current edition of this book, I wrote for more information on several products I either saw advertised, found exhibited at a meeting, or read about in advertisements I received in the mail. I was struck by the absence of anything more than advertisements. I was also struck by the fact that three of the companies I wrote to "for more information" offered to allow me to be the exclusive salesperson for the product in my area. I was told how much good I would do for children by making them aware of this treatment.

I list below those products I know of now that provide no research in the packaging to defend the claims made. Testimonials were common in the packaging. Large technical words were used, often undefined. The copy created a feeling that if I as a parent did not give the product to my child, I was preventing him or her from making progress. This list is meant to inform parents of the most common products available at the time this book was finalized. It is not a complete list. I'm sure there are others.

God's Recipe: This is a mixture of colloidal minerals, antioxidant with ginkgo biloba, and multienzymes.

Pedi-Active ADD: This is "phosphatidy/serine" and is stated to be the "most advanced neuronutrients available," including a diversified combination of other ingredients.

Kids Plex Jr: The ingredients are multivitamins, amino acids, a mixture of "Ergogens and Krebs Cycle Intermediates and Lipotropics."

Calms Kids: This is a mixture of vitamins, minerals, and amino acids.

Pycnogenol: This is described as a "water processed extract from the bark of the French Maritine Pine Tree . . . [the most] potent nutritional antioxidant discovered by science."

New Vision: This is a mixture of sixteen juices and eighteen fruit blends made into a capsule.

Super Blue Green Algae: This product comes in many forms, and its benefits are stated to be based on the fact that algae is the "very basis of the entire food chain—it is largely responsible for creating and renewing all life on earth."

None of the producers of these products give details of their contents on the package. For example, what vitamins or amino acids? Many of the terms used were not defined and make little sense. I found no evidence to support the claims given. I encourage parents to think carefully before buying these products.

In Summary

There is a relationship between brain function and nutrition as well as between brain function and allergic reactions. These relationships appear to be true for learning disabilities, ADHD, and other neurological disorders. However, at this time we do not understand these relationships and there are no known treatments based on these relationships that are clinically successful.

When you learn of a new treatment or technique, you have good reason for showing interest. We all want a better and faster way to help these children and adolescents. Please take the time to become as informed as possible. Ask yourself why this amazing approach is not used by everyone. If the person proposing the treatment tells you that "most professionals are biased" and do not believe his findings because they are different from the usual treatments, ask to see the data supporting the concept and treatment. Don't accept popular books published by the person proposing the theory or treatment as validated facts. Discuss the approach with your family physician, with the school professionals, and with other parents.

Don't put your son or daughter through something unproven and unlikely to help. Please spend as much time researching these treatments as you probably do at a supermarket when you read every label in detail before deciding which product to buy.

S I X

Special Topics

The Adult with Learning Disabilities and/or Attention Deficit Hyperactivity Disorder

The child with a learning disability becomes the adolescent with a learning disability and then becomes the adult with a learning disability. You know my theme: Learning disabilities are lifetime disabilities. About 50 percent of children with attention deficit hyperactivity disorder (ADHD) will become adults with ADHD. With both disorders, there is about a 50 percent probability of a familial pattern. That is, there is about a 50 percent likelihood that the disorder was inherited and that it runs in the family. It is not uncommon for me to discuss a child's learning disabilities and/or ADHD with parents and then have one say that he or she has the same problems. For some, the problems stopped being an issue in their life after they finished school. For most, the disabilities greatly affected their lives, education, and educational accomplishments and continue to cause difficulties in their career and family life.

Thus, finding a child or adolescent with one or both of these disabilities often becomes a family issue. Not only is it important to address the needs of the son or daughter, it is important to explore what help a parent might need. Or this parent might comment on a brother or sister who did poorly as well or on a nephew or niece who is struggling. It becomes important to explain that these relatives might be informed of the possibility of a familial theme so that they, too, can seek help.

. . .

Some adults seek consultation because they read about learning disabilities or ADHD or saw a television show on these disorders. Others might have suspected that they had these problems for years and finally decided to find out. Still others seek help because they are in trouble on the job or in their educational programs. They might believe their problems relate to something else, but the theme of a learning disability or ADHD becomes clear in the evaluation. Whenever I see an adult with a chronic history since childhood of difficulty functioning, I feel a need to explore the possibility of these disorders.

Another not uncommon story is that this adult struggled through high school, possibly with college, and even through graduate or professional school. Somehow they made it. They seem to pick entry-level positions that maximize their strengths and allow them to best compensate for their weaknesses. For example, someone who is hyperactive finds a job that requires working in the field rather than behind a desk, or the person with reading and writing problems finds a job where most of the time is spent verbally interacting and a secretary helps with the paperwork. The person with language difficulties might find a job where the work is done by hand and minimal interacting is needed. Problems begin when they are so successful that they get promoted to a middle-level position. Suddenly, the need to read, write, follow budgets or math trends, establish work schedules, organize and operate a program, or manage a group of people creates difficulties. It is at this time that they might struggle and perform poorly. For those who get help or who manage to survive until they reach an upper-level position, life might become easier and more successful. Now they can go back to using their knowledge, intelligence, and reasoning abilities along with their other strengths. Now they can bring in other people to handle the tasks that are difficult for them.

What Does Becoming an Adult Mean?

To successfully move from adolescence to adulthood requires that the individual master several psychological and social skills. In general, adults must be able to:

Feel like an adult.
Live like an adult.
Work like an adult.
Relate to others like an adult.

If a child or adolescent has learning disabilities and/or ADHD, how might he or she enter adult life? Will he or she be able to accomplish these four tasks that are required to be successful as an adult? When I work with adults, I often find that they fall into one of three possible groups: (1) those who are successful; (2) those who could be successful with the right help; and (3) those who are functioning poorly in all areas and are unsuccessful. Let me discuss these questions and observations.

In the best of all possible worlds, the child's or adolescent's disabilities were identified early. He or she got appropriate special education services and, if needed, medications throughout the school years. Those who went into the military, a trade, or a job received vocational guidance and training designed to maximize success. Those who went to college got all necessary special services and programs available. The probability that these adults are successful is high. However, in the real world, many of our children and adolescents were not diagnosed early or at all. Any services they got in grade school either disappeared or became watered down by middle school or high school. Few if any efforts were made to help them with the transition to life after high school. Their postsecondary world of work or college provided little of what is needed. The probability that these adults reached their full potential or were successful is low.

Let's look at the four characteristics of an adult and how these disabilities might affect the ability of the individual to successfully master each.

Feel Like an Adult

To feel like an adult requires a good self-image and good self-esteem. In general, self-image refers to how you feel about your self, and self-esteem refers to how you feel *others* feel about you. Self-image is based on a lifetime of positive experiences within the family, in school, and with peers. For the individual with learning disabilities and/or ADHD, it is important that these disabilities be accepted, understood, and integrated as a positive into this image of self. Research on self-esteem with children and adolescents shows that it is based on two factors—academic success and peer acceptance. A person must experience each as positive to enter adulthood with good self-esteem.

Ideally, students with learning disabilities and/or ADHD are identified early in their school experiences so that they receive services, counseling, and appropriate medications as necessary. Further, as each student moves from grade school to middle school to high school, he or she continues to receive services as needed and has learned to understand what special accommodations are necessary and how to advocate for them both in school and with out-of-school activities. By high school, each student knows how to be assertive as a self-advocate.

Ideally, each family of a student with learning disabilities and/or ADHD is educated about the student's abilities and disabilities. They, too, learn how to be an informed and assertive advocate for the child. They learn to help him or her begin to take over some of the advocacy roles so that by high school the child can comfortably accept the role of self-advocate. This family knows how to select home activities, peer activities, sports, and other important experiences for the son or daughter that build on the child's strengths while compensating for and minimizing the effects of the weaknesses. Therefore, each student has had successful experiences in the family and with peers.

Ideally, then, this student would leave high school with comprehensive self-knowledge, a good self-image, and a positive level of self-esteem. He or she would move into any postsecondary world with the maximum chance of success.

Unfortunately, most school systems do not provide this ideal world. Most families are not fortunate enough to be taught what they need to know to be successful parents and siblings. All too many high school graduates do not have adequate knowledge of self or experiences with success, resulting in a poor self-image, low self-esteem, and limited self-advocacy skills. Too many high school students give up and drop out of school. (Fifty percent of students identified by school systems as having learning disabilities quit school! We do not know the figures for those who are not recognized and identified.) These students enter their postsecondary world neither psychologically, socially, nor academically prepared. They are forced to pay the price of a lifetime of underachievement, often along with few personal or social successes.

It is critical for parents to know how to accomplish all that is needed in this "ideal" world. You need to apply the information in each chapter in this book to help assure that your son or daughter will leave high school with the maximum chance of success as an adult.

Live Like an Adult

Adults must be able to live independently. They must learn such basic life skills as getting up on time, eating right, getting to work or school, having clean clothes, maintaining good personal hygiene, keeping the environment "liveable," and planning meals. This might mean getting to a cafeteria or planning a menu, shopping, and cooking. Adults need to know how to manage money—budgets, checking accounts, charge cards, bills. They need to know how to manage time so that everything gets done on time and they show up where they are supposed to be on time. For some, it means knowing how to use public transportation or how to find and use needed public services. I'm sure you could add to this list.

Most adults learn these skills while living at home. Some learn from life experiences and from watching how things are done within their family. Some skills are learned because the parents felt they were important enough to teach. Allowances lead to budgets. Eating leads to shopping and cooking. Activities lead to planning. Children expand on these life skills with peers and in school. Certain learning disabilities can interfere with certain life skills, so people with learning disabilities need to be taught remedial and compensatory skills. Some may need help with using money properly—how much to give the person, making change—or with balancing a checkbook. The same organizational strategies taught to keep a notebook and papers in order might apply to other areas of life.

An adolescent who enters adult life without these essential life skills cannot live independently. There are excellent day and residential programs that focus on teaching these skills. Seek them out.

Work Like an Adult

Adults must be capable of earning a living. Anyone planning to end formal education after high school must have a transitional plan in place during these last years. The student should start vocational or other job training so he or she is capable of starting a job or entering a next-level vocational program. If the student goes on to college, he or she needs to choose one that can provide all needed services.

Adolescents or adults might need vocational guidance to help identify which careers best match their learning strengths as well as to identify any accomodations they might need. I'm met many young adults who haven't worked since high school and are still living at home. They have a great challenge to overcome: They must deal with years of failure and lack of confidence along with the reality that they might have no skills to offer a possible employer.

Once on the job, the adult needs certain work skills: getting to work on time each day, being dressed and groomed appropriately, working and producing up to an employer's expectations. It will be essential to relate to customers or clients or to peers and supervisors. Many jobs require follow-through with other assignments using time planning, the ability to meet a production quota or to find new clients, anticipate problems, and prevent them.

We can teach people specific skills. We cannot teach them specific strategies for thinking and problem solving for every problem they might face, only general techniques. We cannot teach attitudes or work ethics on the job; these should be in place before entering work. For some, these are learned "intuitively" through life experiences. For others, they must be clarified and taught, ideally prior to the student leaving high school. Some might need to find a postsecondary program that can teach these essential skills.

Relate to Others Like an Adult

We know how children and adolescents relate to adults. They do not relate as equals. They are dependent on these adults for certain needs and experiences. These adults can tell them what to do. Adult-to-adult relationships must be different. Adults must relate as equals. They are interdependent. Each leans on the other for support and comfort. Each shares certain life tasks to the benefit of both. Each helps to fill some of the other's needs. Each, however, is able to function independently with his or her own adult identity. We call this adult type of relationship intimacy.

Adult relationships require closeness and intimacy. Closeness is the ability to be near or to live with another person. Intimacy is the ability to be one's true self with someone and the ability to allow that other person to be his or her true self with you. Closeness requires effort. Intimacy requires a comfortable feeling about self and taking risks. Intimacy also requires the maturity to understand and accept another as he or she really is.

Many adults are able to create closeness. Not as many adults ever reach a level of intimacy in their relationships. For those who can, life is very fulfilling. For those who are less successful, relationships always seem to be "missing something."

Adults with a poor self-image or low self-esteem do not feel safe taking the risk of sharing their true self with others. Even successful adults might have the old fear from childhood about disclosure. "If I really tell this person about my learning disabilities, he or she will think I am dumb or incompetent and no longer like me." If life has been a constant struggle, with most energy focused merely on survival, an adult might not have an "other" orientation. He or she may not know to consider others feelings, thoughts, or needs. It's not difficult to see why many adults with a lifetime of learning disabilities and/or ADHD have great difficulty with relating to others like an adult.

Intimacy usually evolves as a natural next step following psychosocial development if the person has mastered all previous steps. Otherwise, adolescents grow up to become adults who are too dependent, who expect much and give little, who need to be taken care of, who cannot understand or identify with a companion or a companion's needs. Many lead a lonely life with limited relationships. Some go from one unsuccessful relationship to another or stay in ungratifying or harmful relationships.

Adults who have problems with intimacy need help. Often, they'll need to go back and work on the underlying issues relating to earlier developmental stages or to the reasons for their poor self-image or low self-esteem. These efforts take time. For some, individual psychological help is useful. For others, group experiences help them become aware of the tasks to work on or of the need for further help.

Most adults master these four tasks and succeed as adults. Even adults with learning disabilities and/or ADHD can be successful if they get everything they need during childhood or adolescence. Other such adults with these disabilities will have to work as adults to master these tasks.

How Do You Define These Disabilities with Adults?

The earliest definitions for learning disabilities referred only to children. In recent years, these definitions have been revised to stress that learning disabilities are chronic and lifelong. These newer definitions focus not only on the impact in school but on the impact on self-esteem, vocation, socialization, and daily living activities. Now that we understand that up to 50 percent of children and adolescents with ADHD will continue to have this disorder all their lives, it has become necessary to recognize that adults can have this disorder. The criteria for diagnosis are the same for adults as for children.

The United States Rehabilitation Services Administration developed a definition of learning disabilities for use in vocational rehabilitation programs. These programs facilitate the employment of individuals whose disability interferes with employability; thus, the definition of learning disabilities goes beyond verbal and academic problems and includes such issues as social competence and emotional maturity. This definition reads as follows:

> Individuals who have a disorder in one or more of the central nervous system processes involving perceiving, understanding, and/or using concepts through verbal (spoken or written language) or nonverbal means. This disorder manifests itself with difficulties in one or more of the following areas: attention, reasoning, memory, communicating, reading, spelling, calculation, coordination, social competence, and emotional maturity.

The difficulty with this definition is that it does not take into account all of the effects of learning disabilities on employment.

There is no standard or accepted definition of learning disabilities for colleges. Each may use its own criteria for offering special admission standards or services. California established guidelines for its community colleges. This was done because of the significant increase in the number of students applying to and attending the community college system and the inconsistency within this system. A student could be diagnosed as having a learning disability and be eligible for services in one college and not in another. This California standard is given here.

Learning disability in California Community College adults is a persistent condition of presumed neurological dysfunction which may also exist with other disabling conditions. This dysfunction continues despite instruction in standard classroom situations. Learning disabled adults, a heterogeneous group, have these common attributes:

1. Average to above-average intellectual ability
2. Severe processing deficit
3. Severe aptitude-achievement discrepancy or discrepancies
4. Measured achievement in an instructional or employment setting
5. Measured appropriate adaptive behavior in an instructional or employment setting

These last two factors refer to the vocational training programs offered by many of these community colleges.

If your son or daughter is going to college, you will need guidance on how to select the best school and how to get the needed services. If your child needs vocational guidance and possible vocational rehabilitation—or if you do—you will need guidance on how to utilize the services of your state and county vocational rehabilitation services. I will provide basic information on how to do this later in this chapter.

How Do You Assess Adults?

There will be many reasons for an adult to seek an evaluation. The underlying reason is to establish or to verify a prior diagnosis of learning disabilities and/or ADHD and to develop a plan of action that will help the individual achieve his or her goals. That is, perhaps of more importance than establishing the diagnosis is learning what can be done with the information gained to do career planning and/or to design necessary interventions.

Depending on the need, the assessment might focus on the traditional areas relating to learning disabilities—educational or academic functioning. A fuller vocational assessment would require evaluating social and interpersonal abilities and employment and life skills. I will describe first the assessment for the college-bound student and then the assessment for vocational rehabilitation.

Assessment for the College-Bound

This assessment should include the essential features of the psychoeducational evaluation discussed in Chapter 13. It's especially important to clarify what residual problems may affect the student's success in college. Often included are measures of receptive and expressive oral and written language, reading skills, mathematics reasoning and computation, and verbal and nonverbal concept formation. Also assessed are auditory and visual perception, memory, sequencing, analysis, and synthesis. Of equal importance will be the assessment of study habits and attitudes and study skills and strategies. The student's information must be current. If your school system only does testing every three years and the last studies were done in ninth grade, you might find that the school will not retest your child in the senior year. You'll be left with test results that are too old to use.

The assessment will clarify which academic demands of college are most likely to cause difficulty and what interventions would be needed to remediate, to compensate for, or to accommodate these areas of difficulty. These results will give parents and adolescent clues as to which study skills and strategies this adolescent already has and which new or expanded ones he or she might need. The assessment might clarify which required courses might need to be waived since the student would have tremendous difficulty mastering the course. The purpose of the assessment is to help the parents and student select the right college and define what services will be needed. This information will be necessary to help the college professionals implement the needed services.

Assessment for Vocational Rehabilitation

The vocational rehabilitation assessment must first establish that the person has a learning disability and/or ADHD, using the criteria for learning disabilities listed earlier and the criteria in the diagnostic manual for ADHD. Then, it is necessary to determine the person's eligibility for services and to develop a suitable vocational plan. To do this, the examiner must ascertain the individual's strengths and functional limitations: What would limit his or her employment success. For example, would an adult with a reading disability have difficulty reading the classified ads, a job application form, or certain manuals necessary for job success? Would being on medication be considered unacceptable in certain work situations?

The assessment of social skills, work skills, and the ability to relate to coworkers and supervisors is essential. An adult might have all of the abilities and strengths to perform the job yet be unable to keep the job because he or she can't interact well with others.

The first task is to identify a potential field of interest for the individual. Then the team needs to be sure the individual has all the on-the-job, vocational, or educational experiences needed for that job, keeping in mind any special services or accommodations. Finally, the individual will need job placement with all special accommodations in place.

The Americans with Disabilities Act (to be discussed in Chapter 21) requires that any individual with a disability receive all necessary accommodations to allow that person to be successful on the job. This act does not require that services be provided, only accommodations. It requires that if an individual's disabilities can be accommodated, he or she must be given an equal opportunity to compete for a job and to maintain that job. If the area of disability would prevent that individual from doing a job, even with accommodations, it is not necessary to allow for equal opportunity to work. For example, it might be considered that an individual who is blind could not perform the essential tasks for being a police officer. Thus, this individual would not qualify for this position.

The Needs of Adults with These Disabilities

Some adults may have known they had learning disabilities and/or ADHD since childhood. However, once out of school, they might not think their disabilities still exist since they're no longer challenged in a classroom situation. Others might be aware that they still have disabilities, but think that nothing can be done. Still others might not find out about their learning disabilities and/or ADHD until adulthood.

Specific interventions may need to be redefined to address the needs of adults. Clearly, interventions must address work, family, and other life situations.

I know adults who still cannot calculate money in their head. They have major problems with purchases. For example, how much money do I give the salesperson or how much should I expect back? One man in his forties told me that he tried to carry large bills with him. If he gave the salesperson a twenty-dollar bill, he did not have to worry about giving the proper amount. He just trusted that he got the correct change back. Salespersons can have these same problems. Today's registers that do the math for you are of great help. For these adults, targeted remedial interventions might focus on this specific area of difficulty, relieving them of a major worry. A similar approach might be used for adults who cannot manage a checkbook.

I remember having dinner with a very successful attorney, now a judge, who had learning disabilities. We often compared notes on how to survive. He shared with me that he still had tremendous trouble reading. He joked about a problem he has had all of his life with restaurants and menus. "What is worse is if you are in a restaurant with atmosphere. I hate it. The lights are so low that I can't even see the menu. And then there are the fancy restaurants that write in French, Italian, or Spanish to impress you. I have enough trouble reading in English." He told me how he survived. His first strategy was to fall back to a safe selection. He had a favorite food for each type of restaurant. If he went to an Italian restaurant, he would always order his favorite veal dish. In a French restaurant, he had one favorite that every French restaurant served. And so it went. His other trick was to get into a conversation with the serving person. "Tell me about your chef. What is his or her specialty? What do you like? What would you recommend?" Here is a very successful and very competent professional still living under the fear that he will not be able to do something and that other people might see him as "stupid."

This attorney illustrates a key concept for adults. It is important to learn how to improve on weaknesses as well as how to use strengths to minimize the impact of the weaknesses. But, as an adult, it's equally important to learn how to compensate when you cannot avoid the areas of weakness. Each adult must find his or her own survival skills.

When adults learn for the first time that they have learning disabilities and/or ADHD, they have more to do than get a diagnosis and find the proper interventions. They may need to rethink their self-image and their past. These adults might at last understand why they did so poorly in school or in college or on the job. They might have to explore and rethink memories of childhood, adolescence, and adulthood, and reconsider deep feelings of being a failure or of disappointing parents. It's not unusual to feel anger about not being diagnosed earlier, and to have to cope with memories of all of the failures and pain caused by not having the problem picked up.

For some, going to or completing college isn't realistic. They may have had a lifetime of underachieving. They are working in jobs they feel are below their ability, or they have never advanced despite their sense of competence. Some share with me that they will never see themselves as "smart" unless they finish college. They have a lifetime of disappointments in their work and in their personal world.

For others, the unrecognized disabilities have led to other life problems. Their spouse or partner constantly complains of their disorganization or inability to complete what they start. They are told that they just never seem to listen or pay attention. Many parents hear me describe their son or daughter and sadly say, "That's me . . . I do the same things." The spouse is only too quick to agree.

The adult interventions for learning disabilities are targeted to the specific needs of the adult at that time. For some, the services might be the same as in high school because they're still in college or want to return to college. For others, the areas of frustration and failure have yet to be addressed. Some professionals who used to tutor children and adults have "retooled" themselves to work with adults on these targeted areas. They often call themselves coaches rather than tutors.

Adults with ADHD should consider medication. The same medications that work with children work with adults. Everything discussed in Chapter 16 on medications for ADHD is equally relevant for adults. Unless the hyperactivity, distractibility, and/or impulsivity are addressed, the adult may continue to experience difficulties in college, on the job, or in the family. Let me illustrate.

John, a thirty-five-year-old attorney, came to see me after reading an article in the paper. He told me that he had been on a medication from age nine to sixteen because of overactivity and trouble concentrating. He remembered that two of his sisters took the same medication. At my request, he contacted his parents who contacted their family doctor. He had been on Dexedrine.

During college and law school he occasionally was able to get this medication from friends. When he took it, he studied better and more efficiently. He was now working for a law firm and having great difficulty staying on task and getting his work done. He reported frustration with his performance. He knew he could do the work. But it was not getting done. Often, he stayed late at the office, finding that he did more work when no one else was around. He described great difficulty staying organized and keeping track of his billable hours.

I placed him on Dexedrine. At a dose of 5 mg every four hours he reported a dramatic improvement. He was able to concentrate and stay on task. His thoughts were more organized. He became effective and efficient at work. His supervisor noted the change and wondered what he had done. His wife was so excited about her husband's ability to relax and stay with a conversation that she called me to thank me.

The need to fight for necessary accommodations may start with the PSAT and SAT examinations—but it may not end there. The same accommodations may be needed for teacher certification examinations as well as for legal bar, medical licensing, or medical specialty certification examinations.

In Summary

Learning disabilities will continue into adulthood. ADHD might continue into adulthood. Since many professionals who work with adults are not yet as aware of these disabilities as are professionals who work with children and adolescents, you might have to be the person who first recognizes the need for assessment and help. This effort might be for you, for your adult son or daughter, for your spouse or partner, or for a brother or sister, cousin, or nephew or niece.

If college or graduate studies are a goal, seek out counselors who specialize in helping individuals with these disabilities to find the right programs.

If vocational planning or training is needed, contact your county office of vocational rehabilitation. The professionals at this office are trained to do assessments and interventions.

Whatever direction you or someone you care for needs to take, be aware of the impact that these problems have had throughout life. Help from a mental health professional might be as important as the educational and vocational interventions.

20

The Gifted Student with Learning Disabilities

The possibility that a child or adolescent could be gifted and have a learning disability at the same time has often been ignored or disbelieved. Some professionals even believed that having learning disabilities and being gifted were contradictory terms. Today, many school systems accept that students with learning disabilities can also be gifted (and talented), and programs are available for identifying and educating them.

Part of the difficulty in recognizing this relates to the way being gifted is measured. One approach is based on high levels of academic performance in the classroom. Students with learning disabilities may be of superior IQ but, because of their disabilities, not be at an equal level in certain areas of academic performance. Another approach is to use scores from standardized tests. For example, to be eligible for gifted programs, one might need a full-scale IQ of 120 or higher. Because of the processing problems found with learning disabilities, many students with learning disabilities score high in one of the IQ areas (performance or verbal) and lower on the other. For this student, the full-scale score reflects the approximate average of these two scores and the lower score pulls down the higher score. It is clear that many very bright and capable students with learning disabilities would not meet one or the other of these criteria.

In 1972, the U.S. Department of Education established criteria to identify an individual as gifted: an IQ of 130 or higher, a high level of task commitment, a high level of creativity, and an exceptional ability in one or more of the following areas—artistic, leadership (social), specific academic aptitude, or athletics. Since that time, other definitions have used lower IQ expectations. Concern with the impact of cultural factors on IQ testing has led to alternative models for assessing intellectual ability.

Many states use a broader definition. To give an example of one state's definition that provides a greater opportunity for students with learning disabilities:

> Gifted and talented children are those identified by professionally qualified persons [and] who by virtue of outstanding abilities are capable of high performance. These are children who require differentiated educational programs and services beyond those normally provided by the regular school program in order to realize their contribution to self and society.

> Children capable of high performance include those with demonstrated achievement and/or potential ability in any of the following areas: general intellectual ability, specific academic aptitude, creative or productive thinking, leadership ability, and visual and performing arts.

This concept of assessing not only intellectual ability but unique talents has led to the expanded term *gifted and talented* to cover these programs.

The Problems Associated with the Concept of Giftedness

The word *gifted* can create several problems. It implies its own opposite. If you are not gifted, what are you—worthless? dumb? In addition, the label may be of such importance to parents that the pressure to qualify might place pressure on the child. This pressure can create competition that sets learners against each other instead of joining them in the common goal of learning.

Some families move to a different school district, where their child can qualify for the gifted program. As one mother explained, "In my township you have to be 125 [IQ] to be gifted and my child is 123. Two towns away, you only have to be 120."

Children and adolescents with learning disabilities have difficulty because they can see that they do not do some academic work as well as their classmates. Yet, they often sense that they are as smart as their classmates. If some children are selected for the gifted program and this student is not, even though he or she might be as capable, it strikes one more blow to self-esteem.

I have had parents tell me how angry they become when they see those car bumper stickers that read "I am proud of my child who is an honor student at . . ." They feel just as proud of their student with a learning disability and resent having only those students who can excel academically identified as worthy of pride.

How Should Students with Learning Disabilities Be Evaluated?

Although the formal definitions of giftedness do not automatically eliminate the student with learning disabilities, in practice the operational definitions used by many school systems do exclude many if not most of them. The experts in this area believe that the reason for this is that most professionals recommend the use of individual measures of intelligence such as the Wechsler Intelligence Scales. Schools then tend to screen for gifted students on the basis of group measures of intelligence or achievement tests, often in conjunction with teacher nominations or recommendations. (In some programs, self, peer, or parent nominations are also considered.) Using this approach, many students who are gifted and who have learning disabilities are overlooked because their performance on standardized group tests of achievement are not two or three years above their grade placement.

Professionals in the field of gifted education are moving toward a more sensible approach to identifying gifted students. They propose a wide variety of psychological tests that measure specific abilities (called psychometric testing) and nonpsychometric measures to initially screen as many students as possible for consideration for the available programs. Evidence of academic ability or potential can be assessed by nonverbal measures of deductive reasoning and some measurement of creativity might be evaluated in a way that allows the child with problems in areas of reading, spelling, or handwriting to compete for recognition in other areas.

Clearly, any approach to identify the student with learning disabilities should assess the strengths of the child as well as the weaknesses. The key is for the classroom teacher, the specialist in the area of giftedness, and parents to be aware of the existence of students who both are gifted and have learning disabilities. With this awareness and a sensitivity to the need to modify the screening models, more students with learning disabilities will be found to be gifted.

How Should These Students Be Educated?

The answer to this question can be the problem for some students. In some school systems, it is not clear who should be responsible for their education. Should these students be considered a subset of children and adolescents with learning disabilities and identified and taught under the direction of programs for students with learning disabilities, or should they become the primary responsibility of educators and programs within the area of gifted and talented education? This concern is not a minor one. Basic to the answer is where the money will come from for the program. Some school systems would rather not hear about the existence of our students if it means that they must provide them with more testing and more special classes. If the programs are within the gifted and talented programs, there might be a concern that adding special programs for the gifted student with learning disabilities might have to come out of the existing budget and take away from the other programs. It seems clear that the best programs would involve cooperation between these two administrative groups. Yet, such often does not happen.

Students with learning disabilities who are gifted need elements of both special education and gifted education. Addressing one of these areas without the other or not addressing either usually leads to poor results. To keep a student with learning disabilities in a special education class and add enrichment or to place this student in a gifted class and add supplemental special education tutoring is not the answer. The answer is a program that addresses both factors equally.

Another problem in answering this question is that teachers of the gifted are not typically trained in the special education methods needed for students with learning disabilities. And teachers for children and adolescents with learning disabilities usually have not been trained in gifted education.

There are no accepted models or programs for educating students who are identified as intellectually or academically gifted. Most schools offer one of two types of programs—enrichment and acceleration. Some programs emphasize enrichment of the student's education by providing curricular content above and beyond the basic school program. For example, fifth-graders studying Mexican culture might attend an exhibit of Mexican art. Some programs allow students to progress rapidly through existing curricular content in an acceleration model. For example, fifth-graders finish fifth-grade math in seven months and then move on to sixth-grade math. A few programs integrate both models. Most school systems focus on enrichment activities rather than acceleration. Yet, even in these programs, the added enrichment curriculum is managed by accelerating the regular learning program.

Acceleration models for the gifted are usually not very realistic for gifted students who have learning disabilities. Most such programs require the student to learn a fair amount of material on his or her own in one way or another but probably primarily through reading textbooks. If a student is permitted to skip a grade, he or she must be able to learn the content of the skipped courses by some method, again, probably by reading a textbook on his or her own. Some who are permitted to skip courses must learn the courses on their own to pass such tests as the Advanced Placement Program.

Students with reading disabilities will have difficulty keeping up with the pace of the class. In mathematics, where acceleration is often recommended, students may be required to read the textbook on their own to learn theorems or problem-solving paradigms. Students with learning disabilities in accelerated programs have to be taught differently. What is needed are creative models for teaching materials that build on the student's strengths rather than demand a high level of performance in the areas of weakness.

Gifted students with learning disabilities usually do best in programs that provide for acceleration using learning models based on the student's learning abilities and disabilities, allowing the student to succeed. These programs should provide enriching experiences above and beyond the basic school curriculum. To deny these experiences to the bright student with learning disabilities in order that they may spend more hours trying to master other skills is not right. As one professional put it, "After all, the skills of accessing and communicating information are often the means to the end, not the ends in and of themselves, for many bright people. It is wrong to neglect or overlook the talents and strengths of children in our diligent but perhaps misguided efforts to teach the cornerstones of education: reading, writing, spelling, and arithmetic." To say this another way, reading, writing, spelling, and arithmetic are important. However, if a student has disabilities that prevent him or her from successfully mastering these skills, it is important to find alternative ways to continue the educational process. Reading is not the critical issue. Learning what is in the book is. Writing is not the issue, nor is correct spelling. Getting one's thoughts from the brain onto the page is what is important.

Today, many bright students with reading or writing problems are excluded from enrichment programs for the gifted. Yet, their lack of these skills is, at best, minimally related to the purpose of the course or the content being taught. For example, one student might do extremely well in a creative writing class if he could dictate the story or speak into a tape recorder for someone else to type. Another student might do very well in an advanced chemistry course if she had a note taker in class or had the text on tape. An excellent math student might have no difficulty with complex mathematical concepts or theorems yet do poorly because of problems with simple computations and arithmetic. The ability to use a calculator in class might make all the difference.

Programs for the gifted student with learning disabilities must provide these accommodations for those with special needs. For some students, no matter how bright, no amount of special education remedial help will allow them to totally overcome a spelling, reading, or handwriting problem. Yet, these students should be given access to the advanced courses in high school that they need to prepare for college. They should be allowed to use appropriate survival tools to compensate for their disabilities. They must be permitted to use our modern technologies. They should be able to use a computer, maybe a laptop, in class. They should be able to use tape recorders in class or calculators. If needed, they should be able to use books-on-tape. Adults who are poor spellers can now use word processors with editing programs and spelling checkers, or they can hire a secretary who spells well. Why can't these students use such technical aids or let a parent help with editing (not thinking)?

In Summary

What should you do as a parent? You may be so concerned with your child's learning disabilities that you have never focused on her or his possible giftedness. Ideally, programs for students with learning disabilities should provide guidance to parents for those children or adolescents who are of superior ability. They deserve the enrichment and challenge provided by a gifted program.

You should understand the characteristics of gifted children and those of children with learning disabilities and how these two might merge. You should know what programs exist in your school system and the criteria used for selection. If your school doesn't have special programs for the gifted student with learning disabilities but expects this student to fit into the regular gifted programs, get together with other parents and try to get such programs started.

21

Legal Issues of Importance to Parents

Fortunately for your son or daughter and for you, today laws require school systems to provide services for children and adolescents with learning disabilities. This was not always the case. Before 1975, about half of the children with disabilities of any kind in this country could not get an appropriate education. About one million were excluded entirely from the public school system. For the child with learning disabilities, the situation was worse—about 90 percent were not even identified.

These laws, however, do not automatically assure that your child or adolescent will receive the educational programs he or she needs. This reality is even more true now because of the decrease in federal and state funding for education. As I have repeatedly noted, you must be an informed consumer and an assertive advocate. You must know the laws and know your rights, and then you must work actively with the school while insisting on these rights. The school personnel care about the education of *all* students. You care especially about the education of *your* student.

What are these laws? What do they mean for your son or daughter? What must you know and do to assure the best help you can possibly get? What can you do if you are not pleased with your school professional's effort? Let me try to answer these questions.

Parent Power

The major force behind today's legislation was a consumer move-ment led by organizations of parents of children with disabilities. Later, the people with disabilities themselves joined in this effort. They focused on the lack of an appropriate public education and on the exclusion of children and adolescents from programs provided by the public education system.

In the 1960s, various groups of parents whose children had differ-ent disabilities used publicity, mass mailings, public meetings, and other well-organized, opinion-molding techniques to put pressure on state legislatures. They wanted laws to make educational oppor-tunities for persons with disabilities not simply available but manda-tory. Most states responded with legislation, some more than others. A few states did nothing. Most of the more progressive state govern-ments passed the laws but provided no enabling funds for facilities or trained professionals to carry out their intent. The focus of these pressure groups then shifted toward enactment of a federal law that could have an impact on all states.

In 1971, the Pennsylvania Association for Retarded Citizens filed a suit in that state that directly involved the federal government in these issues for the first time. Citing constitutional guarantees of due process and equal protection under the law, they argued that the ac-cess of children with mental retardation to public education should be equal to that afforded other children. The court agreed. A year later the federal court in the District of Columbia made a similar rul-ing involving not only persons with mental retardation, but those with a wide range of disabilities. This 1972 decision established two major precedents critical to future progress: (1) Children with dis-abilities have the right to a "suitable publicly supported education, regardless of the degree of the child's mental, physical, or emotional disability or impairment," and (2) concerning financing, "if suffi-cient funds are not available to finance all of the services and pro-grams that are needed and desirable . . . the available funds must be expended equitably in such a manner that no child is entirely ex-cluded from a publicly supported education." More than forty such cases were won throughout the United States following these two landmark decisions.

These court actions also had a profound influence on federal legislation. The Rehabilitation Act of 1973, referred to as the Civil Rights Act for the Handicapped, prohibits discrimination on the basis of physical or mental handicaps in every federally assisted program in the country. Public education, of course, accepts federal assistance. Section 504 of this law focuses on the rights of the individual people in these programs, and it has been the keystone of parents' demands and of numerous successful court actions. The most critical issues in Section 504 are described here.

1. As disabled job applicants or employees, handicapped people have the same rights and must be guaranteed the same benefits as nonhandicapped applicants and employees.

2. They are entitled to all of the medical services and medically related instruction available to the general public.

3. They are entitled to participate in vocational rehabilitation, day care, or any other social service program receiving federal assistance on an equal basis with the nonhandicapped.

4. They have the equal rights to go to college or to enroll in job-training or adult post–high school basic education programs. Selection must be based on academic or other school records, and the disability cannot be a factor. (If a person has learning disabilities, the standard entrance testing procedures, the Scholastic Aptitude Test, for example, can be modified, and admission standards can be based on potential as well as on past performance.)

5. State and local school districts must provide an appropriate elementary and secondary education for all handicapped students.

In 1990, this law was expanded to all programs and not just to federally funded programs. The Americans with Disabilities Act ended discrimination against individuals with disabilities in the area of employment, education, public accommodations, and licensing of professional and other activities. It extends the coverage of basic civil rights legislation to a wide range of public and *private* entities. I will discuss this act in detail later in this chapter.

Section 504, especially the fifth point noted, became the basis for

Public Law 94-142, the Education for All Handicapped Children Act. It was passed overwhelmingly by Congress and enacted in November of 1976. It was a final victory for the parents who fought so hard for their children. This landmark legislation capped a heroic effort begun by a few parents who joined with others to form organizations, these organizations then working together to successfully lobby for the needs of all children with disabilities. This law is unique in several ways. There is no expiration date. It is regarded as permanent law. It does more than just express a concern for children with disabilities; it requires a specific commitment. The law sets forth as national policy the proposition that education must be extended to persons with disabilities *as a fundamental right*.

Thanks to these parents, the right of the person with learning disabilities to a good education is now guaranteed by law. (This assurance is not yet as clear for persons with attention deficit hyperactivity disorder, ADHD.) The challenge of today's parents is to insist on the transformation of this promise into reality.

Your need as a parent to educate yourself and to be appropriately assertive is more critical now than ever. With federal, state, and county budget cuts, services to persons with disabilities have been significantly cut. Because of these budget cuts and loss of personnel, some school systems lead parents to believe that their child is not entitled to services or that the minimal services offered are adequate. This crisis in services is compounded by another problem. The initial law, Public Law 94-142, provided services to inform parents of their rights under the law. This knowledge helped parents enter the system and function within it. After this initial funding for parent education ended, most school systems stopped providing such an education. None of the parents of the current public school students have benefitted from this initial educational process. As I lecture around the country, I am distressed by the frequency with which I meet parents who don't know of their rights or how to fight for the services their son or daughter needs.

Public Law 94-142: Education for
All Handicapped Children Act

Because Public Law 94-142 is so important to you, let me review first what the original law included and then explain the many amendments enacted since. I will suggest how you can work within this law to be an advocate for your child or adolescent. This law is your only hope of fighting for services. You must know and understand it.

The initial law listed eleven categories of children with disabilities: mentally retarded, hard-of-hearing, deaf, deaf-blind, speech-impaired, visually handicapped, seriously emotionally disturbed, orthopedically impaired, other health-impaired, *specific learning disabilities*, and multihandicapped. In a 1986 amendment, two new groups were added: autism and traumatic brain injury. Despite the efforts of parent groups, ADHD was not included on this list when the revisions were made.

The phrase *children with specific learning disabilities* is defined as applying to those children

who have a disorder in one or more of the basic psychological processes involved in understanding or in using language, spoken or written, which disorder may manifest itself in imperfect ability to listen, think, speak, read, write, spell, or do mathematical calculations. Such disorders include such conditions as perceptual handicaps, brain injury, minimal brain dysfunction, dyslexia, and developmental aphasia. Such term does not include children who have learning problems, which are primarily the result of visual, hearing, or motor handicaps, or mental retardation, of emotional disturbance, or of environmental, cultural, or economic disadvantage.

This law guarantees children and adolescents with a handicapping condition the following:

1. A *free public education* must be available to all between the ages of three and twenty-one. (The term *free and appropriate public education*, or *FAPE*, is often referred to in school procedures.)

2. An *individualized education program*, or *IEP*, in the form of a written statement, must be jointly developed by the school officials, the child's teacher, the parent or guardian, and if possible by the child her- or himself. It must include an analysis of the child's present achievement level, a list of both short-range and annual goals, an identification of the specific services that will be provided toward meeting these goals, and an indication of the extent to which the child will be able to participate in regular school programs. The IEP must also be clear about when these services will be provided and how long they will last, and it provides a schedule for checking on the process achieved under the plan and for making any revisions in it that may be needed.

3. Handicapped and nonhandicapped children must be *educated together* to the fullest extent that is appropriate. The child can be placed in special classes or separate schools only when the nature and severity of his or her handicap prevents satisfactory achievement in a regular education program. This concept of placement is referred to as being *in the least restrictive environment* possible.

4. Tests and other *evaluation materials* used in placing handicapped children must be prepared and administered in such a way as not to be racially or culturally discriminatory. They must also be presented in the child's native tongue.

5. An intensive and ongoing effort must be made to *locate* and *identify* children with handicaps, to evaluate their educational needs, and to determine whether these needs are being met.

6. In all efforts, *priority* must be given to those who are not receiving an education and to those severely handicapped people who are receiving an inadequate education.

7. In all decisions, a *prior consultation with the child's parents or guardians* must be held. No policies, programs, or procedures affecting the education of handicapped children may be adopted without a public notice.

8. These rights and guarantees apply to handicapped children in *private as well as public schools*. Any special education provided

to any child shall be provided *at no cost to the parents* if state or local education agency officials placed the child in such schools or referred the child to them.

9. States and localities must develop comprehensive *personnel development programs,* including in-service training for regular as well as special education teachers and support personnel.

10. In implementing the law, special effort shall be made to employ qualified handicapped persons.

11. All architectural barriers must be removed.

12. The state education agency has jurisdiction over all educational programs for handicapped children offered within a given state, including those administered by noneducational agencies.

13. An *advisory panel* must exist to advise the state's education agency of unmet needs. Membership must include handicapped people and parents or guardians of those people.

This law guarantees *procedural safeguards.* Parents or guardians have an opportunity to examine any records that bear on the identification of a child as being disabled, on the defined nature and severity of his or her disability, and on the kind of educational setting in which he or she is placed. Schools must provide written notice prior to changing a child's placement. If a parent or guardian objects to a school's decision, there must be a process in place through which complaints can be registered. This process must include an opportunity for an impartial hearing that offers parents rights similar to those involved in a court case—the right to be advised by counsel (and by special education experts if they wish), to present evidence, to cross-examine witnesses, to compel the presence of any witnesses who do not voluntarily appear, to be provided a verbatim report of the proceedings, and to receive the decision and findings in written form.

The rights and safeguards of Public Law 94-142 are critical. Take the time to reread the above paragraph. Each school system is required to provide you with a written guideline explaining your rights of appeal. If you have not received it, ask for it.

Revisions to Public Law 94-142

In September 1986, Congress passed Public Law 99-457. This law, the Education of the Handicapped Act Amendments of 1986, included provisions for children with disabilities of all ages. The upper age was kept at twenty-one. The original starting age of three, however, was lowered to include "handicapped and 'at risk' children between the ages of birth and age six and their families." There are two major components to this law.

The law created a new mandate for state education agencies to serve all three-, four-, and five-year-old children with disabilities by 1991. All rights to an education in the original law for ages six to twenty-one are now required for kids as young as age three. As with the initial law, services for these children in the three-to-six age group are not encouraged but mandated. If a state does not comply, it can lose federal funds.

The second landmark in this early intervention program established by these amendments is the Handicapped Infants and Toddlers Program. This section of the law created a brand-new federal program for children with disabilities and who are at risk, from birth to age three years, and for their families. While the infant and toddler program is voluntary for states—that is, they may elect not to participate—if a state does choose to participate or to apply for funding under this law, it must meet the requirements of the law and assure that services are available for all eligible children.

Public Law 99-457 stresses the importance of a coordinated and multiagency approach to the planning and dialogue needed to implement the new early childhood initiatives. A wide variety of local providers, public and private, must work together to provide the services.

In 1988, the 101st Congress approved a change in the name of Public Law 94-142 from Education for All Handicapped Children Act to Individuals with Disabilities Education Act, or IDEA. This change was in keeping with the increased concept of political correctness. One does not speak of "handicapped children" or "disabled children" but of "children with disabilities."

Changes never cease. IDEA was considered for revision during the 1997 session of Congress. Many of the proposed changes would have significantly weakened the law. Through constant efforts by parent volunteers, the law was saved in a strong form. In April of 1997, the latest amendments were passed by Congress and signed by the president. These amendments provide the following changes:

1. Schools must obtain informed consent from parents prior to a child's initial evaluation to determine the presence of a disability and to do any reevaluation.

2. Parents are now members of their child's eligibility, IEP, and placement teams.

3. The three-year, or triennial, reevaluation no longer automatically requires extensive or prescribed testing. The IEP team (including parents and other professionals) will determine the reevaluation information and testing necessary based upon the needs of the individual child.

4. Children with disabilities must be included in all general and district-wide assessment programs. Appropriate accommodations will be provided when necessary.

5. Alternative assessments must be developed by July 1, 2000, for those children who cannot participate in state- or district-wide assessment programs.

6. To resolve disputes about a child's special education, all state and local education agencies must make available a mediation process. Parent participation in mediation, however, is voluntary.

7. All children with disabilities even if expelled or placed on long-term suspension, are entitled to educational services that meet the standards of a free and appropriate public education.

Your Child or Adolescent and IDEA

Each state has developed its own laws, rules, and regulations for carrying out the intentions of this federal law. You will have to speak to your school officials, other parents, or other knowledgeable people to learn about the specifics as they apply in your state and community.

It is useful to look at the several steps in the process used to help your son or daughter. I will outline the process required by this law.

1. *Search.* Each school system must have a system for seeking out students who might have a disability.

2. *Find.* Once a student with a potential problem is identified, there should be a system for collecting information and designing an evaluation process.

3. *Evaluation.* A comprehensive, multidisciplinary evaluation should be done.

4. *Conference.* Parents or guardians should meet with the school personnel and evaluation professionals to review the evaluation conclusions, any labels or diagnoses established, and any proposed placement and IEP. The details should be presented in writing.

5. *Parents' decision process.* Parents or guardians, with consultation from educational or other professionals and lawyers when needed, decide to accept, request clarification of, request changes in, or reject the proposed placement and IEP.

6. *Appeals process.* If parents reject the label, placement recommendation, or IEP, there should be an appeals process that starts with the local school system and can go to the county or state level.

7. *Follow-up progress reports.* Such reports should be provided to the family. As the end of the school year approaches, a reassessment is done. There should be a conference (see step 4) to plan the next school year. Steps 5 and 6 are repeated before implementation of the next year's plans.

Throughout this book I urge you to be informed and assertive parents. I suggest what you need for your son or daughter and how to get the services from your school system. Please note that what I encourage you to fight for is not based only on what I believe children and adolescents with learning disabilities need. It is based on federal law. This federal law requires every state and every school system within the state to meet the requirements of the law. School systems can only get away with not meeting the requirements of the law if you do not know your rights. Since this is so important to you, let me go into more detail on your rights under this law.

Search

If someone from your school system suggests that your son or daughter might have a problem and needs testing, be positive and agree to the testing. If the tests reveal a problem, you can get help. If the tests find nothing wrong, that should relieve both you and the school. If you are concerned about your child's academic progress and suspect a problem but your school has said nothing about it, speak to the classroom teacher. Share your observations and concerns.

If the teacher agrees with you, the teacher can initiate the process through the principal. If you cannot get the classroom teacher to start this process, meet with the principal yourself. (It is best not to go directly to the principal first because this may antagonize the teacher.) When there are two parents, it is always better for both to be present at such meetings. Explain your concerns again, and ask the principal to start the evaluation process. If the principal does not agree and/or refuses to request such an evaluation, follow up this meeting with a formal request in writing. Under federal guidelines, if a request is made to the principal in writing, the principal must call a meeting of essential people within thirty working days to consider this request. Usually, the school psychologist, special education person, and classroom teacher attend this meeting, which is chaired by the principal. This meeting is usually called an education management team meeting, or EMT meeting.

At this EMT meeting, your request will be reviewed. If the team agrees to do the evaluation, you will be asked to sign a release for such testing. If the team does not agree to do an evaluation or suggests observing for several months first, you can accept this decision or you can appeal this decision to a higher level.

Another option is to get a private evaluation and bring the results back to this team. If the results show evidence of a disability, the team must respond. Such private evaluations are expensive, and many families cannot afford them.

Why is it hard for school professionals to see what parents are concerned about? I find that there are several types of students who are struggling but not recognized. One is the quiet, shy, withdrawn student who is not causing trouble. Unfortunately, the school staff might wait until this child is so frustrated and unhappy that he or she refuses to go to school, cries in school, or gets into difficulty before becoming concerned. Another type is the very bright child who manages to do at least average work in spite of his or her problems. This child may have a superior intelligence but, because of learning disabilities, be performing at a C level. School personnel see the student as "just average," yet actually what is happening is a case of significant underachievement.

In some situations, the parents do two or more hours of homework with the child each night, essentially teaching the child what he or she didn't learn in class or doing the work for or with the child. The child might also have a private tutor. Thus, he or she appears to be doing well in school. I always ask the school professionals, must this parent remove all help and supports and let the child fail before the child is seen as in need of an evaluation?

Find

Once the school personnel agree to the need for an evaluation, make yourself as informed as possible about what the evaluation is and what is being assessed. Find out what is planned, make sure that the plans cover the areas discussed in the chapters on evaluation. Be sure that someone prepares your son or daughter for each step.

For preschoolers, school systems are required to have a multidisciplinary team available to evaluate children who need assessment. In most school systems, this program is called Child Find.

Evaluation

This was covered in Chapters 12 and 13.

Conference

In the next stage, you will meet with school personnel and special educators. If the child has two parents or guardians, be sure both of you are present. You may also bring your own professional consultant to review the results and recommendations and to advise you. You are entitled to receive written copies of each evaluation prior to this meeting so that you can have your consultants review them and advise you. If you feel it necessary, you can bring your lawyer.

Angry, defensive, or demanding behavior won't get you anyplace. Assume that everyone there has the best interest of your son or daughter at heart. In reality, this is true for more than most school conferences. Your school personnel want to do what is best for your child or adolescent. Often, they must weigh this need against the realities of budget and available services. Listen, ask questions, reflect. Even if you completely agree with everything that is advised, ask for time to think and to read the recommendations in detail. On the one hand, anger or defensiveness polarizes the sides. On the other, too quick an agreement may prevent you from asking questions that might occur to you after you have read the reports and reflected on them.

Do your homework prior to the conference. Reread the chapters on evaluation. Talk with other parents or parent advocates who have been in the same situation, and if possible, learn something about what programs are likely to be suggested.

Ask questions during the conference. If someone says that your child has learning disabilities, ask for specifics. You know what learning disabilities are. Let them know that, and tell them you need exact information. Don't let the evaluators overwhelm you with professional jargon. Ask for definitions and clarification in a calm, concerned way. Let them know that although what they say is important, this is *your* child and you need to share your views.

Remember: For the school professionals, the question is not whether your son or daughter has a learning disability—the question is whether he or she is *eligible for services*. Each school system has a definition of eligibility based on a discrepancy formula. That is, how far behind does the child or adolescent have to be in what areas to qualify for services? (It has been my experience that when the budget is adequate, the amount of discrepancy between ability and performance required for the child to be eligible for services is less than when the budget is tight.)

If you do not agree with the findings, don't challenge them just now. Tell the evaluation team that you would like a copy of the test results and the minutes of the meeting so that you can discuss them with a consultant. You wouldn't consent to your child having open-heart surgery or even to being sent to the hospital without a second opinion. Committing your child to at least one year of a special education program or to another year in a regular program without the appropriate help has a different degree of urgency but just as great an impact on his or her life.

You will have to agree to the diagnosis or label; that is, to the name your school gives to the problems they say your son or daughter has. You also will have to agree to the level and type of services to be provided and to the placement recommendations. All of these conclusions should be written in the proposed individualized education program (IEP). Ask for clarifications and definitions. Carefully read the documents and be sure you understand. Only if you agree to and sign the IEP can actions be taken. No school system can act without a parent's consent.

Keep in mind the difference between an emotional problem that *causes* academic difficulties and an emotional problem that *results* in academic difficulties. If your son's behavior problems are due to the frustrations and failures experienced because of learning disabilities, don't agree to having him labeled only as "emotionally disturbed." If the school personnel insist that your daughter has learning disabilities *and* an emotional disorder, they may be correct. In making your decision, consider this possibility. If she is coded as learning disabled first with emotionally disturbed as the secondary diagnosis, the placement will be in a program for students with learning disabilities with supportive psychological help. If she is coded as emotionally disturbed first with learning disabled as the secondary diagnosis, the placement will be in a program for students with emotional disorders with supportive special education help for the learning disabilities. Which do you believe would be best for your child or adolescent? The primary label is critical. Fight for the correct one.

Your school system is responsible for placing your child in an appropriate program within the system. Only if this is not possible will they consider an out-of-system or private placement. You may prefer that your child go into a particular private program that you know about. The school officials do not have to concur, however, if an appropriate placement is available within their own system. You might argue that the private placement is better, and this might be true. But even if it were, the law states only that each child must receive an *appropriate* education, not necessarily the *best* education possible.

There are several program levels of service. You want to find the least restrictive program that still provides the most effective educational support for your child. Remember that this does not always mean being in a regular class program. The least restrictive environment for some children might be the most restrictive environment available. A child may need the security and support of a small, separate, self-contained classroom in order to feel safe enough to relax, take risks again, and become available for learning.

Ask for the details on any placement. Where is it? Will your child have to be transported out of the neighborhood? Ask about the qualifications of the teacher, the size of the class, and the age distribution of the students. Ask for the mix of students—diagnoses, levels of intellectual functioning. Ask to visit the program; even if it is spring and you will see a different group of students, you will get a feel for the teacher and program. Try to speak to parents of several of the children who are currently in the program. If the teacher has not been selected yet or the class makeup established, ask for a written statement of the qualifications that this teacher must have and the probable makeup of the class.

What about the IEP? This is the written plan identifying the instruction designed especially for your son or daughter and listing reasonable expectations for the child's achievement. There should be a specific system for monitoring progress.

At a minimum, each IEP must cover the following points:

1. A statement of your child's or adolescent's levels of educational performance.

2. A statement of goals or achievements expected by the end of the school year for each area of identified weakness.

3. Short-term objectives stated in instructional terms that are the steps leading to the mastery of these yearly goals.

4. A statement of the specific special education and support services to be provided to the child.

5. A statement of the extent to which a child will be able to participate in regular education programs and justification for any special placement recommendations.

6. Projected dates for initiation of services and the anticipated duration of the services.

7. A statement of the criteria and evaluation procedures to be used in determining, on at least an annual basis, whether short-term objectives are being achieved.

In addition to an appropriate placement and IEP, your child or adolescent may need other services. These are called related services. They are to be provided at no expense to your family. The formal definition of related services is:

> transportation and such developmental, corrective, and other supportive services (including speech pathology and audiology, psychological services, physical and occupational therapy, recreation, and medical counseling services, except that such medical services shall be for diagnostic and evaluation purposes only) as may be required to assist a handicapped child to benefit from special education, and includes the early identification and assessment of handicapping conditions in children.

These services are usually provided by the school system by school professionals.

Related services are expensive. Your school personnel might make many *suggestions* about getting the child or adolescent into psychotherapy but never formally *recommend* it verbally or in writing. If they recommend a service, thus identifying it as a needed related service, the school system must pay for the service.

Parents' Decision Process

After the conference, you are entitled to a full transcript of the meeting. You can also get copies of all tests that were done. The placement and the IEP recommendations must also be provided in writing.

Read all of the documents. If necessary, ask for clarification or for more details. If you see something in writing that was not mentioned at the meeting, ask for an explanation. If you need help, seek advice from other parents or from professionals.

If you are comfortable with the school's plan for your child, you may agree to it and sign the necessary documents. If you do not agree and cannot get the school personnel to modify their proposals, inform them that you wish to appeal. Ask that they review with you their appeals process. Remember that you are entitled by law to due process of appeal.

Appeals Process

The appeals process differs with each state and local school system. Your school system is to provide in writing the step-by-step process of appeal. Many school systems require a mediation process first. You and appropriate school personnel meet with a competent and neutral person who tries to resolve the differences. Only if this mediation process fails may a parent start the formal appeals process.

If you feel that you need legal guidance, try to find an attorney who works in the area of special education law. Ask other parents to recommend an attorney who is good and who knows your school system. If you go before a hearing officer, you will need an attorney. This is a formal legal process, and the school system will have an attorney to represent it. You need the same.

The final step in this appeals process is a meeting between you and your school system representatives before a hearing officer. This officer is a professional knowledgeable about learning disabilities, school law, and school procedures. The officer is not employed by the school system and acts independently. Both sides present their arguments. Often the decisions are based on the needs of the individual as well as on procedures of law. The decision of the hearing officer is binding. If a parent loses at this level, the only other option is to appeal under civil law (Americans with Disabilities Act). This process involves the court system and might take years.

This appeals process may go quickly or may take months. Meanwhile, your son or daughter must attend school. In this situation, the usual procedure is for the child to be placed in the program proposed by the school system until the appeals process is complete.

Implementation of Decisions

The best designed plans of April and May might fall apart in September. Be observant when school opens. Be sure the placement, the teacher, the related services, the makeup of the class, and the implementation steps for the IEP are correct and in operation. Be concerned, ask questions, but try not to be a nuisance. If you believe that some departure from the agreed-upon plan has been made, ask about it.

Be sure that the regular classroom teachers are aware of any special needs or programs and accommodations. Check to find if the regular and special education personnel are interacting with each other.

Programs begun in September may get changed or diluted as the year progresses and the case load for each professional involved increases. Ask your son or daughter to keep you informed or check this for yourself. Does each person see your child or adolescent for the amount of time noted in the IEP? Are more children being added to the program during the time when your youngster receives services? One hour of individual time twice a week might become thirty minutes twice a week in a group of three to five other children. Know your child's IEP, and insist that he or she gets what is promised. Remember that no changes can be made without a written notification and your concurrence. If you hear such things as "we just don't have the personnel to do what is on the IEP" or "our budget is less than expected," inform the principal that you have great empathy for the school's problems. However, these are the school's problems. Your problem is that your son or daughter is not getting what he or she is supposed to get.

Other Thoughts

You must keep your son or daughter informed about your actions. How much you share, what you explain, and how you explain it will depend on the child's age. If you need help, ask the professionals involved to meet with you and your child or adolescent. If you think it would be helpful, make it a family session.

You may need help in dealing with a son or daughter who resists or refuses special help or being in a special class. Another problem you might have to deal with is stigma. Other children can be cruel, sometimes on purpose, sometimes by carelessness. They might call the special programs "retard" or "mental" classes and the children in them "retards" or "speds" (for "special education"). It all hurts. Speak to the teachers. Ask that they talk to the offending students. Perhaps these teachers could discuss the theme of being different with the whole class. Alert the teacher if his or her insensitivity contributes to the teasing. If necessary, speak to the parents of an offending child in as positive a way as you can. (Here, as elsewhere, hostility won't get you very far.) Support your child and empathize with his or her feelings. Don't be afraid to show your own emotions, and don't be afraid to have a good cry together. You would do anything in the world to spare your child these problems, but they exist. Make sure the child knows that you care too much to ignore what is going on and that you will do everything possible to support and help him or her. Keep at it until the teasing is minimized or stopped.

Work closely with your school personnel. And make them work closely with you. As a team, both the school people and the family can do the best job of helping your child reach his or her maximum growth and potential.

As you read this chapter, you might feel that I ignored the needs of students with ADHD. Unfortunately, this disability is not listed under education law. Thus, the only way to get help is through civil law, using Section 504 discussed earlier in this chapter. The details for doing this were discussed in Chapter 16, on treatment of ADHD.

In Summary

You are standing on the shoulders of many parents who went before you. I have great respect for those parents who fought so hard in the 1950s and 1960s to get what we have today. Without their efforts and the resulting legislation, our children and adolescents with learning disabilities would have no rights within school systems. Other parents have taken their place on the front line in the years since.

In the spring of 1997 there was a real danger that Congress would change IDEA in ways that would weaken or destroy its effectiveness.

I was part of a major effort by parent volunteers who met with their members of Congress and who reminded critical people in the House of Representative and the Senate day after day of the need for IDEA. I am more than convinced that it was the effort of these parents that saved IDEA in its present form for your son or daughter.

Try to find a way to take your turn as a parent volunteer, fighting for services. Find a way to be active in a parent organization at your local, state, or national level. I list these organizations in the appendix. You will learn much from other parents and from the materials available. You will find informed parent advocates to help you. You will find much to be done. It is my hope that you will join the ever-present need to fight the next windmill.

Conclusion

Perhaps you remember Victor, the boy whose victorious story opened this book. Let us for a moment look at another young man who had the same extent of learning disabilities. Bob struggled through elementary school, did poorly in junior high school, and finally quit school at age sixteen. Early on, his parents tried to get the school to provide help. Later, they gave up in frustration. Once Bob quit school, they lost control and lost track of him.

The next time they heard of Bob, he had been arrested for killing two policemen while trying to rob a bank.

The newspaper coverage was painfully revealing. The psychiatric report noted "Every time he struggled hopelessly with a math problem, every time he stumbled over a sentence from his first reader, every time his brother beat him in a fight . . . [he] grew a little more hostile, a little more withdrawn, a little more convinced of his worthlessness. . . . He thought of himself as stupid and worthless and developed intense anger at himself and the world."

Bob's parents were professionals. His older brother was an honor student. Bob had been labeled "slow" in elementary school, but the first testing was not done until eighth grade. It revealed learning disabilities and an IQ in the bright range. No programs were offered. The high school counselor never knew of these studies. After Bob quit school, he moved from job to job. He spent more and more time riding his motorcycle and getting into trouble with the police.

The bank robbery and killings were an almost inevitable outcome of his lifestyle.

Bob is now in prison.

You have probably heard all of this before, but let me mention a few other people with learning disabilities. Leonardo da Vinci often wrote backward; his writing shows evidence of perceptual problems. Woodrow Wilson didn't learn the alphabet until he was eight years old. He didn't read until he was eleven. At school, he excelled only in work that was related to speech. He was labeled "dull and backward."

Auguste Rodin, the famous sculptor, did poorly with math and spelling. He was described as "ineducable" and "an idiot." General George Patton had significant learning disabilities and could not read or write at age twelve. A special reader worked with him all through his time at West Point. Winston Churchill had learning disabilities. Albert Einstein did not talk until age four or read until age nine. He was considered backward and made progress only after his family moved him to a special school where he could learn using his own style. My editor tells me that Hemingway was a poor speller.

Thomas Edison couldn't learn anything in public school. He entered at age eight and was removed three months later by his mother, who decided to teach him herself. His autobiography is revealing. Edison wrote, "I remember I used never to be able to get along at school. I was always at the foot of the class. I used to feel that the teachers did not sympathize with me and that my father thought I was stupid." Later, he added, "It was impossible to observe and learn the processes of nature by description, or the English alphabet and arithmetic only by rote . . . it was always necessary to observe with my own eyes and to do things or to make things." To see for himself, to test things for himself, he said, was "for one instance . . . better than to learn about something I had never seen for two hours." His mother noted that he never learned to spell. His grammar and syntax were appalling. He was hard to teach. Whatever he learned, he learned in his own way. In fact, she said, she only inspired him—no one ever taught him anything. He taught himself.

There are others. Perhaps you have met successful people who overcame or learned to compensate for their learning disabilities. Perhaps you are one. I know that I am. You should have seen the first draft of the first edition of this book—spelling errors, letter reversals, illegible handwriting. But I had something then that I didn't have when I was in school. I had a secretary who learned to read my handwriting, who could spell, and who did not laugh at my errors. That was compensation. By the time I started the second edition, I had discovered a miracle—the computer and the word processor. I can now type almost as fast as I think. (How exhausting it is to have to slow my thinking down to the rate my hand can write.) I can use a spelling checker. The printout can be read by everyone. I think back at the pain of writing that first edition first draft by hand at such a slow rate and with such fatigue.

But I did not always have such help. My grades in elementary and junior high school were less than good. The principal recommended to my mother that I would be happier in a vocational high school. My mother refused and insisted that I go to the regular high school. She won—or I should say, she gave me the chance to win. Somehow I got my act together in high school. I taught myself how to learn and how to pass exams. I figured out that I could not just read. I had to read, think, and then take notes. It took a long time, but I learned what was in the books. I never learned to spell, but I became better at finding other words to use or at writing so small the teacher could not read the misspelled word. My grades improved in college. Medical school was a mixed blessing. My strengths plus learned study skills permitted me to do well and to graduate. For the first time in my life, I finished near the top of my class. But I still remember the chief of surgery calling me in during my senior year. I had just completed my required rotation on surgery. My visual motor and fine motor skills are at best poor. He said to me, "Larry, if you promise never to go into surgery, I will pass you." I agreed and I passed. It is no surprise to me that I chose a specialty of medicine that requires listening and talking.

My inability to sit still for more than a second has always been a point of humor in my family. If not my wife, then my kids will say, "Can't you sit down and relax?" I guess the answer is no. I still remember a fifth-grade teacher who tied me in my seat and a fourth-grade teacher who made me sit on my hands so that I would not fidget. I also remember the sadness and the embarrassment as my classmates looked at me.

All of this was the beginning. The ending never comes. I still face new frustrations and challenges. When I was the acting director of the National Institute of Mental Health, I attended a congressional hearing on our budget with the director of the agency. I needed to pass information to him so that he could answer a senator's questions. When the hearing was over, he handed back my note. On the top he had written "Thanks"—then he had proceeded to correct two spelling errors and one letter reversal! Writing notes will never be a comfortable thing for me. I always have the fear that I will show someone that I cannot spell. And, of course, everyone knows that if you can't spell, you must be dumb.

Why is it, then, that some children and adolescents make it and some do not? It seems to me that the outcome depends on the interaction of several factors:

1. The types and extent of the learning disabilities.

2. The level of one's intellectual potential.

3. The point at which these disabilities are recognized and an appropriate program developed. If this is not done early, the child develops additional academic and emotional problems and falls further and further behind.

4. The kinds of help provided by the school and in the family.

5. The child's or adolescent's personality. Does he or she take on the disabilities as a challenge, accept the need to work harder, develop styles of coping? Does he or she relate in a way that makes people want to reach out and help or in a way that pushes them away?

6. The parents' and the whole family's ability to be supportive and caring.

Current research efforts will someday give us the knowledge to minimize or to prevent learning disabilities and attention deficit hyperactivity disorder (ADHD) and to improve the existing problems through education, medication, and/or special nutritional approaches. For now there is little we can do to "cure" the learning disabilities or the ADHD that your son or daughter has. His or her intellectual potential is established. You can only work for programs that will maximize this potential.

Our best hope for achieving the best outcome is to work on the other factors that affect the child or adolescent—those factors that we can influence.

By being an informed consumer and an assertive advocate, you can work to get the necessary evaluations and school interventions. Through your own understanding, you can help your child or adolescent understand and maximize strengths rather than magnify weaknesses. You can help with his or her self-image and personality development. You can help your family understand and support the child. You can support your other children. And, equally important, you can support yourself.

There is a saying that you never know how good a parent you have been until it is too late to do anything about it—until your child is an adult. Perhaps this saying is true for those delightfully "normal" children. But it cannot be the philosophy for our children with special problems or disabilities to overcome. We must stop and assess ourselves at they grow. If everything has been done to help them get through the challenges of their current stage of life, we must then look ahead for the challenges of their next stage of life.

I truly hope this book has given you a better understanding of your child's world. I hope that it has suggested a new way of thinking and some ideas that will help you help your son or daughter reach his or her full potential as a happy, healthy, productive adult.

This challenge will never be easy. I wish you the best of success.

Organizations Related to Learning Disabilities

Learning Disabilities Association of America, Inc.
The Learning Disabilities Association (LDA), formerly called the Association for Children with Learning Disabilities (ACLD), is a national parent association with state and local chapters. Membership is open to parents and professionals. Through a network of national, state, and local programs, parents receive educational programs, parent advocacy advice, and support systems for individuals with learning disabilities throughout the life span.

> 4156 Library Road
> Pittsburgh, PA 15234
> (412) 341-1515
> Fax: (412) 344-0224
> Website: http://www.ldanatl.org

International Dyslexia Association
The International Dyslexia Society (IDA), formerly called the Orton Dyslexia Society, is for parents and professionals. The primary focus is on individuals with dyslexia, also called a language-based learning disability.

> 8600 LaSalle Road
> Suite 382

Baltimore, MD 21286
(410) 296-0232 or (800) 222-3123
Fax: (410) 321-5069
e-mail: info@interdys.org
Website: http://www.interdys.org.

Council for Exceptional Children

The Council for Exceptional Children is the branch of the National Education Association for educators in special education. The Division on Learning Disabilities is the specific group within the council concerned with learning disabilities.

1920 Association Drive
Reston, VA 22091
(703) 620-3660 or (800) 845-6232
Fax: (703) 264-9494
Website: http://www.cec.sped.org

National Center for Learning Disabilities

National Center for Learning Disabilities is a foundation-like organization with extensive fund-raising efforts. This money is used to further public education about learning disabilities and for specific areas of research. Information is provided to parents and professionals.

381 Park Avenue South
Suite 1401
New York, NY 10016
(212) 545-7510
Fax: (212) 545-9665
Website: http://www.ncld.org

Organizations Related to Attention Deficit Hyperactivity Disorder (ADHD)

Children and Adults with Attention Deficit Disorder

Children and Adults with Attention Deficit Disorder (CHADD) is a national alliance of parent organizations that provides information and support to parents of individuals with this disorder.

499 N.W. 70th Avenue
Suite 101

Plantation, FL 33322
(954) 587-3700
Fax: (954) 587-4599
Website: http://www.chadd.org

Attention Deficit Disorder Association
Attention Deficit Disorder Association (ADDA) is a national alliance of support groups that provides referrals and information to parents and to support groups.

8091 South Ireland Way
Aurora, CO 80016
(800) 487-2282

Professional Organizations

American Academy of Child and Adolescent Psychiatry
3615 Wisconsin Avenue, N.W.
Washington, DC 20016

American Academy of Ophthalmology
1101 Vermont Avenue, N.W.
Washington, DC 20036

American Academy of Optometry
5530 Wisconsin Avenue
Chevy Chase, MD 20815

American Academy of Pediatrics
P.O. Box 927
141 Northwest Point Road
Elk Grove Village, IL 60007

American Medical Association
535 N. Dearborn
Chicago, IL 60610

American Occupational Therapy Association
P.O. Box 31220
Bethesda, MD 20824

American Psychiatric Association
        1400 K Street, N.W.
        Washington, DC 20005

American Psychological Association
        1200 17th Street, N.W.
        Washington, DC 20036

American Speech, Language, and Hearing Association
        10801 Rockville Pike
        Rockville, MD 20852

National Association of School Psychologists
        8455 Colesville Road
        Silver Spring, MD 20910

National Association of Social Workers
        7981 Eastern Avenue
        Silver Spring, MD 20910

Sensory Integration International
        1402 Cravens Avenue
        Torrance, CA 90501

Legal Organizations

Many law schools have special units or programs offering reference materials or counsel on children with disabilities. If you or your attorney needs such help, contact your nearest law school and find out what they offer. The following national programs may be of help or may provide a local resource.

Children's Defense Fund
        122 C Street, N.W.
        Fourth Floor
        Washington, DC 20001

Mental Disability Legal Resource Center
        American Bar Association
        1800 M Street, N.W.
        Washington, DC 20036

Information Centers

The National Information Center for Children and Youth with Disabilities

The National Information Center for Children and Youth with Disabilities (NICHEY) provides extensive information and literature on all areas of disability.

> P.O. Box 1492
> Washington, DC 20013
> (202) 884-8200 or (800) 695-0285
> Fax: (202) 884-8441
> Website: http://www.nichy.org

HEATH Resource Center

HEATH provides resources, services, and information on adults with disabilities, including information on postsecondary education, including vocational preparation programs, adult education, and college.

> One Dupont Circle, N.W.
> Suite 800
> Washington, DC 20036-1193
> (202) 939-9320 or (800) 544-3284
> Fax: (202) 833-4760

Parents of Gifted/LD Children

This organization provides resources and services and an opportunity to interact with other parents.

> (301) 986-1422
> Website: http://www.geocities.com/athens/1105/gtld.html

Recording for the Blind and Dyslexic

Resource for loan of tape-recorded textbooks, books, and other materials.

> 29 Roszel Road
> Princeton, NJ 08540
> (609) 452-0606 or (800) 221-4792
> Fax: (609) 987-8116
> Website: http:///www.rfbd.org

Directories

The Directory for Exceptional Children

> Porter Sargent Publications, Inc.
> 11 Beacon Street
> Boston, MA 02108

Directory of Facilities and Services for the Learning Disabled

> Academic Therapy Publication
> 20 Commercial Boulevard
> Novato, CA 94947

The Schoolsearch Guide to Private Schools for Students with Learning Disabilities

> School Search
> 127 Marsh Street
> Belmont, MA 02178

INDEX